RURAL SOCIETY AND
FRENCH POLITICS

MICHAEL BURNS

RURAL SOCIETY AND FRENCH POLITICS

BOULANGISM AND

THE DREYFUS AFFAIR

1886-1900

PRINCETON UNIVERSITY PRESS

PRINCETON, NEW JERSEY

Library of Congress Cataloging in Publication Data will be
found on the last printed page of this book

ISBN 0-691-05423-1

Publication of this book has been aided by a grant from
the National Endowment for the Humanities

This book has been composed in Linotron Baskerville

Clothbound editions of Princeton University Press books
are printed on acid-free paper, and binding materials are
chosen for strength and durability

Printed in the United States of America
by Princeton University Press
Princeton, New Jersey

*For Frank, Mary Lou,
and Pamela*

PREFACE AND
ACKNOWLEDGMENTS

I came to France by way of England. In 1969 a friend urged me to read Leonard Woolf's autobiography, and a year later we toured the Sussex Downs over which Leonard and Virginia had hiked decades before. In 1975 I crossed the Channel for the first time to visit David Garnett, novelist and octogenarian survivor of the Bloomsbury group then living in southwestern France near the small village of Moncuq, a place as charming as its name. On my walk up the steep, unpaved road which linked Garnett's house in the hinterlands to the village, I looked out to a patchwork of green and yellow fields. My impressions were aesthetic, those of a tourist who appreciates the scenery but knows little about French peasants living on isolated farms, and still less about the land they till, their traditions, their politics. A year later, in a California classroom, I would be inspired to learn more about that rural world by a new guide who had also come to France by way of England (and Rumania); I am indebted to Eugen Weber for his support and encouragement.

At Yale, three eminent historians of modern Europe directed this work through its dissertation stage: John Merriman, with his expert grasp of social change in nineteenth century France; Peter Gay, who patiently urged me to look beyond my narrow village boundaries and consider rural political cultures in a broad European context; and Robert Herbert, a distinguished art historian with a superb understanding of French social history to complement his knowledge of pigment and provenance. The willingness of an *éminence grise* to plod through my early drafts was matched only by her desire to introduce me to the people and potables of France she knows so well: Susanna Barrows, a fine historian and dear friend, took care of my shyness abroad and my passive voice at home.

A Fulbright Grant and Tocqueville Award from the French-American Foundation enabled me to begin research in Paris and four *départements* in 1979-80. I returned to France in 1982 for further work in the Vendée and Orne thanks to a National Endowment for the Humanities Summer Stipend and a Mount Holyoke College Faculty Grant. During both visits, I received gracious and expert assistance at the Archives Nationales, Archives de la préfecture de Police, Paris, Bibliothèque Nationale, Musée national des arts et traditions populaires, Musée Carnavalet, and the departmental archives of the Isère, Gers, Marne, Orne, Savoie, and Vendée. M. Dupraz, assistant archivist in the Isère, was an excellent critic and delightful dinner companion; and M. Lemée, director of the Gers archives, kindly invited me to his home adjoining the ancient monastery which now contains the historical documents of the Gers. I also wish to thank my other French hosts: Jeanne Innes Kaqueler, Margitta Matthes, and Jacqueline Weber in Paris; the Debas, Longo, and Fiard clans in Chambéry; and, above all, Pierre Delaunay and his family for so many enjoyable fall and winter weekends in the Savoie.

At home, two friends and former co-workers, Brenda Vaccaro and Sandy Dennis, helped ease my transition from one career to another, and for more reasons than I have space or eloquence to list I am grateful to them both. Martine Richard did an excellent job of deciphering my revisions and unraveling my bizarre bibliographical notes. Ted Margadant offered many insights into the complexities of structural transformations in the nineteenth-century countryside, and Patrick Hutton taught me a great deal about Boulangism and mass politics. Ingeborg Day, an accomplished writer and editor, and a granddaughter of Austrian peasants, helped shape the form and content of these pages. The Sterling Library at Yale, the Williston Memorial Library at Mount Holyoke College, and the New York Public and Yale Club libraries in New York provided important materials in friendly settings. Finally, I have dedicated this book to my father, mother, and sister because they have been unflagging in their support and because T. S. Eliot was right, "Home is where one starts from."

CONTENTS

LIST OF ILLUSTRATIONS

ABBREVIATIONS

RURAL SOCIETY AND
FRENCH POLITICS

. . . l'historien ne doit jamais oublier que sa mission est de faire à chacun sa part; le malheureux et le riche sont égaux devant sa plume; pour lui, le paysan a la grandeur de ses misères, comme le riche a la petitesse de ses ridicules. . . .

BALZAC

INTRODUCTION

One Sunday night in August, 1899, an elderly Parisian gentleman stopped at the Gare de l'Est to greet friends returning from a holiday in the countryside. On the platform he encountered a "brave campagnard" who stepped down from an arriving train and, in a "most simple and ingenuous manner," called out "Tiens! mais c'est donc la fête ici." Perhaps the peasant was reacting to the huge crowds in the bustling station, to newspaper hawkers crying out headlines of the Dreyfus retrial taking place in Rennes, or, simply, to his first glimpse of Paris. Whatever the case, our Parisian witness went on to describe the consequences of this "naif" shout in an angry note to the police prefect: the peasant "had barely set foot on the platform when police agents punched him smack in the face, then in the chest, sending the good man flying against an iron gate. At the same moment, a pack of guards . . . bullied a few harmless onlookers." And there, with a few nasty remarks about police brutality, the story ends.[1]

The peasant's fate is unknown; nor can we fathom what precisely motivated his attackers. It is clear, however, that after years of anarchist assaults (in train stations), and, more recently, bloody anti-Semitic riots surrounding the Dreyfus Affair, Parisian police abided no strangers in search of "fêtes." Just arrived from Champagne, Alsace, or another region serviced by the Gare de l'Est, the peasant might have picked himself up, taken the next train home, and warned countrymen that Parisian fêtes are not only different but dangerous.

Richard Cobb says of social history that there "must be a wide element of guesswork. It is like attempting to sound the unsoundable and to penetrate the secrets of the human heart."[2] This brief tableau of a peasant in Paris—incomplete and reported by a city dweller—typifies the impressionistic evidence available to the historian of the peasantry; it provides more information than most documents, but still requires guesswork. Police and prefectoral reports, diaries and letters, newspapers and novels, parliamentary debates and poetry, record the perceptions of those who have the time, desire, and equipment (from literacy to sufficient light) to upstage those who "miss their share of the credit . . . until they can write the despatches."[3] A peasant's life is infinitely more difficult for the historian to investigate than, say, the lives of General Georges Boulanger or Captain Alfred Dreyfus, because the latter two can be heard, the former only felt. History is a selective affair.

Yet, starting with Marc Bloch and Lucien Febvre and continuing through the recent work of historical sociologists, cultural anthropologists, and others, new methods have been developed to probe elusive rural subjects. Demography, oral traditions, farm tools, folklore, cadastres, statistics of elections, fluctuating food prices, and much more provide important insights into the peasant's world. The historian's stage is now more crowded than ever, the plot more complex, and yet, despite this modernization of methodology, the majority of players remain silent. The guesswork continues. If Montaigne was right, however, and the journey matters more than the arrival, then a history of rural France which offers tentative conclusions—and there can be no other kind—is as valuable as that scholarship which stands on firmer, usually urban, ground.

Most historians of nineteenth-century rural France have focused on the crucial years between 1848 and 1851: on the revolution, on the insurrection and its aftermath. From broad and thorough studies of Montagnard politics, collective action, and government repression to detailed regional accounts including the magisterial work of Maurice Agulhon, we have learned a great deal about social, economic, cultural, and political change in rural bourgs. In these studies the 1840s and 50s mark the pivotal time when national political organization penetrated the countryside and significant numbers of hitherto ignorant or indifferent rural folk turned their attention to new issues and ideologies. The horizons and priorities of peasant politics had changed.[4]

Meanwhile, the less numerous accounts of the early Third Republic in rural France have examined transformations unfolding in specific departments from the Deux-Sèvres to the Loir-et-Cher and Var. Some highly quantitative studies probe rural economies and the growth of the national market system, whereas others have an especial interest in the impact of phylloxera and the political organization of wine-growing communities between the 1870s and the Midi strikes of 1903-1907. The leitmotif is the radicalization of a peasantry for the most part already politicized.[5]

Finally, arguments concerning the time and manner of rural politicization and national unification stretch into the mid-twentieth century. Rural sociologists, historians, and even a recent President of France have insisted that the character and culture of the nation did not fully coalesce until the development of sophisticated mass communications after World War II.[6] But these are minority opinions. It is the mid-nineteenth-century which continues to enthrall most scholars who consider the fin de siècle better territory for devotees of urban intellectual decadence or those interested in strikes and union organization in Lille, Lyon, Limoges, or Decazeville,[7] and feel that enclaves of peasant atavism in the twentieth century—in, say, the Massif Central—are vestigial and relatively insignificant.

A few years ago, Eugen Weber, who considered all these arguments "plausible" but none "overwhelming," and who did not believe that the peasantry had been fully politicized at mid-century or at the dawn of the Third Republic, placed the "modernization" of rural France in the "two score years on either side of 1900."[8] Through a rich analysis of a dozen largely undeveloped departments, Weber charted the major "agencies of change"—education, communication networks, the military, the national market economy—which gradually but decisively unmoored peasants from archaic local habits and brought them into the mainsteam of the nation. Weber's book was "a suggestion of the work still to be done,"[9] intentionally broad in scope and provocative in interpretation.

And provocative it was. Critics applauded and attacked *Peasants into Frenchmen* (usually in the same review), commending it as ambitious, lively, brilliantly presented; criticizing it as too reliant on the folklore of backward regions, too incognizant of the fundamental transformations which had occurred early in the century.[10] The most thorough response came from sociologist-historian Charles Tilly, who insisted that the "cake of custom" had already been broken by the final decades of the nineteenth century. Large-scale industrial capitalism had long before upset traditional rural ways and proletarianized much of the European peasantry. Tilly stressed that the "magic mentalism" so important to Weber "is not only wrong but unnecessary. The analysis of capitalism and of state making offers a far more adequate basis for the understanding of change in nineteenth-century Europe."[11]

Long ago G. M. Young reckoned that a central theme of history is not only what happened, but "what people felt about it while it was happening."[12] The story which follows—an account of how country folk in face-to-face communities responded to the two major political watersheds of the early Third Republic, Boulangism, and the Dreyfus Affair—hopes to show, among other things, that structure without people, the *longue durée* without the everyday, the mainstream without the marginal (and, of course, vice versa), can make for provocative sociological analysis or engaging historical narrative, but that it is a meeting of both which brings us closer to an enriched understanding of the past. We shall see that structural changes in agricultural communities in the 1880s and 90s had a decisive but uneven impact on rural inhabitants; as Maurice Halbwachs pointed out, they did not touch "all members of a group uniformly like raindrops or sunrays which fall on all the trees of a forest."[13] Although the grand issues surrounding Boulangism and the Dreyfus Affair are familiar, we know little or nothing about their impact, their reception, in the villages and hamlets of France. A close look at peasant communities in the final decades of the century will show that the architecture of national politics changed from village to village.

Few events in the history of modern France have been more exhaustively explored than Boulangism and the Dreyfus Affair. Between the *seize mai* crisis of 1877 and the separation of church and state in 1905, they stand as the quintessential turning-points of the pre-World War I Republic. In 1886, with France immersed in profound economic crisis, and with the moderate Opportunist Republic under attack from Left and Right, General Boulanger, the enormously popular Minister of War, attracted the attention and hopes of the discontented. Georges Clemenceau and his Radical allies were the first to sense the political uses to which Boulanger could be put. But when republicans began to fear plebiscites which smacked of Bonapartism, new supporters—including royalists and Bonapartists—emerged to coopt and finance the General's burgeoning popularity. By 1888-89, Boulangism (and the threat it posed) was at the center of Third Republic politics. The circus-like nature of Boulangism has attracted simplistic and serious scholars alike who have analyzed nearly every aspect of the movement, from the charismatic quality of its blond-bearded leader to the significant political realignments which followed in its wake. In the end, the Republic battled Boulangism and survived, strengthened, until the Dreyfus Affair.[14]

In the fall of 1894, the army arrested and court-martialed Captain Alfred Dreyfus, assigned to the French General Staff and accused of transmitting military secrets to the German attaché in Paris. Dreyfus was innocent, but for the next three years few believed the protestations of the Jewish "traitor" imprisoned on Devil's Island. Later, when another staff officer discovered forged evidence in a secret army file, and when Emile Zola published "J'Accuse," his scathing indictment of the General Staff in January, 1898, the case became an *affaire*. The profound and varied issues surrounding Dreyfus—nationalism, militarism, anti-clericalism, anti-Semitism, and more—continue to fascinate those who consider the Affair a "historic drama, unique of its kind, a drama in which thousands of characters played their parts and whose stage was the whole world."[15] A complete bibliography of the Affair published in 1970 listed 551 titles; and the list has grown longer.[16] It was an event which crystallized the problems of its time, and timeless problems.

Yet, unlike the historiography dealing with 1848-51, studies of Boulangism and the Dreyfus Affair continue to reflect an urban *parti pris*; they are, of course, considered "national" events, but their impact on the majority of French men and women—rural men and women—is rarely, if ever, examined. In that massive bibliography of the Dreyfus Affair, not one title deals with rural reactions.[17]

Boulanger and his surrogates stood in local and national elections in dozens of departments garnering hundreds of thousands of votes. Campaigns reached into the smallest rural communes, but this crucial aspect of the movement has been overshadowed by the celebrated Nord victory in 1888 and, above all, by the January 1889 triumph in Paris. In March, 1888, in a decision it would later regret, the military released the mischievous General from service, thereby freeing him to engage in forthcoming elections throughout France. Most were marginal sorties designed to discredit Opportunists and keep the protest plebiscite for Dissolution of the Chamber of Deputies and Revision of the Constitution alive; but if a better understanding of Boulangism and national politics in the 1880s is desired, then the nature of rural reactions in scattered departments deserves as much attention as do Parisian responses.

For tens of thousands of industrial workers in Paris, the Nord, and other provincial centers, the General represented the (absent) hero of Decazeville: the enlightened War Minister whose troops had exchanged rations not bullets with striking workers in 1886.[18] The Radical image which so pleased Georges Clemenceau early on had not yet been tarnished by revelations of monarchist support, deceit, and untrammeled personal ambition. The General's victory in the Nord legislative election, says Jacques Néré in our only thorough analysis of the movement in provincial France, was due to the massive support of urban workers in textile, metallurgy, and, above all, maritime industries.[19] The Decazeville myth held strong and worked to Boulanger's political advantage. Socialist organizations in the Nord, especially the Parti ouvrier, underestimated the General's popularity, and were unable to prevent workers from turning to this seemingly radical and dynamic candidate who stood out from the dull coterie of unresponsive Opportunist republicans. In the end, however, Boulangism would help Guesdists and others by detaching "a large number of workers from the republican parties which they had supported up to that time," and by preparing the "future triumphs of socialism." Despite contemporary assessments, Boulanger was not the peasants' candidate in the Nord; indeed, one finds a "marked repugnance against the Boulangist adventure" among rural inhabitants, many of whom voted republican for the first time in April of 1888. If Boulangism served as the last stop on the road to socialism for a great many industrial workers, it reinforced the tendency of peasants to rally to the Republic.[20]

Above all, Néré wanted to go beyond the myth of Boulangism as a "burlesque" complete with songs, imagery, and hapless politicians, and examine it as an expression of serious popular sentiment fueled by the economic crisis of the period. But Néré studied urban, industrial France and focused on economic and political changes in cities like Lille, Roubaix, and Dunkirk. His observations on election results in rural areas are instructive, but we are left with little insight into how Boulanger addressed the peasantry—if, indeed, he ever did—and why most rural communities rejected his appeals although a few others gave their support.

Election results from other regions show which rural communes rallied to the General, and shed new and different light on the interpretation of Boulangism as a "chronic urban protest."[21] But momentary victories or defeats in rural areas tell only part of the story. The avenues by which Boulangism arrived in the countryside, the short- and long-term effect it had on the politics of rural people, the campaign methods and propaganda (including songs and popular imagery) used by traveling agents should be central, not peripheral, to any study of Boulangism. One must look not beyond, but into, the "burlesque"—after all, it was Friedrich Engels who said of Boulangism, "After the farce, the tragedy."[22] Popular political propaganda, used to an unprecedented degree by Boulangists in rural France, contains a key to how country people learned about Paris-based events in the 1880s. When studied in conjunction with local histories and pressing economic issues, it offers a better notion of national politics in rural settings.

The long, labyrinthine history of the Dreyfus Affair is dramatic and familiar; from the Captain's arrest in 1894 through his trial, imprisonment, retrial, pardon, and reinstatement in the army in 1906, it abounds with genuine heroes, villains, and martyrs. Any attempt to revise our view of this tragic *affaire* should not be construed as an underestimation of its significance. Bernard Lazare, Emile Zola, Georges Picquart, Dreyfus's dedicated and combative wife Lucie and brother Mathieu bravely faced every adversary, from militant anti-Semites to apathetic politicians, and prevailed. The Affair was indeed a major turning-point in the history of the Third Republic.

But did it tear all of France "to pieces"? Did it cause a "schism in all groups of Frenchmen," splitting the nation "from top to bottom"? Was the "whole country" pervaded by virulent anti-Semitism, "consumed by blind hatred and intolerance . . . hopelessly and hysterically divided"? Had France become an "anarchic mob" riven by a "moral cataclysm"?[23] An over-enthusiastic historian whose account of the Affair remains one of the most widely read, insists that "France . . . went out of her mind. Normal life stopped."[24] Nations don't have minds, of course, and normal life stops only once for most mortals, but during the feverish months of the Affair did "Europe [stand] still to watch with thrilled pulses"?[25] If so, why? If so, how?

"The crowning attainment of historical study," Lewis Namier maintained, is to achieve "an intuitive sense of how things do not happen."[26] We know much about what happened in Paris and provincial cities during the Dreyfus Affair,[27] nothing about its reception in villages and hamlets, nothing about the degree to which anti-Semitism, for example, was a significant issue in rural France. Was the whole country "hysterically divided"? If it was not, why did contemporary observers and scores of historians feel compelled to assume it was?

We shall see that though national politics in cities and the countryside had much in common, small, rural communities in the final quarter of the nineteenth century still shared many features which support Robert Redfield's belief that "peasant society and culture has something generic about it. It is a kind of arrangement of humanity with some similarities all over the world."[28] So it went for peasant politics too. Responses to the Affair and to Boulangism will show that political issues originating in Paris underwent so many permutations on their journey to the countryside that all-encompassing "national" definitions of these events must be reassessed. As Richard Hofstadter put it, "politics can be a projective arena for feelings and impulses that are only marginally related to the manifest issues."[29] Paris, the central arena of these political affairs, was also the home, the seedbed, of the manifest issues. Politicians, army officers, literati, Boulanger and Dreyfus themselves, were principal actors in the central arena. Other urban participants in and out of Paris—workers, students, petty bourgeois shouting "Vive Boulanger!" and, later, "A bas les juifs!"—populated the arena's periphery, grafting their demands onto a situation which was physically near and, for many, directly relevant. In the countryside, the different feelings and impulses of rural people frequently altered national issues and Parisian events became "marginally related," if related at all. An

examination of kindred scenes unfolding at the same moment on dispersed stages will help define what sort of nation was "torn asunder"
by the major political upheavals of the late nineteenth century.

Until recently, many historians, cultural anthropologists, and others
have tended to pass over the indigenous achievements of given societies
for anticipated signs of primitiveness or, in the vocabulary of another
time, "barbarism."[30] Binary systems—primitive/advanced, wild/domes-
ticated, and so on—are often, if not always, value-laden and ethno-
centric. But these "vague dichotomies," used carefully, can provide a
mechanism for investigators probing motive forces of change and continuity.[31] For example, anthropologist Jack Goody believes that in many
cases "it is 'oral' and 'literate' that need be opposed rather than 'traditional' and 'modern.' . . . 'Traditional' societies are marked not so
much by the absence of reflective thinking as by the absence of the
proper tools for constructive rumination."[32] At the end of the nineteenth century the majority of French peasants were literate, though
some barely, and others only recently. They were also members of
intimate *sociétés d'interconnaissance* in which oral tradition and an intricate series of communicative acts continued to play principal roles.
"Differences in the mode of communication," Goody concludes, "are
often as important as differences in the mode of production, for they
involve development in the storing, analysis, and creation of human
knowledge, as well as the relationships between the individuals involved."[33] In order to grasp the ways in which rural people learned
about national events—to examine the words and pictures, sounds and
sights, transmitted from Paris to the countryside, along with the artic-
ulation (and transmutation) of those communicative acts by local personalities—we must try to unravel a mystery of meaning by placing
(abstract) words and pictures in their (concrete) social context. When
a Boulangist leader in the Loir-et-Cher cried "Vive la République dé-
mocratique et sociale!" he was sounding more like a mid-century Montagnard than a *Belle époque* reactionary.[34] Was he? Or was he intentionally manipulating radical words (and memories and desires) for
reactionary ends? Moreover, the impact of his shout must be considered in light of his local influence. We shall see that a spokesman's
position in a village—his class, status, family ties, historic involvement
in long-standing feuds and rivalries, and more—added a crucial element to the formulation of political opinions. Personalities in the nineteenth-century French countryside, like rural patrons and Holy Men

in Late Antique Roman villages, can be used "like a mirror, to catch, from a surprising angle" how people on the spot influenced local political cultures and molded national political meanings.[35]

Yet another discourse will require close study and reassessment: the language of French officialdom, the vocabulary of police, prefects, and local politicians, especially their litanies on rural "indifference" and "naiveté." Urban definitions of rural behavior taken at face value may lead not only to inaccuracy but to one-sidedness: the wrong side. Perceived "indifference" and "naiveté" may, in reality, be difference and sagacity. Whenever possible, however possible, country people must be allowed to speak for themselves.

Peasants, country people, rural folk; village communities, the countryside, rural France—it is hard to avoid T. S. Eliot's "general mess of imprecision" when discussing a population as variegated as the peasantry, a mosaic as complicated as the French nation. A century ago the archetypal "peasants" in Millet's painting *Angelus*, so popular with town folk, were, in reality, a complex amalgam of overlapping professions: day laborers (*journaliers*) who owned small plots of land; proprietors (*propriétaires*) and cultivators (*cultivateurs*) who might also have been artisans or industrial workers; sharecroppers (*métayers*); tenant farmers (*fermiers*); rural servants (*domestiques*); plowmen (*laboureurs*), and on and on. Let Emile Guillaumin who lived and worked in the Bourbonnais describe the complexities:

> The daily task, the milieu, the climate, shapes the individual. And the role of men on the land is infinitely diverse according to regions, soil, cultures. There is a great difference of character and appearance between the Flamand and Gascon, the Breton and the Dauphinois, the Beauçeron and the Provençal. . . . When setting off on a general study of peasant life, it helps to point out the arbitrariness of generalizations. . . .[36]

Marc Bloch echoed Guillaumin when he told of that "large and complex country," rural France, where the "villages of Lorraine surrounded by their long open-fields, the closes and hamlets of Brittany, a Provençal village like an ancient acropolis, the irregular plots of Languedoc and Berry—speak also of very profound human differences."[37]

Do all these complex geographic and human differences render the generic term "peasant" absurd? Is it yet another example of urban prejudice to say that small-holding farmers in Isère hamlets can be studied along with sharecroppers in the Gers, wine-growers in the Marne, or Savoie mountainfolk, and that they are all somehow different from citizens in Paris, Grenoble, or Reims? And how do we solve the thorny problem presented by those rural laborers whose work often placed them *mi-chemin* between agriculture and industry? Tentative generalizations on peasant culture are possible if one believes there was something *sui generis* about rural life, something which distinguished small agrarian communities and the men and women who inhabited them from good-sized bourgs and cities. Shortly after the turn of the century, a sensitive observer of rural France believed that a "profound difference" still existed "between the social organization of agriculture and industry"; and a half-century later a leading rural sociologist stated that rural societies exist "in opposition to urban societies."[38] They were speaking not only of the hard facts of economic taxonomy—producers and consumers—but of distinctive mentalities which survived despite occasional cross-fertilization.

Ted Margadant entitled his magnificent study of the 1851 insurrection *French Peasants in Revolt*, then proceeded to investigate the major roles played by artisans, rural industrial workers, and other non-agricultural inhabitants of the countryside. Often, though not always, peasants stayed home while their rural neighbors marched off to bourgs and market towns to protest Louis Napoleon's coup d'état.[39] The temptation to subsume all the inhabitants of villages, hamlets, and farmsteads into a "peasant" population is great, and, as I hope to show in Part One, not entirely inappropriate in the final decades of the nineteenth century.

French officials had established the somewhat arbitrary but enduring definitions of "urban" and "rural" in 1846: communes with agglomerated populations of over 2000 were designated "urban," all others "rural." Following these distinctions, 62.6 percent of a total population of more than 38 million was still "rural" in 1891.[40] A few years later, Paul Meuriot pointed out that 72 percent of those country people were directly engaged in agriculture, but insisted that other factors, including the physical configuration of communities, the differences between nucleated villages and dispersed hamlets, must also be considered when defining urban and rural characteristics.[41] In the 1880s there were 3.5 million farms in France—a record number—and fourteen million people lived outside agglomerated settings. Of the entire population 60.5 percent still resided in the commune of their birth; an even higher percentage in rural communes. In addition, rural depopulation in the second half of the century led to a proliferation of very small communes: between 1851 and 1896 those with fewer than 500 souls rose

from 15,684 to 18,054, whereas communes with 500 to 5000 inhabitants dropped from 8,756 to 7,657.[42] Cities, of course, continued to
grow, largely because of the influx of provincial immigrants. Although
such statistics tell us nothing about the behavior or beliefs of country
people, we shall see that many rural folk residing in small, dispersed,
agricultural communities were like those described by an observer in
1911: "living inwardly," holding to local customs, memories, work routines, and old political habits.[43]

For Eric Wolf the peasant resides at the center of a series of con-
centric circles, understanding and sharing common experiences with
those closest to him. This inner circle, or "positive reference category,"
may also include artisans who are not yet "so removed from the life
experience of the peasant that they appear as outsiders or strangers."[44]
With the continuing encroachment of the state into a formerly autarkic
world—including the growth of the national market economy and other
factors—the peasant (food producer) and his neighbors are gradually
integrated into a new and broader society. Still—and this is essential
for our story—traditional social relations, ties of kinship, long-standing
customs, ceremonies, and rituals are maintained, not for folkloric purposes, but as vital signs of distinction, as mechanisms used to "ward
off the penetration of outside demands and pressures."[45]

For reasons we shall explore in detail in Part One the great majority
of rural inhabitants at the end of the last century were, in fact, "peasant"; in other words, directly engaged in agriculture. By the 1880s and
90s the countryside had become, in a sense, homogenized, and rural
folk, including those non-agricultural members of small societies who
stayed on the land, maintained particularisms which distinguished their
communities—and their politics. For example, in later chapters dealing
with the dissemination of news concerning Boulangism and the Dreyfus Affair, we shall see how the unique structures of urban and rural
societies required different modes of propaganda; population density,
like literacy rates and local customs, helped determine the form and
impact of national political propaganda.

Meanwhile, popular urban views of rural life rarely bothered with
nuance. In the nineteenth century "peasant" was a loaded word, usually
pejorative and synonymous with "lout." If no longer "savage," peasants
remained for many "rude" and "coarse." Using a vocabulary reminiscent of colonial views of African "natives," observers considered peasants "resigned" and "childlike." But, alas, they were French too, and
therefore "ferociously individualistic."[46] Some were. So were many city
folk. They were often quaint as well. But these clichés reveal more
about the observers than the observed. Peasants themselves preferred

the more neutral terms *cultivateur* or *agriculteur* until the beginning of the new century when *paysan* became acceptable. Today many French farmers proudly call themselves "peasant." With that important qualification I shall do the same.

In 1790, officials subdivided the ancient provinces of France into *départements*. Bureaucracy was facilitated, and, in most cases, the new departments comprised functional regions based on complementary exchange of produce between smaller *pays*. For the historian, however, the advantages of taxonomy must be weighed against the dangers of treating the administrative unit as something homogeneous. One must look beyond the department to individual localities and consider specific economies and cultures to understand better how country people viewed the immediate and distant world: the village, the region, France.[47]

The economic and political histories of each locality are essential considerations, but there is much to learn, too, from Paul Sébillot, Arnold Van Gennep, and others who stress folkloric divisions. The perils of fossilization through folklore are many, but such methods, used carefully, can provide advantages for the historian of rural France. Small societies studied on their own merits with their own customs may be woven into the regional and national picture revealing similarities as well as differences in the countryside. For example, when it came to national politics, we shall see that dispersed villages and hamlets hundreds of kilometers apart often had more in common with each other than they did with nearby cities and towns in their own departments. Perceptions of space, definitions of boundaries, are vital to an understanding of the workings of rural politics.

That blend of arbitrariness and reason which marked the original choice of *départements* has informed my selection as well. Among the recent histories of rural France cited above, some have examined a single province, department, or village; others have explored a dozen or more localities. I realized early on that a comparison of only two departments—one rural-agricultural, the other urban-industrial—might perpetuate the myth of "two nations." Too many villages in departments throughout France at the end of the nineteenth century remained on the penumbra, with, for example, rural industries surviving in the face of rapid urbanization. My two choices quickly became six: the departments of the Gers, Marne, Isère, Savoie, Orne, and Vendée. Although the story which follows includes evidence from all these areas, I have focused in Chapter III and elsewhere, on a representative quartet: the agricultural Gers in Gascony and Orne in Normandy; the

Marne in Champagne, with its large cities, industries, and wine-growing communities; and, finally, the Isère in the Dauphiné, a department
with scores of semi-agricultural, semi-industrial communes.

How did depopulation and entrenched Bonapartism in the Gers and
industrialization, Radical republicanism, and population growth in the
Marne influence rural reactions to Boulangism and the Dreyfus Affair?
The Isère falls between these two poles: active industrial centers with
developing socialist organizations shared departmental space with poor,
isolated, and conservative mountain villages. What, if anything, did
politics in the pre-Alps of the Isère and neighboring Savoie have in
common with the politics of the plains? How, why, and with what results
did Boulangists and, later, political anti-Semites adjust their propaganda to fit the diverse needs, desires, and backgrounds of men and
women in the Orne, a center of much Boulangist organization, or in
the Vendée, with its long history of militant Catholicism? What did
images of a General on horseback or shouts of "Death to the Jews"
mean to country people in the Marne, close to Paris, and the Gers,
600 kilometers to the southwest?

The three parts of this study, in their broad outlines, move from
the general to the specific. Part One offers an overview of rural customs
and politics in late nineteenth-century France. It includes material from
a number of departments, then moves on to a detailed investigation
of the geography, economics, politics, and people of the Gers, Orne,
Isère and Marne on the eve of the Boulanger and Dreyfus Affairs.
Part Two deals first with the dissemination of Boulangist propaganda
from Paris to the provinces—and, again, discusses many regions—then
focuses on the impact of the movement in four departments. Part
Three, on the Dreyfus Affair, follows a similar course: after a general
survey of religious, economic, and political anti-Semitism throughout
rural France—the myths, legends, people, and publications mobilized
for and against Dreyfus—it concentrates on the Affair in specific villages and hamlets. Here, in Chapter VI, the four-department format
used to study Boulangism is replaced by a more impressionistic view
of rural responses to the Dreyfus Affair in other departments. Boulangism, a political movement with reams of propaganda, campaign
speeches, and election statistics, provides more data for the historian
of the countryside. Reactions to the Dreyfus Affair, on the other hand,
are harder to grasp for three reasons: a misreading by officials of the
workings of rural politics (a confusion of local differences with political
indifference); sparse evidence in some rural areas; and a genuine lack
of interest in the Affair in others. Significant numbers of country
people paid little or no attention to the Dreyfus Affair, but their silence

can be as telling as their impassioned moments of interest and involvement.

Studies from the French Revolution and Terror, through 1848-51 to the Communes of 1871 have stressed the checkerboard nature of provincial responses to national events. On the political map of France areas of intense engagement have always been surrounded by patches of ignorance and indifference. We shall see that such rural diversity persisted in the late 1880s and 90s, as did skewed urban views of what rural politics was all about. Only close analyses of individual localities can make sense of what seems so arbitrary. Reactions to politics and propaganda in the countryside have never been so uniform as urban politicians (and some historians) would like to believe.

In a German wood during the Thirty Years' War, musketeers ordered a strange hermit to lead them out of the forest's maze. Simplicissimus complied: "To get rid of these unfriendly guests as soon as possible, I led them by the nearest road to the village. . . . Truth to tell, that was the only road I knew."[48] Two centuries later French peasants enjoyed many contacts with the outside world, but their roads were still marked by ancient memories and habits. Rural responses to national politics followed a particular road not because peasants were simple-minded, but because, truth to tell, it was often the only road they knew.

PART ONE

———————

THE RURALIZATION OF
MODERN FRANCE

CHAPTER I

COUNTRY PEOPLE,
COUNTRY WAYS

---

*Parce que les paysans ont cessé de danser la
bourrée et qu'ils abandonnent leur vieille blouse
bleue, il ne faut pas nous figurer que tout est
changé.*

MICHEL AUGÉ-LARIBÉ, 1912

On a May market day in 1895 socialists in the Isère mining town of
La Mure held a meeting to attract visitors from the countryside. Addressing 400 inhabitants "de tous environs," a deputy began his political
appeal with "Vous paysans." There it ended. The audience jeered,
shouted, hissed, and ignored all attempts to restore order. The deputy
and his colleagues tried to calm the crowd but, says the mayor, the
meeting degenerated into a ludicrous *bouffonnerie* and had to be quickly
terminated.[1] The mayor might have held a political or personal grudge
against these visiting socialists—the audience reaction might have been
less farcical than depicted—but it is the truncated introduction which
concerns us here. What type of rural inhabitant attended the meeting?
Unhappily, the evidence hides more than it reveals. Given the nature
of the Isère, most were probably small-holding farmers come to market. But did field hands, domestics, artisans, wine-growers, or peasants
who worked in the local mining industry also attend? Was the politician's inflection condescending—the offhand slur of an imperious deputy—or was "Vous paysans" uttered straightforwardly, even sympa-
thetically, and still to no avail? Crucial questions, never to be answered.
But who were these folks "de tous environs"?

Tidy definitions of the countryside are impossible. One finds many
blurred distinctions, many exceptions, to the strict "city versus country"
rule at the end of the century: butchers in the inner city of Limoges
maintained ancient traditions commonly associated with atavistic peas-

ants, while workers in outlying faubourgs, many of them recent rural migrants, developed a class consciousness and led the way to modern political organization.[2] Daniel Halévy, traveling through the Centre, mentioned those towns—"half urban, half village-like"—which were set off from isolated peasant hamlets, yet removed from bustling provincial cities.[3] Industrialization and urbanization in the Lyon region did not completely destroy rural industries in outlying bourgs and villages; on the contrary, as in Limoges, there was an important interlacing of the rural and urban industrial worlds. Throughout the century France consisted of many "cities without borders," many "towns still countrified."[4]

Marx characterized the separation of city and country as the first division of a population into two classes;[5] and, with Engels, said that the bourgeoisie "agglomerated the population, centralized means of production, and concentrated property in a few hands." Political centralization followed, and "independent, or but loosely connected provinces . . . became lumped together into one nation. . . ."[6] State centralization and the growth of large-scale industrial capitalism were two of the most important and pervasive motive forces of change in the nineteenth century. Yet we shall see that the state could centralize, industry could grow, and urban and rural populations could proletarianize without destroying crucial aspects of rural culture. In much of France, despite blurred distinctions, the town-versus-country conflict had not yet been "confined to historical museums."[7]

The size, location, and economic activity of a rural community helped determine the impact the locality had on immediate and nearby residents. "Proto-urban" centers—bourgs and market towns in rural regions—facilitated the spread of Montagnard politics in 1851;[8] and, at the end of the century, new ideas and political movements, still traveled more easily through nucleated communities.[9] Peasants who became porcelain workers in the faubourgs of Limoges, for instance, could be distinguished from their distant countrymen in outlying agricultural hamlets. Topography continued to be an essential factor in shaping human differences, much as it had been 300 years before in the Mediterranean region so exquisitely painted by Fernand Braudel.

In the late nineteenth century both contemporary travelers and peasants stressed a difference between villages and the world beyond. Emilie Carles in the Hautes-Alpes emphasized the tightly knit world in which she lived,[10] and Emile Guillaumin in the Allier reckoned that "one can divide rural people into two categories: those of the region and those of the village. . . . Personalities of a region" who travel extensively and often; "petits gens" of a commune who rarely venture far from home.[11] Auguste Santerre, a laborer who worked on large, sophisticated farms in the north, said that he "would like to see something other than the fields. . . . I was born in 1889 and since my childhood I have only seen the fields. And still it is the soil that I gaze upon, because I hardly have time to admire the landscape."[12] In the twentieth century, peasants working in a forest clearing did not know an area less than ten kilometers away. They were aware of the village where they sold wood twenty kilometers down the road, but "outside a specific line, they were unaware of space."[13]

On rural fields and roads conceptions of space and time differed from those on city streets and in urban factories. In agricultural communities frenetic work was concentrated in a few summer and fall months, and the rest of the year was reserved for no less back-breaking maintenance, repairs, feeding of livestock, and sporadic oases of leisure. This "milieu naturel" contrasted within the "milieu technique" in cities and industrial towns where artificial schedules replaced natural cycles, indoor work shifts supplanted dawn-to-dusk labor, and seasons lost their significance (though the poor were no less cold in urban tenements than in rural shacks). Leisure industries and fashion designers found new uses for sunshine and snow. Land, the essential ingredient of agricultural life, was bought, used, and sold in the city with little—or at least different—attachment. Zola's avaricious Beauce peasants displayed heartless greed for land at the end of the century, but this had evolved in a unique time and place, shaped by legacies of *morcellement* and intense family rivalries which we shall explore in more detail below. While town and country moved closer together, the different ways in which peasants and bourgeois lived and worked—including how they addressed politics—survived as the new century approached.[14]

Much has been written about rural exodus and the economic crises which fueled the flight from the countryside; about decaying villages like Chaudan in the Hautes-Alpes with its closed inns, empty stables, abandoned fields, and, in this case, families exchanging property for land in Africa. "The village of Chaudan will soon disappear and become an African colony."[15] A strong and numerous peasantry sent not only food to the table but (many believed) right-minded politicians to the Chamber, and these decades were marked by entreaties, as Jules Méline put it, to "return to the land." The *Georgics* had been written to hold peasants to the soil, and late nineteenth-century appeals waxed as enthusiastic (if not as rhapsodic) as Virgil's. Still, they had little effect. Rural decline provided an important theme for doomsaying politicians, including, as we shall see, Boulangists and, later, anti-Semites. But in

order to grasp the nature of rural communes in the 1880s and 90s—
and how their inhabitants might or might not react to Boulangism or
the Dreyfus Affair—we must know more about who left, who remained, and most importantly, how the latter viewed national politics.

Traditional accounts of rural exodus and depopulation rarely venture beyond sentimental laments about the world we have lost, and
many overstress the glittering attractions of the city, especially fin de
siècle Paris. The capital, a "modern Babylon" for Stendhal's characters
earlier in the century, stands as a beacon of opportunity in the literature
of peasant exodus. Most country people, however, never got that far.
Only detailed regional studies can adequately explain complex migration patterns and the forces behind local economic and demographic
changes in the countryside.

In general, both emigration and low or falling human fertility led
to rural decline. Paul Hohenberg tells us that the excess of births over
deaths fell from "some 60,000 per year in 1876-81 to *minus* 8,000 in
1891-96 in fifty-eight departments covering most of the *campagne*."
Enclaves of high or stable fertility remained, but the falling birth rate
which so worried contemporary observers was—no less than emigration—a striking and pervasive feature of rural France.[16]

Meanwhile, new roads and railroads, facilitating communications
and spreading urban goods and services to country people, helped
change the structure of French agriculture. In Calvados, as in other
areas, railroads and the competition of new markets meant that farmers
lost their age-old "geographic privileges." Distant economic centers
became "more and more indispensable" and eclipsed local markets.[17]
This development, combined with rural deindustrialization, acceler-
ated exodus.

While polyculture remained the base of French agriculture, increasing numbers of peasants in Normandy, Gascony, Dauphiné and elsewhere responded to new economic pressures by turning to animal
husbandry. "He who marries has a lovely day," said peasants near
Toulouse, "He who kills a pig has a beautiful week."[18] Livestock raising
and dairy farming saved many former cereal growers who felt the
impact of a declining labor force and national and international competition (linked, again, to the railroads). The Paris basin—that rich
expanse of agricultural land where thousands of hectares of wheat
spread across the horizon interrupted only by a windmill or the spires
of a cathedral like Chartres—the Paris basin had long been a cereal-
producing region serving the capital. But it could not become the major
commercial "bread basket" that it is the twentieth century until structural transformations reshaped French agriculture. Although the proc-

esses of mechanization after 1900, and *remembrement* after 1945, go far beyond the scope of this study, it is important to note that the origins of these structural changes date from the late nineteenth century, and that rural France in the 1880s and 90s was not a static society made up exclusively of decaying villages and unemployed agricultural laborers in search of the first train out.

In fact, contrary to conventional wisdom, agricultural workers did not always move *en masse* to cities, towns and industrial centers. Many, perhaps most, did, but along with village artisans suffering dislocations brought by large-scale industrialization, significant numbers of rural workers acquired land and became peasant farmers.[19] Small holdings of five to thirty hectares increased in number down to the last decade of the century, above all in the West and South. The declining number of large farms is associated with a fall in the number of agricultural laborers, which suggests that while many workers moved to cities and towns, others bought or rented land.[20] Again, the French countryside, like French history, is a landscape of exceptions. There is no doubt that rural populations declined rapidly, and specific examples of that decline will be presented in the next chapter. Broadly speaking, however, many longtime rural residents also stayed on the land (at least temporarily) to pursue agricultural activities which, in turn, had been reshaped by the growth and impact of new communications networks and competition.

The "modernization" of rural France brought by the "agencies of change" so expertly outlined by Eugen Weber,[21] led to an ironic consequence in the final decades of the century: the "ruralization" of modern France. Philippe Pinchemel's comments on Picardy apply elsewhere:

> villages became exclusively agricultural communities with, here and there, a merchant and a few other non-agricultural workers; this impoverishment of the socio-professional structure, this 'ruralization' of the countryside, is in fact recent, dating from the second half of the nineteenth century.[22]

Early Third Republic observers, and many historians, oversimplify the scenario when they describe tidal waves of "peasants" sweeping out of isolated villages into industrial centers. Exodus had indeed become a "neurotic worry,"[23] but working farmers very often stayed on the land while many of their neighbors—rural bourgeois, artisans, shopkeepers, workers in small industries, and others—left. Pinchemel continues:

Rural communities where *cultivateurs* . . . lived in a variegated social structure alongside artisans, factory workers, and merchants, were eclipsed by villages comprised almost exclusively of *cultivateurs* and agricultural workers; the evolution led, in a sense, to a simplification of the social structure, to a "ruralization."[24]

Southwest of Picardy in the Norman countryside, and farther south still in the hinterlands of Toulouse, depressed land prices at the end of the century prompted many rural bourgeois to sell out to local peasants and, to a lesser degree, agricultural workers. A "hierarchical structure," says Roger Brunet speaking for others, was replaced by "an egalitarian community" dominated by small landowners.[25]

The decline of rural industry, along with the type of exodus described above, helped create "an agrarian world which resembled the 'traditional' countryside. . . ."[26] Traditional in the sense that agriculture dominated while rural industry diminished; yet far from traditional in light of widespread advances in education, new roads and railroads, and a generally improved quality of life. The heterogeneous villages of 1800 or even 1850—with their rich patchwork of rural notables, notaries, artisans, peasants, and laborers—had become more exclusively agricultural societies. This "pastoralization" of rural France—its economic and demographic transformation—had important cultural and political consequences which would shape the mode and timber of peasant reactions to Parisian events.

Peasants who stayed on the land were, on the average, older than town- and city-dwellers. A mayor in the Lot in 1889 grieved at the sight of youths setting off for the city, leaving, he reported, villages filled with old people and children. A decade later, the socialist Emile Vandervelde described a void created by the flight of the young and the strong: "only the aged remain." In Picardy the "departure of young people" had a severe effect on the birthrate in the countryside; it was a period marked by an "aging of the rural population." Exodus from the Southwest also drained rural regions of young adults, and led to an overall population decline. In some areas only a "few good old folks" (*quelques bons vieux*) worked the land.[27] The next chapter will offer more examples of this "aging" process, but these descriptions and others confirm that the emigration of young men and women became more and more frequent between 1870 and 1914. There were exceptions of course—septugenarians and juveniles did not completely overrun peasant communes—but, beyond doubt, the young and active left the countryside in great numbers. Fictional characters in nineteenth-century *Bildungsromane*, newly arrived in Paris from the provinces, had thousands of real-life (and more humble) counterparts: young country people moving to cities and towns in search of a better life. "The loss of manpower is killing agriculture," warned a Norman peasant in 1884. "If workers were less assured of being aided in case of unemployment or sickness in the city, they would not desert villages as often. As it stands now, very few young men return among us after their military service: they are staying in the cities."[28]

Those who remained on the land were not doddering illiterates condemned to a relentlessly static life; isolated villages in the Massif Central, Alps, or Upper Var were exceptions (though no less important for that). Yet, in agricultural villages and hamlets throughout France, the memories and habits of the predominant older generations, less challenged by youthful harbingers of change, would continue to influence the actions and reactions of rural people. The "routine" of peasant life, said Marc Bloch, is formed and perpetuated by grandparents tending and instructing children while parents work (or move away); in this way, traditions persist.[29] When older people abound and many young adults depart, a society will reflect the world view of the dominant generational unit. Considered along with the geographic and economic distinctions of agricultural communities, and the ongoing routine of rural life, we can see that changes would come slowly, skirmishing as they must with entrenched conventions.

"Generation location," said Karl Mannheim,

is based on the existence of biological rhythm . . . the factors of life and death, a limited span of life, and aging. Individuals who belong to the same generation, who share the same year of birth, are endowed, to that extent, with a common location in the historical dimension of the social process.[30]

But that is not enough: there must be a similarity of location, "one must be born within the same historical and cultural region." And an additional factor is needed to make a *Generationszusammenhang*—generation as an actuality—useful for the historian: there must be a "*participation in the common destiny* of this historical and social unit."[31] Mature members of rural communities shared a complex of experiences which set their generation apart from those which preceded or followed. French conscript "classes," like African "age-sets," were only the most obvious manifestations of this subtle process. One finds no strict unity of thought or action, only a common participation in certain events and changes. "Obviously all generations are overlapping," remarks H. Stuart Hughes, "all are somewhat arbitrarily defined. But at the same time they tend to shape their own definitions through common experiences."[32] French men and women born between 1825 and 1835 might recall the political upheavals of mid-century—a few might have participated in them—but by the late 1880s the great majority knew only the Empire and early Republic. And many peasants who stayed on the land knew and cared most about the history, politics, and people of their own locality.

Positions of power and influence once filled by local nobles and notables—political activism once the domain of, among others, young rural artisans—were giving way to farming communities dominated and administered by seasoned peasants.[33] Personal pressure, rivalries, and feuds—always important features of rural politics—still played a crucial role. Now, more and more, peasants alone participated in the "common destiny" of their locality; and they continued to address national politics sometimes with avid interest, often as an irrelevance, but always in their own style formed by their own priorities, their own past and present. An analysis of the workings of rural politics in the late nineteenth century must consider the significance of this interplay of exodus, falling birth rates, aging, and the "agriculturalization" of the countryside. Peasants stayed to cultivate the land while others left, and their traditional political cultures stayed with them.

A painting by Lhermitte of 1883 entitled *La Moisson* shows a weathered farmer pausing from his work in the fields, one arm raised to wipe sweat from his brow, the other cradling an immense and ancient scythe (see fig. 1). His clothes, tools, and wooden clogs would soon be catalogued by folklorists eager to capture a vanishing rural world. In the 1880s, however, this old but active peasant was, in many respects, typical of rural France.[34]

Factors other than the size and economic activity of a community shaped rural routines and influenced residents' views of each other and the world beyond. Small agro-towns and villages with worker-peasant populations could maintain a cultural cohesion similar to that found in pure farming centers. The number of peasants, wine-growers, mine-workers, day laborers, sharecroppers, or wood-cutters in a village can tell us much about hierarchies, class and status divisions, and possible sources of influence and resentment. But the physical proximity of a limited number of residents coupled with generations of shared experiences also helped distinguish rural localities. Villages with residents of long standing, and with large local kin groups, sustained specific identities longer than those undergoing constant social and structural changes, and far longer, of course, than cities.[35] Marx's ob-

1. *La Moisson*, Lhermitte

servations on an "identity of interest" and a "local interconnection" among peasants apply to individual communities a generation after Louis Bonaparte's coup.[36] With few exceptions, those residents who stayed in the countryside remained closely bound to their villages and to each other. Theirs was an "identity of interest" based sometimes on ignorance and isolation, but more often on familiarity, shared experiences, and, often, kinship.[37]

In a Lorraine village in our century differentiations between local metallurgy workers and farmers have not led to irreconcilable social differences. A cultural unity persists "based essentially on *l'ancienne appartenance* of each member to the village, and on a communal equality not yet disrupted by the state and the political ideologies which it conveys."[38] Similar face-to-face societies survived at the end of the last century, and invariably recast local and national issues into the mold of indigenous culture. "As long as a culture possesses some vitality, external pressures . . . can be integrated into . . . the universe of the community without totally upsetting" the uniqueness of that special world.[39] Profound changes accompanied state centralization and the development of large scale industry at the end of the century, and countryfolk often felt those changes as acutely as any other sector of the population; after all, their land was overtaxed by a distant government, their family members left home, and (on the positive side) they too enjoyed new comforts. Peasants knew that *la politique du clocher* must give way to a new and broader focus, but an expanding horizon did not immediately destroy age-old rural boundaries.

The point is this: rural societies held to a constellation of economic, geographic, cultural and human characteristics which rendered their politics—local and national—a reflection not only of externally imposed changes but also of internally conditioned realities. To remark that this or that village was "reactionary" or "radical," "Boulangist" or Dreyfusard," is to employ a traditional urban vocabulary which obscures more often than it instructs. In order to grasp how and why rural French men and women rallied to Boulanger or considered Dreyfus a remote irrelevance, a different vocabulary is needed; one which includes the internal peculiarities of rural communities and explores how local people addressed national politics on their own specific and often very narrow terms.

Country people from diverse regions have composed village portraits which share what we might call a common iconography of rural life. Reflecting on the years preceding World War I in the Beauce (a region, like the Champagne, close to Paris and noted for expansive farms and early mechanization), one peasant said that "people knew only those who shared the world of the village."[40] Reports from other communities from Brittany to the Alps also stress the survival of strong local attachments which influenced their views of life outside the village.[41]

But local cultural unity is not synonymous with harmony. Bitter battles, political and social, could rage among residents who detested each other, yet whose larger universe was populated by remarkably similar heros and villains. Local class divisions must be sorted out with care. "Startling" distinctions continued between day laborers who owned plots of land and "the agricultural worker who will never be a landowner and knows he will never be."[42] Employees who lived in the community and maintained close contact with individual farmers, for example, should be distinguished from transient laborers migrating from distant locales. One close observer confirmed that "a lack of cohesion characterizes the agricultural working class."[43]

The interrelationship of workers and owners—permanent residents in a single village—suggests that hierarchical distinctions could coexist within a local cultural unity: not "agrarianism" or "corporatism"—a strict commonality of peasant interests as against the urban industrial world—but familiarity among diverse peoples which could, in turn, influence the ways a society viewed external events. During the wine-growers' protests of 1903-1907 in the Midi, large landowners felt the wrath not only of the workers, but of entire communities marching in concert. Early political organization emerged in the context of "traditional social unity among villagers. . . ."[44]

At mid-century Emma Bovary's small town rewarded an old rural domestic for many years of faithful service to one family. Four decades later in the Isère, workers still received agricultural medals for "bons services" of thirty years or more on the same farm.[45] To the north, in the Vosges, festivities honored domestics and shepherds who had served a single household for up to forty years: Jean Robert "was so much a part of the Lalloué family for whom he worked that no one in the village knew his real surname. For years they had called him Jean Lalloué."[46] Workers were often integrated into the household to such a degree that employers considered them relatives, and employers' children called them "uncle" and "aunt." A fermière from lower Normandy described the intimacy that reigned at veillées and in the fields among workers and landowners who comprised a "true family."[47] In the Marne and other departments, owners and field-hands commonly worked, ate, drank, and socialized together: an intimate, if not idyllic society in which everyone lived "under the eyes of his neighbors."[48] In 1899 in parts of the Dauphiné and Gascony, peasants might be "day laborers and small proprietors at the same time . . . the same workers are employed by the same owners [and] this aspect of permanence engenders excellent social relations. . . ."[49] Idealized portraits to be sure—such relations could also engender hostility—but the fact remains that rural proletarians must be considered not as statistics on a long list of the disinherited, but as integral members of face-to-face communities.

In regions where farmers hired temporary labor at harvest time, moissoneurs often worked for the same owner from year to year. Proprietors and permanent laborers left specific chores to hired hands— mowing, for example—but all joined in a traditional feast at the close of the season. In 1891 in the Southeast workers still marked the end of their seasonal employment by forming a procession and setting off for the owner's house. Once there they offered a gift (usually a decorated cross of corn) then sat down to a copious feast. In mountain regions of the Isère and Savoie, neighboring communes constrained by short summers and difficult harvests worked together for a few feverish days, then gathered for a huge meal attended by a hundred or more local peasants and workers.[50] *Fête de la moisson* was a feast and more; it was "harvest home," words which tell much about the close, domestic nature of rural sociability.

This is not to describe peasant life as a joyous gambol complete with festivities and mutual respect. All was not harmonious. Harvesters staged periodic rural strikes and demanded higher wages and better conditions. But strikes waged by laborers who migrated to large farms must be distinguished from grievances expressed by local workers who shared time, toil, space, and perhaps family ties with proprietors;[51] especially when those proprietors also worked the land.

Long-standing feuds between villages or hamlets also helped form and perpetuate a community's self-image. We shall see that communal rivalries presented a problem during the annual drawing of military lots (*tirage au sort*) at the time of the Dreyfus Affair. Here, let three examples suffice. At the end of the century Gimont was one of the few agglomerated communities in the Gers. Almost 2,000 inhabitants resided in the town center, with 350 scattered in outlying hamlets. In 1888 the police commissioner described a marked difference in attitude and political involvement not only between these distinct sectors, but between residents in the upper and lower town as well. Rivalries were so acute that politicians of every persuasion had to maintain separate offices and appeal to separate geographical interests in dispersed and nucleated sections of the commune.[52] In 1890, the Vendée commune of Sainte Florence was divided into two warring factions. The small section of L'Oie had asked to become a separate commune, thereby so infuriating the mayor (a resident of Sainte Florence) that he planned to make the poor, old, and indigent of L'Oie trek twelve kilometers to fetch their traditional July 14 bread. Politics, local and national, would be colored by this bitter communal feud.[53] Far to the southeast in the Savoie, the residents of Saint François complained in 1902 that the neighboring village, Montgellafry (the commune's *chef-lieu*), had pressured and threatened them during recent legislative elections: "the inhabitants of Montgellafry, who are absolutely hostile to the government, while the section of Saint François is devoted, exert a veritable terror on residents who no longer dare to vote at the Montgellafry town hall."[54]

In rural societies where personal and family ties were extensive and daily contact the rule, politics, like gossip, traveled through this maze of complex relationships taking on particular characteristics which localized the issue at hand. Outside events, grafted onto existing alliances or feuds, were imbued with extra meaning: complicated not simplified.

If an unpopular mayor declared himself a Boulangist, a beneficent schoolteacher a Dreyfusard, rivals or allies might use that added information to formulate or solidify political and personal opinions. To stress the importance of personalities in rural politics is not to deny the significance of ideology or to underestimate the peasant's ability to comprehend abstractions inherent in national events. It is, instead, to understand that country people could share the concerns of city dwellers while maintaining unique and intimate avenues of political exchange. It is a question of learning how external issues arrived in rural communities, how they were received, rejected, or acted upon, by residents who knew much more about their neighbors than most city folk knew about theirs. As André Siegfried put it, any attempt to define "political temperament" must concentrate not only on opinions, but on the way opinions are formed.[55]

Frequent contact with villagers privy to information about outside events made the discussion of those events as subjective as it was sociable. Strategic positions occupied by mayors, priests, teachers, and innkeepers contributed not only to the dissemination of news but to its interpretation and impact as well. The importance of priests and schoolteachers is well known and will be discussed in more detail later, but other local officials continued to exert pressure and influence on peasants in outlying hamlets and farmsteads at the end of the nineteenth century: rural guards, town criers, and postmen await their historians.

A decree of 20 Messidor, Year III, called for the appointment of one rural guard in every commune to patrol property and report untoward activity to the *Conseil général*. After 1884, mayors nominated local guards (with the consent of the prefect and subprefect), and they came increasingly from the ranks of the "most devoted partisans of the mayor." One manual published in Grenoble in 1887 maintained that the post of *garde-champêtre* had become far too politicized and, not infrequently, corrupt. Meager salaries of 100 to 800 francs a year did not help discourage foul play.[56]

The guard often doubled as local farmer or day laborer. Although recruitment of men over 60 years of age was discouraged, many communes had guards in their seventies or eighties. Guidelines recommended, but did not require, that they be literate.[57] Obligations to the mayor, and constant contact with peasants living away from the village center, made rural guards ideal political messengers. Though they were technically prohibited from discussing politics, little had changed since mid-century when guards in the Alpine region played an important role in the repression of republican propaganda; or since 1876 when a guard in the Haute-Garonne went "from house to house . . . speaking especially to women, reading them a Bonapartist brochure . . . accompanying it all with diatribes against the Republican candidate."[58] In the Vendée in 1888, for example, officials reprimanded one guard for calling republicans "canailles" and "voleurs," and for tracking down peasants on election eve with promises of liquor in return for "reactionary" votes.[59] And similar reports come from other communes.

Instruction manuals warned guards to avoid familiarity and all knowledge of the "secrets of certain persons or certain families."[60] They would not have bothered with such regulations had the dangers not been real. The evidence suggests that guards followed these orders about as well as they adhered to strict rules against "drunkenness, intemperance, and overexcitement." The prefect of the Marne was inundated with complaints about the constant state of drunkenness of gardes-champêtres in communes like Binarville in 1890, where one guard submitted his retirement papers to the municipal council in the same condition he had been conducting his daily rounds for years: drunk.[61]

"Abstain from all interference in elections and remain extremely circumspect," advised one instruction manual. Many did, but for others temptations or pressures were too great. As late as 1900 in the Marne commune of Cormontreuil, residents protested "acts of pressure and intimidation."[62] A decade earlier in the same department, the mayor of Sainte-Marie-à-Py had refused to certify a local guard. Politics and personalities were at the root of the problem, compounded by the mayor's unfortunate habit of abusing hunting laws the guard had tried to enforce. In Trépail, the republican mayor accused the guard of conspiring with his reactionary predecessor. But the guard denied the charges, alleging that he had been badgered ever since he had arrested the mayor's brother and other family members. The crime is not revealed, nor is the fate of the guard, but the report shows that his job entailed more than daily protection of rural property.[63]

Nominally, gardes-champêtres were servants of all the people; but they were dependent on the mayor and the municipal council, and a close watch on the political predilections of rural residents was as much a part of their agenda as were border disputes and stray sheep. In the Gers, guards and postmen carried Paul de Cassagnac's conservative politics to peasant communities. The patronage system, widespread and sophisticated in the Bas Armagnac, required most local officials to serve as emissaries for Cassagnac, patroling the politics of his flock of sharecroppers and tenant farmers.[64] In the Vendée, the illiterate, often drunk, and always violent garde-champêtre of Tardière sold "reactionary politics" as well as *eau de vie* to village residents. Local officials fired him after he knocked out the front teeth and broke the legs of the wife of a client whose liquor bill was past due. Interestingly, villagers considered the guard's teen-aged sons even more frightening than the father: the young women of Tardière lived in constant fear. There is little here to suggest an arcadian country life or an ideal environment for calm and measured rural politics.[65]

Other visitors frequented peasant homes. After 1863 all communes theoretically enjoyed daily delivery of the mail, and postal officials boasted that their hearty *facteurs ruraux* trekked an average of 11,000 kilometers a year, or the equivalent of seven times around the world in a career.[66] Most important, however, were the few kilometers they walked each day from the *chef-lieu*, "reading newspapers along the way" and recounting news events upon arrival in outlying communes.[67] If Roger Martin du Gard's portrait of village life is correct, postmen read not only the news but the letters they carried as well, and reported "little secrets"—personal and political—to their ally the mayor. For a price.[68] Like rural guards they were scrutinized by agents of the state. In the Gers, officials considered postmen scandalous subjects worthy of close investigation prior to elections. In 1888 a police commissioner reported that three of the five local postmen were drunk and reactionary, the other two (it is assumed) sober and republican. *Facteurs ruraux* also played a role in the spread of Boulangist propaganda in the countryside, along with peddlers, *chanteurs ambulants*, even barbers. Furthermore, news still reached many country people through the town crier whose tone, inflection, and personal opinions must have shaded the meaning and interpretation of local and national political issues.[69]

Still other relationships crept into rural politics and prejudiced village residents. In September 1899, while "the eyes of the civilized world" were upon Captain Dreyfus at Rennes,[70] police arrested two women in a field near the village of Clelles (Isère) for throwing stones at each other. One pressed charges and the other accused her opponent of loose morals. The reason for the skirmish is unclear, perhaps because the case proved impossible to adjudicate. All the witnesses—local peasants, tenant farmers, wheelrights—were related to one of the two combatants.[71] Family ties influenced organized politics as well as personal scuffles. In 1890 municipal council members in Jâlons (Marne) nominated a "reactionary" rural guard, to the displeasure of republican residents. The appointment was especially dangerous, said one villager, because the guard had a number of relatives in the commune, including a son-in-law running a local café, who would assist in the dissemination of frightful pressure and propaganda. Inhabitants might fall victim to "vengeance and hatred"; besides, the guard was a notorious "sinner and poacher."[72]

Municipal councils were often small coalitions built on family ties as well as political opinions. In the Isère commune of Auris two brothers and three brothers-in-law sat on the same council. Other members complained that politics had become far too incestuous.[73] In the nearby village of Venosc, 90 percent of the 570 residents had been born in the commune, and most others came from neighboring localities. Of nineteen councilmen, nine belonged to the Balme family, and a glance at Venosc's register reveals no fewer than 80 Balme and 35 Roux residing in the small commune.[74] In 1888 the rural guard of Cernay-les-Reims (Marne) was unable to perform his duties because too many of the 705 residents had family members on the municipal council. He told the prefect that "more than half the population is related . . . to local officials."[75] In the Gers, where the majority of rural inhabitants resided in the commune of their birth, powerful family networks commonly associated with nationally known figures like Cassagnac could be found in the smallest communities. The political life of Saint Brès, for instance, was dominated by a father and son who served as the commune's mayors for 53 years, from 1852 to 1905.[76] In neighboring Tarn-et-Garonne "consanguity is widespread," said one observer, and census lists show village families dating back three centuries. A local proverb advised that you should "Prends la fille de ton voisin / Que tu vois passer chaque matin."[77] You could, of course, take your neighbor's daughter and leave his politics, but family ties were bound to color the opinions of intimate village members.

In 1884 the republican mayor of Sère (Gers) sent letters to two political rivals saying that their daughters were rumored to be "in an interesting condition." He demanded a doctor's report within 48 hours. The young women were in no such condition, and their fathers complained to the prefect. Hoping to convince the rural population that the republican government would rise above local feuds and protect villagers regardless of political views, the prefect dismissed the mayor. In the same department the mayor and schoolteacher of Saint Arailles arranged for the tricolor to be flown from the church tower. Within two hours it was stolen, taken to the grave of the mayor's daughter, and torn apart, the red strip being hung around the tomb's cross. Officials never found the culprit, but the mayor accused his reactionary predecessor who had once vowed that a tricolor would never fly from the church.[78] Finally, Emilie Carles said that in the Dauphiné her father and the mayor were bitter enemies, not for ideological reasons, but because "old rivalries had forever pitted the two families against each other."[79]

Family ties, familiarity, personal pressure, and indebtedness of every sort became inextricably linked with politics. The historian attempting to understand national issues in the countryside must consider human relationships which cut across or obscured ideological lines. As late as the 1930s Guillaumin maintained that

> old families in each village still form a type of tribe, sharing the same work methods, anxieties, language, and cast of mind; with an identical feeling of defiant reserve, if not hostility, toward the outsider.[80]

And the insider as well. A generation later, during municipal council elections in Lorraine, one candidate lamented "I have no family ties, and one has to be a superman in this village to be elected without a family."[81] Such communities were not unique to the east, and the survival of this phenomenon—as in a Creuse village in 1974 where 149 residents were "linked by common relations" and 82 others shared at least a first cousin[82]—suggests that kin groups have long been a critical factor in French rural life.

How and when personal relationships merged (or converged) with political issues is as essential to explore as it is difficult to pinpoint. Boulangism and the Dreyfus Affair mixed with private feuds and rivalries of long standing, but given the priorities of local officials, they were often ignored, passed over for traditional definitions of political alignments. We can only bear in mind that in many rural communes at the end of the century, families and personalities contributed, *pace* André Siegfried, to the "political temperament" of country people. The historian of the countryside does well to remember T. S. Eliot's belief that "Between the idea / And the reality / Between the motion / And the act / Falls the shadow."[83]

In the late 1880s when Boulangists set out to garner support in departments from the Nord to the Isère—and a decade later when Dreyfusards and anti-Dreyfusards attempted to export the Parisian event to the provinces—rural communities were in the midst of startling transformations. Peasant societies continued to display an "individual entelechy" and "tempo" very different from the cities'; but they were no longer "slowly changing" or "largely static."[84] Instead, they were a complex amalgam of movement (exodus, education, increased literacy, the stirrings of mechanization and new political organizations) and cultural survival (agricultural villages with long-time residents clinging to work routines and traditional patterns of sociability and politics). Those who remained on the land had not yet broken from the constellation of forces we have described as essential to an understanding of peasant communities. Differences between cereal farmers and wine-growers, sharecroppers and day laborers, wood-cutters and domestics, persisted; but common residence in a rural community still played an important part in shaping views of external events.[85] Much of rural France was like the Var, where, after 1880, communities grew "ever more homogeneous" and a "strong sense of shared concerns and common enemies" continued.[86] Some maintain that distinctions between town and country survive to this day. Perhaps. But our concern is the early Third Republic, and during those crucial years the politics of Paris and the politics of the countryside were, in many ways, as divergent as they had ever been.

The conservation of local customs had little to do with political conservatism. In fact, cultural tenacity could provoke political radicalism in a traditional framework: a case of modern politics on rural terms, not "primitive" but different. For example, the continued use of patois need not indicate atavism or an inability to comprehend national issues. It can instead be a symbol of self-definition, of distinction. The man whose shout "Vivo lo socialo!" resounded through the streets of (French-speaking) Limoges at mid-century, may or may not have been well-versed in the complexities of Montagnard politics. His patois, at the very least, indicates that his politics were defined by local realities expressed through ancient language.[87] "Language and accent," says Mannheim, "offer an indirect indication as to how far the foundations of a person's consciousness are laid, his basic view of the world stabilized."[88] Henri Mendras adds that the "duality of language strongly marked the distinction between peasant societies and national societies, and the recent diffusion of French is one indication, among others, of the slow penetration of the national society into the peasant society."[89] Finally, Eugen Weber says that "French was a foreign language for a substantial number of Frenchmen, including almost half the children who would reach adulthood in the last quarter of the century."[90]

Peasants who remained on the land were more likely to adhere to local habits, including patois, than those who fled. After all, French was often as essential part of a traveler's baggage. But country people could be *patoisant* and politicized; and in so being they retained distinctive features which set them, and their politics, off from city dwellers.[91]

A society may constitute a "universe within a universe," says Claude

Levi-Strauss, a world with special divisions, hierarchies, and laws, and may produce a body of work (*oeuvres*) which "reflects its own image. . . ."[92] His description may be extended beyond the instructive fossils of artisanal culture to the opinions and politics of small communities. Rural responses to national events were, in a sense, works of art. Each locality brought unique designs, intricate variations, to common themes. At the end of the nineteenth century, rural cultures were less varied than they had been a century before; but people and politics in the countryside remained complex. France was a canvas composed of simultaneous images converging in one corner, diverging in another, contained by a frame, the nation, that was as arbitrary in reality as it was durable in myth.

In 1892 the mayor of Tréminis (Isère) warned conscripts not to "confuse the Fatherland with the village where one is born. For a Frenchman, the Fatherland is all of France (*la France entière*)."[93] The issue must have been vague enough to warrant a reminder. In the final two decades of the century, Paris-based Boulangists, followed by Dreyfusards and anti-Dreyfusards, sent peddlers and popular imagery, politicians and vague promises, into communities where agricultural changes, rural exodus, and a falling birth rate had served to "reinforce rather than break the solid traditions of routine."[94] An increasingly homogeneous world of peasant farmers continued to operate on the basis of local concerns, beliefs, and rivalries. Before examining Boulangism and the Dreyfus Affair in these rural communities, a closer look at the economics, politics, and peasants of individual regions will confirm the diversity of "la France entière" and help us understand how national events were shaped by (and shaped) local perceptions of the "village" and the "Fatherland."

CHAPTER II

TOUR DE FRANCE: GERS, ORNE, ISÈRE, MARNE

*Geography . . . helps us to rediscover the slow
unfolding of structural realities . . . it helps us
to discover the almost imperceptible movement
of history, if only we are prepared to follow its
lessons and accept its catagories and divisions.*

FERNAND BRAUDEL

Lucien Febvre described facts as hooks on which we hang ideas.[1] An investigation of rural France would, ideally, consider facts from scores of departments, hundreds of cantons, thousands (at least) of France's over 30,000 communes, from the Nord to Provence, Brittany to Alsace. The portrait would be finely brushed but never final. In the end it might only reveal the pretensions of a historian who believed that the quality of his ideas could be measured by the quantity of his hooks. It is the historian's business to select representative examples with care. In this case, the *tour de France* which follows will focus on the rural regions of four very different departments in order to illustrate the nature of change and continuity, of diversity, in the countryside on the eve of the Boulanger and Dreyfus Affairs.

Shaped from the old Gascony province, the Gers is best known as the birthplace of Armagnac, foie gras, and Paul de Cassagnac. Situated between Toulouse to the east and the Pyrenees to the south, it has long been an out-of-the-way department, attracting little interest and fewer visitors. It is also the home of unpredictable politics and a huge rural population.

In 1891 over 83 percent of the department's 261,084 inhabitants were designated as "rural." Seventy-one percent of the active population was engaged in agriculture, only 11 percent in industry. The Gers had no large towns (Auch, the capital, was 158th on the list of French cities), and the great majority of Gersois lived in dispersed communities linked (barely) by inferior roads and railways. The Southwest did not enjoy the benefits of massive public-work projects which had transformed many parts of the North, East, even the West in the nineteenth century.[2]

A village like Bascous in the Eauze canton was typical: 210 souls lived in twenty-three villages, hamlets, and farmsteads with only forty-one in the commune's *chief-lieu*; the population was overwhelmingly peasant. Berdoues in the Mirande canton had 423 farmers and day laborers in twenty-nine hamlets and farmsteads and fifty-two residents in the central village. Three hundred and one inhabitants lived in Gavarret in the Fleurance region, but they were spread over eleven hamlets with no concentrated population whatsoever. In 1891 only fourteen of 465 communes had a population exceeding 2,000 inhabitants. Scattered hamlets and farms was a dominant characteristic.[3]

In the late 1880s when General Boulanger began his political career and captivated Paris, almost 90 percent of the Gers' population still lived either in the commune of their birth or in a neighboring locality. Older than most—at least four years older than the national average—rural Gersois suffered the ravages of phylloxera and the general agricultural crisis which began early in the decade and continued to the end of the century.[4] The entire area was so hard hit that a student of "rural neurasthenia" chose the Southwest to explore the psychic effects of rural poverty and isolation. Although his conclusions are suspect, his laboratory was apt.[5]

Paul de Cassagnac, the powerful Bonapartist leader of the Gers, predictably accused the Republic of bringing "black misery" in the guise of phylloxera to the economically depressed department.[6] Insects which had already touched 119 communes by 1883 caused wine production to fall from 734,751 hectoliters in 1886 to 578,000 a decade later. The vine was a crucial economic factor in the Gers, and at the turn of the century only 48,000 hectares remained of the 108,000 harvested in 1873. Wheat production fared no better, declining by almost a half million hectoliters between 1886 and 1896. The region had enjoyed high cereal prices through the early nineteenth century, but after 1860 the impact of national competition, bad harvests, and a shortage of manual labor changed the structure of agriculture in the Southwest as it had done in many other areas. More land was given over to polyculture—including sheep, cattle, and poultry raising—in an attempt to diversify in the face of economic crisis.[7] "Paradoxically," says one historian of the region, rural areas were becoming "less oriented toward commerce." This pervasive "form of regression"[8] contributed to another transformation which would influence political culture: active, socially variegated market towns—crucial networks of rural political mobilization in 1848-51—lost their vitality in the final decades of the century.

Rural exodus surged on, the birthrate dropped, and between 1881 and 1896 the department's population fell by 30,000, to 250,000. Marginal peasants and rural bourgeois made up the great majority of emigrants, but the crisis was widespread, touching, for example, the small building industry in Gimont. Construction workers chose a more exotic exodus than most: by 1888 forty had left with their families for Buenos Aires.[9] The common route, however, was out of unproductive villages to industrial centers in nearby departments, or on to Paris. The tiny agricultural commune of Saint Brès northeast of Auch lost 32 percent of its inhabitants in the second half of the century (a staggering 72 percent between 1862 and 1955), and its transformation was not unusual: wage-laborers, artisans, and rural bourgeois fled, leaving a preponderance of farmers.[10] In the Gers as elsewhere, the countryside deproletarianized, manual labor became rare indeed, and those field hands who remained demanded ever increasing wages. Too often, however, hired help was almost impossible to find and, if available, difficult to afford.[11]

Primarily a department of small-holding peasants, many share-croppers also resided in the Gers, "tied to a system of isolated farms" and now facing the danger of eviction. Conversely, proprietors, stripped of capital and unable to avoid expropriation, were often forced back into sharecropper status.[12] Constant movement, frequent ruin, continuing agricultural crises, villages drained of productive young adults through migration and low fertility—these were the striking characteristics of the Gers in the 1880s and 90s.[13] Those too old, young, or poor to move, and those survivors too stubborn to flee, now dominated rural communities. Hard times might have distracted them from the distant complexities of national politics; on the other hand, angry people could be attracted to appeals from the Left and Right—if those entreaties had local meaning. And now, with universal manhood suffrage, more country folk could fight at the polls, as well as in cafés and along village streets where popular politics in previous decades had been so crucial.

The political history of the department in the nineteenth century is marked by two seemingly contradictory phenomena: first, the traditional image of local notables administering the fiefs of Cassagnac,

molding the politics of impressionable peasants;[14] and second, the spec-
ter of popular revolt in 1851 when country people rose up against
those who had abrogated the constitution and destroyed the future
dream of 1852: peasants, politicized and modern.[15] The two views are
not incompatible. Montagnards had great success in many proto-urban
centers in the Gers for the very reason that local personal influence
had always been an important factor in the department's politics. In
1851 a significant number of peasants had no notion (or the wrong
notion) of what they were rebelling against, but many others were clear
in their convictions and committed in their politics.[16]

Essential to a study of peasant societies late in the century, however,
is an understanding of how politics evolved in the Gers and how the
legacy of 1851 influenced rural populations one and two generations
later. Ted Margadant explains that a "differentiation of artisans from
cultivators, proto-urban bourgs from entirely rural communities, was
the basis of the social geography of revolt in the Gers."[17] Almost four
decades later, more and more rural communities had taken on the
characteristics of those which had remained calm in 1851: largely agricultural, denuded of artisans and rural bourgeois, dominated by cultivators and, now, aging. Earlier in the century active bourgs with
frequent markets and fairs provided a setting for animated exchanges,
political as well as commercial, as Louis Napoleon would learn. Lively
politics continued in the 1880s and 90s, but without the participation
of many traditional notables or artisans who, by then, had departed;
and without the benefit of some proto-urban centers which were dying
along with the economy.[18]

At mid-century the Montagnard movement owed much to the
"youthful vigor" of men in their twenties and thirties. "For them
the politics of conspiracy was the politics of youth."[19] By the 1880s the
"veritable evaporation" of young human resources had turned the
Gers, especially rural Gers, into a "country of old people."[20] The department had become strongly conservative in its politics, often Bonapartist, and radical appeals would have to follow a long, slow course
led by the moderate socialist Thierry Cazes in the 1890s. The repression following 1851 had done its job exceptionally well. But force can
stifle actions without destroying memories and desires. In December
1889, *La République des paysans* tried to rekindle the fervor of 1851,
but conceded that the Gers was now rife with Bonapartism led by "our
awful Cassagnac."[21] Generations had changed and so had the political
complexion of the department.

Memories of 1851, like those of 1789, must have influenced the
political attitudes of some country people at the end of the century.

But forty years is a long time, and enough had transpired in the interim to create new needs and desires, new political preferences and targets.[22] Older inhabitants undoubtedly clung to memories of the insurgency, but the late 1880s—Boulanger's most active years—was a time of discontent and deprivation for many country people in the Gers, and immediate economic crisis and rural exodus placed new demands on their political agenda. On the other hand, by the time of the Dreyfus Affair the crisis was abating and the Republic was winning its long battle with entrenched anti-government forces. Though not yet "extremely favorable,"[23] the situation in the rural Gers was, beyond doubt, an improvement over the black decade of the 1880s. These factors, coupled with legacies of 1851 and more, must be considered when charting the penetration of Boulangism and the Dreyfus Affair into that remote department nestled between Toulouse and the Pyrenees.

In the lower Normandy region west of Paris and on the threshold of Brittany, the department of the Orne, like the Gers, has long been surrounded by better-known provincial centers. Caen to the north, Rennes to the west, and Chartres due east overshadow the modest Orne towns of Argentan, Mortagne, and Alençon, the capital. During the late 1880s, however, small peasant communities in the department attracted legions of Boulangist agents led by the General's powerful supporter, Baron Mackau. An expert political organizer, and for many years an influential deputy from the Orne, Mackau played a principal role in Boulangist campaigns in his home department and, as we shall see, elsewhere throughout France.

In 1891, 85 percent of the Orne's residents had been born in the department. Nearly 80 percent were still "rural," with over half directly engaged in agriculture. Alençon, like Auch in the Gers, could hardly be considered a bustling provincial capital: it numbered barely 18,000 inhabitants. In the hinterlands the rural landscape varied from small, enclosed holdings in the *bocages* areas to large and expansive farms in the Perche region. But, over all, more than half the total population of 354,387 still lived in scattered villages and hamlets away from communal centers.[24]

In the second half of the century country folk left those communities in increasing numbers. Between 1836 and 1901 the department's population fell by 120,000. A few cities and towns in the region grew, while the countryside suffered the consequences of exodus and a falling birth rate. In one brief period, during the Boulangist years, the urban population rose by over 1,000 while rural communes lost almost 4,000 inhabitants. The Orne vied with the Gers, the Lot-et-Garonne, and a few other departments for the dubious distinction of highest and most rapid depopulation.[25]

Better times were not a distant memory. At mid-century, rural industries employed thousands of country people who, as we have seen elsewhere, balanced work on the land with work in small textile, glove, nail-making and other industries. A "rapid multiplication of artisanal activities" made rural areas genuine "usines polyvalentes."[26] But in the final decades of the century, 25,000 weavers alone lost or left their jobs. Along with workers from other dying rural industries, they moved to nearby Le Mans, Chartres, Laval, or Evreux. Some traveled the fairly short distance to Paris. The same general forces fueled depopulation in the Orne and Gers: deindustrialization, competition from new markets served by rail lines, and a loss of "local privileges."[27] The location of the Orne, however, offered emigrants more choices than those available to country folk in the remote and isolated Gers. We shall see that it would also offer them better access to Parisian propagandists.

One study of rural industry in the Orne across the nineteenth century confirms changes we have found in other regions. At mid-century, peasants, artisans, shopkeepers, industrial workers and others still shaped the complex socio-professional structure of rural communities. By the end of the century, deindustrialization and the structural transformation of agriculture left many villages and hamlets to peasants and agricultural workers.[28] Changes occurred at different times in different regions, but the pattern is undeniable here and elsewhere in rural France, and these transformations would have an impact on the workings of rural politics.

The events of 1848-51, coupled with the economic crisis of that period, sparked some agitation in the Orne countryside. After 1849, secret societies in bourgs and market towns attracted the interest of weavers, shoemakers and a few farmers. This, in turn, drew the attention of the forces of order. On the eve of the coup d'état the prefect stressed that peasant villages did not worry him, though some bourgs "étaient livrés à l'esprit démogogique."[29] He mobilized three infantry companies to meet any eventuality. A year earlier Louis Napoleon had traveled through the Orne countryside preaching peace, prosperity, and stability to anxious peasants looking for relief. At the same time, republicans made their appeals to country folk. Near Aigle they found an ingenious, if perverse, way to convince peasants to vote against Louis Napoleon. "You don't like the Republic?" they asked local Bonapartists, "Then vote against Louis Napoleon. . . . By voting 'no' you'll help him attack the Republic he hates as much as you do, and he will become Emperor." How many country people fell for these studied confusions, or for Bonapartist promises, is unknown. But the 1852 plebiscite reveals that the Emperor received 95,000 of 99,000 votes cast in the Orne.[30]

More significant than the final tally is the fact that 1848-51 proved to be a period of political acculturation for some rural inhabitants. The period was brief, however, and much popular interest seems to have come from artisans and rural industrial workers, many of whom would leave villages and hamlets in the coming years. Political initiatives in the countryside were often met with only a halfhearted, "very mitigated enthusiasm" among peasants whose long days in the fields prevented them from attending evening meetings where agents from all sides tried to instruct them in the new political ways of the world. At midcentury, outside a few market towns and small industrial centers, peasants and visiting agents rarely found common ground on which to construct an organized political movement.[31]

Early Third Republic elections would draw more and more peasants into the national political process. We shall see that a pivotal moment came in the late 1880s when local Boulangists, familiar with the personalities and political culture of the department, and armed with a canny blend of old and new propaganda, entered agricultural communities. Witnessing the decline of regional industries and the impact of rural exodus, and in the midst of yet another economic crisis, Orne peasants paid attention to Boulangist agents. Republicans, fearing the consequences of this popular, well-organized challenge, responded, and country people in lower Normandy, as in other regions, found themselves at the center of an intense national political battle.

The Isère has been called a "geographical nonsense."[32] Industrial centers and farms scattered across its plains, and mountain villages in the pre-Alps, serve as a striking contrast to the rural Gers and Orne. The Dauphiné province had been divided into three departments in 1790: the Drôme, Hautes-Alpes, and Isère. The latter became a curious unit of seemingly unrelated parts. Any study of the department—especially in the late nineteenth century when it was undergoing extraordinary social change—must consider two panels of a diptych: the flat stretches of the lower Isère, with industrial towns like Vienne, Voiron, La Mure, and Bourgoin; and the upper Isère to the southeast, where isolated mountain villages still resembled those in Balzac's *Le Médecin de campagne*. "Civilization has not made much headway hereabouts," said one character. It was a region which lay "completely beyond the limits of social stir and change," an inaccessible country where "political events and revolutions never reached."[33] The novelist has a right to exaggerate: Balzac did not consider migrant labor, the moving of livestock, and peddling, which had connected some mountain regions to the outside world for centuries. But his description of remote villages carried more than a grain of truth, and, as we shall see below, still applied in the final quarter of the century.

In 1886, the Isère had twice the population of the Gers: over 580,000, with 52.8 percent engaged in agriculture and an impressive 26.1 percent in industry. The distribution of dispersed and nucleated communities was more like that of the Orne than of the Gers: half the population lived in scattered hamlets and farmsteads. Contrasts with the overwhelmingly rural Gers and Orne, however, were pronounced. The Isère had 38 communes with a population exceeding 2,000 inhabitants, and its capital, Grenoble (population 60,449 in 1891) was almost five times that of Auch. An important administrative, judicial, military, and university center, as well as a commercial and industrial town, Grenoble enjoyed a sophisticated communications network which linked this active city to Lyon to the north and to Italy southeast across the Alps. Its most celebrated visitor, Napoleon I, passed through on his journey back from Elba (and, if local innkeepers are to be believed, slept in every Grenoble hotel during his one-night stay). Throughout the century his route and others were used by migrant laborers, peddlers, politicians, merchants, and, later, an increasing number of tourists on their way to the baths of Uriage and the ski slopes of the Alps. If the Gers and Orne were out of the way, the Isère was central and heavily traveled.[34]

Between 1886 and 1891 the Isère had a net population loss of 9,000. However, while the urban population of the Gers fell by 1,500 during this period, it increased in the Isère, as it did in the Orne, by 1,000.[35] Rural inhabitants in the Isère did not have to search beyond their borders for new employment: they could travel to the mines of La Mure, the silk industry of Voiron, the ironworks of Vienne. The population of many villages and hamlets, especially in the mountains, decreased as larger towns and cities grew rapidly. Eighty-nine percent of the population had been born in the department, but intradepartmental mobility made for a very different situation from that found in the Gers and Orne.[36]

Many laborers maintained rural domiciles (and plots of land), working *in situ* or traveling five, ten, or more kilometers to industrial towns. An example of this complex interplay can be seen in the glove industry, which started in Grenoble, expanded to the countryside to make use of rural labor, then returned to the city. In Voiron, silk workers came from outlying rural communes on Monday morning, worked through the week, and returned to their villages on Saturday night. Of course Vienne, La Mure, Grenoble, and other towns had concentrated worker populations, but these and other localities could also be temporary homes for part-time peasants. Ironworkers in Vienne, hard hit by the economic crisis, were not confined to the city; they could return to the countryside and easily find work among local peasants who might be family members or former neighbors. The Great Depression of the 1880s and early 90s contributed to this constant mobility and inter-lacing of rural and urban worlds.[37]

Yet many localities were now almost exclusively agricultural. Signif-icant numbers of artisans and workers had moved to cities and bourgs— many never to return—and Isère peasant communities resembled those in other departments. This was especially true of mountain regions where exodus was pronounced: "Industrial centers in the plains," ob-served a local historian, "were growing at the expense of less favored mountain communities."[38] Small textile and other rural industries in the pre-Alps of the Isère and neighboring Savoie had a long history of selling to the exterior. In addition, large numbers of mountain folk moved down to the wheat-fields of the plains for temporary employ-ment each year. Renowned peddlers from the rugged hinterlands of the Southeast traveled throughout the region, throughout France and beyond, and, like migrant workers, returned periodically to their mountain homes. In the second half of the nineteenth century, this pattern changed, gradually but decisively. As we have seen in other areas, new communications networks and the competition of growing industrial centers severely undermined traditional rural work, and this new organization of commerce also "asphyxiated" peddling. More and more, permanent exodus replaced centuries-old patterns of temporary movement in and out of rural communities.[39]

Villages and hamlets throughout the Isère underwent changes seen in other departments. In 1851, the Dauphiné village of Morette had 528 residents; by 1901 the population had dropped to 402, a result of emigration and the falling birthrate due to the aging of the population. In 1896 this commune, too, was almost purely agricultural. Only five artisans remained.[40] Changes unfolded gradually in this complex re-gion; nevertheless, growing contrasts set agricultural villages apart from towns. The rural world had become, in many ways, "a profound unity."[41]

One traveler visiting the Southeast shortly after the turn of the cen-tury remarked that "the inhabitants of each area form communities distinct from their neighbors, and have practically no contact with those around them."[42] This could be an urban observer's misreading of rural life, but reports from local officials confirm the view. The commune of Courtenay, for example, in the extreme north, was purely agricultural and "made up of only a few hamlets of little importance scattered far from one another." Saint Chef was another farming community "situated far from any contact with large towns." The commune of Chezeneuve, near Vienne, had no important roads nearby, and resident cultivators had very few visitors. No one passed through Mazennes, "neither city folk nor other peasants"; in Solaize, close by Lyon, one found no industry, no workers, no urban visitors. All these communes are located in the relatively rich and "industrialized" northeastern part of the Isère; to the south, in mountain communes stretching from Grenoble toward Savoie and the Hautes-Alpes, semi-autarkic communities were more severely isolated, especially during long winter months.[43]

Small-holding peasants dominated the agricultural Isère, with a decreasing number of tenant farmers and sharecroppers. Day laborers dropped from 36 per 100 *exploitations* in 1882 to 25 per 100 in 1892 (when the national average was 55 per 100). Some became landowners, most fled the countryside for cities near and far. Agricultural products included wheat, wine, walnuts, and livestock; fervent prayers offered by pilgrims at the shrine of Notre Dame de la Salette to the south or by priests of Chartreuse to the northeast could not prevent the economic crisis from penetrating the Isère as it had the Gers and most of France. Between 1882 and 1895 the entire department underwent a profound economic depression which touched every sector of agriculture. Again polyculture offered almost no refuge.[44]

On the surface, the situation in the 1880s and 90s resembled that of mid-century when peasant indebtedness and economic upheaval helped shape rural reactions to the national political events of the era. In the late 1840s, economic misery throughout the Alpine region led many peasants into debt or total ruin.[45] Later in the century, however, new forces, including phylloxera and international competition, fueled the crisis. Moreover, when the population of the Isère peaked at mid-century,[46] villages maintained that complex character they would lose one and two generations later: an abundance of local notables, rural industrial workers, artisans, day laborers, domestics, full-time and part-time peasants.[47] By the final quarter of the century the continuing deindustrialization of the countryside and the flight of artisans and workers had created a very different rural world.

The contrast between political reactions to Louis Napoleon's coup in the Isère and Gers could not have been more striking. Thousands of rural Gersois participated in the insurrection of 1851, but peasants in the Isère, unlike their immediate neighbors in the Drôme and Hautes-Alpes, "did not budge."[48] The weakness of organized Montagnard movements, along with the strong hold of local Bonapartists, stifled action in the Isère. This department, long proud of its reputation as "the cradle of the French Revolution" (the first rumbles were allegedly felt in the town of Vizelle in 1788) was marked by moderate republicanism which helped allay the diffusion of secret societies. In 1851, with the Vaucluse, it was the least revolutionary department in the Southeast.[49]

During the Second Empire, the Isère countryside, like most of rural France, remained quiescent and fairly prosperous. Republicanism persisted, especially in the towns, and with the coming of the Third Republic it is not surprising that Gambetta chose Grenoble to herald the *nouvelles couches sociales*. With some notable exceptions, moderate republicanism and Radicalism would thrive throughout the Isère at the end of the century. For example, except for a few communes to the south and southeast, much of the population, including the peasantry, remained staunchly anticlerical. Some of the most heated battles occurred not only among urban secular forces and religious personalities like the popular Monsignor Fava, but among peasants of every persuasion in the most remote rural communes.[50]

The mid-1890s marked a turning-point in the economic crisis which had been destroying crops and people for almost two decades. Between 1895 and 1914 the situation of the Dauphiné farmer clearly improved. Wheat and livestock prices rose, and phylloxera, though not eradicated, was under control. By 1898, when the Dreyfus Affair threw Paris into another kind of crisis, the small holding farmer in the Isère was starting to enjoy a certain prosperity, a trend not unlike that found in the Gers.[51] Meanwhile, industrial centers entered their most tumultous decades. The weavers and metallurgists of Voiron and Vienne, the miners of La Mure, and the glovemakers of Grenoble had a long tradition of worker organization, and by the end of the century *Bourses de travail* were instituted in a few Isère towns.[52] By 1900 Grenoble had tapped its abundant water sources and had become "the Water Power Capital" of France. A huge metallurgy industry developed, attracting more workers, including growing numbers of migrants from nearby Italy. After the 1890s, strikes increased throughout the department, often marked by conflicts between xenophobic locals and newly arrived Italian laborers. Socialists fared well in the Isère, and by the eve of the

First World War they had strong bases in Grenoble, Vienne, and the semi-rural regions to the north.[53]

When Boulangism and the Dreyfus Affair arrived in the department, rural and urban areas were undergoing massive social, economic, and political changes. Yet one man from Trièves—a conscript in 1889, Boulanger's most active year—said that he and others in the country-side never bothered with politics. *Boules* on Sunday was their favorite pastime, followed by a "joyous return to rugged work in the fields on Monday, without a thought of other things."[54] If he was referring to "politics" associated with arcane debates over church and state, or the advantages of Sadi Carnot over Jules Grévy, his recollection was probably correct—though it is hard to believe that Monday morning labor was ever "joyous." If, however, he included local politics in his assessment—politics which often merged with national issues—then either his memory served him poorly, his desire to romanticize his rural past served him well, or his commune was an outstanding exception.

We shall see that politics in Grenoble, Vienne, and Voiron differed from those in rural communities throughout the department. At the end of the century needs and desires differed and so did modes of political expression. But country people, with the exception of some *montagnards* tucked away in the Bourg d'Oisans, were not unaware of national events. Their interest or indifference would be based on the relevance of Parisian issues in their individual localities.

The 600 kilometers separating the Marne and Gers could well be 6,000. Almost every aspect of rural life in the Gers—scattered hamlets with peasants rarely venturing farther than a local fair; poor communications; emigration and population decline; a paucity of cities and industry—all these characteristics made the Gers and Marne two of the most dissimilar departments in France. Close to Paris, bisected by the important national route linking the capital to the eastern frontier, the Marne was among those departments *to* which country people fled in the second half of the century. Nucleated villages dominated the landscape, and the industrial city of Reims (the largest subprefecture in France; population 98,107 in 1891), with Epernay and the capital Châlons-sur-Marne, added to the urban character of the region. In our departmental quartet, the semi-rural Isère stands between the relatively static Gers and Orne, and the active, urbanized Marne.[55]

Unlike its counterparts due west and to the south and southwest, the population of the Marne grew, from 429,494 inhabitants in 1886 to 434,692 five years later. There was to be a slight downturn at the

The Departments of France

end of the century, but for most of the period which concerns us, the
department was more than holding its own. In 1891, 55 percent of
the population was "rural" with only 38 percent of the total population
engaged in agriculture and 31 percent in industry—highest among our
departments. Between 1886 and 1891 the urban population increased
by 15,713 while rural communes lost over 10,000 inhabitants. A quarter
of the department's residents had been born elsewhere. Compact villages and bourgs surrounded by vineyards or fields of wheat, rye, and
oats, contrasted with small, dispersed settlements found in much of
the Isère and Orne and most of the Gers. Over 375,000 people lived
in agglomerated communities in 1891, barely 39,000 in scattered hamlets and farmsteads. The topography alone—flat expanses of farming
land which, decades later, would become part of France's "bread basket"—distinguished the Marne from the rugged Alpine region, the
rolling hills of the Gers, and the *bocage* areas of the Orne.[56]

Reims and Epernay conjure up images of magnificent cathedrals
and tastes of the finest champagne. By the late nineteenth century the
champagne industry had become one of the most important economic
activities in the department; its workers among the best-paid and least
politically active. Other workers—above all in the Reims woolen industry—felt the economic pains of the 1880s and 90s, heightened in
this department by competition from industries in the north of France
and in Germany. It is not surprising that official reports cast a suspicious eye on urban workers, a sympathetic one on remote and quiescent
peasants, including wine-growers. Things were to change a great deal
after the turn of the century.[57]

Phylloxera came late to the Marne, taking time to pillage its way
north. By August, 1890, however, the first vines had been touched,
and after 1893 viticulture in the region entered a crisis which would
last into the early years of the twentieth century. As usual, winegrowers
organized early in the battle against plodding government policies; but
the real fight was to begin after 1900. Significantly, in the 1880s, when
Boulanger formulated his populist appeals, the champagne industry
was "flourishing"; wages were high, unemployment low, and phylloxera a potential not present threat. A decade later, during the Dreyfus
Affair, the situation deteriorated. At a moment when economic conditions were gradually improving in many rural areas troubles were
just beginning in the Marne; not a few malcontents would searched
for scapegoats among Jewish "capitalists" and "conspirators" who, they
thought, surrounded Dreyfus.[58]

Vineyards require only a small percentage of tillable land. Cereal was the major crop in the Marne, the domain of small-holding peasants as well as large landowners overseeing farms of 150 hectares and more. The Marne had fewer tenant farmers than the Isère, and virtually no sharecroppers, but scores of rural communes listed day-workers and manual laborers: not surprising in a department with large *exploitations* on the eve of full-scale mechanization which would deal the final blow to the rural proletariat. But many of these workers were themselves small-holding farmers—yet another example of that shifting rural world where the stated profession conceals the nuances of peasant labor.[59]

Differences between the Marne and other departments are mitigated when we look closely at the structure of rural communities. Urban centers grew at the expense of villages and hamlets, a classic pattern found throughout France. Twenty-two of 32 Marne cantons lost population between 1840 and 1880; only the populations of industrial or wine-growing cantons increased.[60] In 1885 the prefect set the following unhappy scene: property values have diminished by half; no buyers can be found; farms are being abandoned and villages deserted. More than a decade later, officials informed communes near the Meuse border that soldiers would help with the harvest: too few laborers had stayed in the countryside for local farmers to go it alone.[61]

Cities had taken "the young and vigorous" from the Marne countryside, and, in the words of one observer who spoke for many, "destroyed them" in the process.[62] The horror of an "unhealthy" urban life was a constant theme among those who wished, for various reasons, to curb the flow of rural emigrants. In this department with industrial centers like Reims and Epernay, and with direct rail lines to Paris, emigration to the cities was extensive. This, in turn, benefited many of those who remained on the land. The prefect stressed that "rural workers had no difficulty procuring jobs and demanding an adequate salary." An exaggeration perhaps, but one often repeated. The situation differed from one village to the next, but many rural proletarians could find work and decent wages—if they stayed.[63]

Many villages and hamlets were now almost exclusively agricultural. Peasants tended their own parcels of land, worked on large farms, or did both. Wood-cutters lived and worked in a few rural communes near Châlons-sur-Marne, and small industries survived in some areas at the end of the century (tile-making in Thiéblemont, paper works in Fismes), but most communities followed the course taken elsewhere: the countryside was deindustrializing, workers and artisans were departing, and villages were the domain of seasoned peasants.[64]

When the Marne prefect noted sophisticated railways and roads linking his department to nearby Paris, he touched on one theme important to an understanding of politics in the region. Newspapers, politicians, ideas, and, too often, soldiers coming from Paris and other northern cities, traveled with great regularity through the Marne.[65] Châlons-sur-Marne had long been a crucial military post. From Attila the Hun (whose final encampment was in the environs of Châlons), to Valmy, 1870, the "taxis" of 1914, and the maneuvers of the Second World War, the destiny of the Marne was closely bound to that of the Fatherland. Belgium was just to the northeast across the fields of Verdun and the Argonne forest, and Alsace and Lorraine were due east. The physical proximity of the Marne to these strategic centers—Paris on the one side, the frontier on the other—made the patriotic appeals of successive governments more immediate than they would be in the distant Gers or west of Paris in the Orne. In the Isère most citizens were acutely aware of their closeness to Italy,[66] but the Alps provided a natural fortress as sprawling fields in the Marne could never do. No Maginot line would be needed in the Southeast. Issues of nationalism and militarism surrounding Boulanger, and, later, Dreyfus were not abstractions for Marne peasants who recalled a succession of wars which had always been too close to ignore. Indeed, village architecture in the region turns its back on passersby for a reason. "The life of the house is nearly always directed inwards," noted one observer, and few windows face the street. For too long, and too often visitors proved foreign and hostile. *Revanche* had special relevance on this "battlefield of France."[67] So, as we shall see, did anti-Semitism.

If the "republican idea" had arrived slowly but definitively in two-thirds of the municipalities by the early 1890s, the reality was altogether different in 200 other communes.[68] Some were "reactionary" indeed, with mayors, priests, rural guards, and others battling over a variety of issues, local and national. Meanwhile, in urban centers, the continuing organization of socialists, secular and Christian ("Notre Dame de l'usine"), challenged moderate republicanism. "The socialist danger," warned the prefect, "is in Reims, and it is serious and imminent."[69] In addition, anarchism, found periodically in the Isère and almost never in the Orne or Gers, was a menace in the Marne: dangerous though desultory.[70]

Strong *revanchisme*, urban worker discontent, wine-growers and other peasants facing agricultural crisis—all these factors and more made the 1880s and 90s in the Marne an era when local problems intertwined with heated national issues. Country peple did not remain untouched. But here, too, rural reactions to Boulanger and Dreyfus will show that issues important in nearby cities, including Paris, had to be adapted to the politics and priorities of the village.

———————

This departmental quartet had rough equivalents throughout France at the end of the century. Large-scale industrialization, urbanization, rural exodus, falling birthrates, and economic crises touched some regions later and more pervasively than others; but in much of France, rural communities underwent strikingly similar transformations. Country people in most regions continued to live in or near the commune of their birth, very often in scattered villages or hamlets removed from communal centers. Deindustrialization and structural changes in agriculture—largely a result of new communications networks and increased national and international competition—meant that fewer rural communities enjoyed that rich mix of artisans, industrial workers, rural bourgeois, and others who had dominated village life and village politics at mid-century. Working peasants stayed on the land and became the new notables of the countryside at the end of the century. Even in the Marne, with its nucleated villages and relatively stable or growing population, and in the Isère where small silk, glove, and other industries survived, rural communities "simplified" as they did in the Gers and Orne when huge numbers of country folk left for cities and towns and entered new worlds with different customs. In thousands of villages "aging" peasant populations maintained distinctive routines, including political routines, that had shaped their world for generations. These were among the many consequences of the "ruralization" of modern France.

Balzac's closed villages "at the end of the world" had all but disappeared and deserved the attention of folklorists. Civilization was indeed making much "headway hereabouts." Yet while cultural and political changes do not follow economic ones at some remote remove, there is a shadowy *décalage*, a moment when routine coexists with novelty. Boulangism and the Dreyfus Affair did not always mark the pivotal moment in the political evolution of the peasantry—we have seen that France was too variegated for that—but rural reactions to these events will show that many a peasant was still "bien de son pays"; not a "simpleton" as the phrase now implies, but a rural inhabitant whose political culture was shaped by a combination of contemporary local interests and ancient local customs, and whose "patrie" was not always synonymous with the national definition, the urban definition, of "Fatherland."

PART TWO

BOULANGISM

CHAPTER III

SIGHTS AND SOUNDS

Dans son programme il peut tout se permettre,
Tout proposer, réformer, reviser . . .

Il faut flatter les raisins en Champagne . . .
On doit en Beauce admirer la campagne . . .

En politique il n'est rien d'impossible.

ANTI-BOULANGIST SONG, C. 1890

"There is no way of stemming the Boulangist tide," the French socialist Paul Lafargue wrote Friedrich Engels in 1888. "The country is demented." Engels agreed, adding that Henri Rochefort, Boulanger's most active propagandist, "seems off his head." As for the peasants, they are "mercenary soldiers [*lansquenets*] who will always serve in the conqueror's army by choice. . . ."[1] A police informant shared Engels' assessment: "Peasants, tenant farmers, and all those who are tied in some way to rich conservatives are today perfectly won over [by Boulangists]. When the efforts of the clergy are also considered, one has an idea of the situation."[2] One observer described the "veritable intoxication which has seized the peasantry,"[3] and another insisted that "peasants are the real supporters of Boulanger." They may "appear indifferent," he warned, but in reality they detest the Opportunist Republic and know that the General understands the most basic desires of *le peuple*: "Peace, Order, Thrift, and Work."[4]

These commentators were, after all, voicing well-worn truisms about the peasantry. With war and defeat a recent memory, and economic crisis an immediate reality, peasants quite naturally desired peace and prosperity. But the popular view had changed little over four decades: for many urban observers, peasants were still the unthinking masses on whose back Louis Napoleon rode to victory at mid-century. They would undoubtedly support Boulanger, the new Caesar of the fin de siècle.

Like most populists, the General was considered a "river into which fed many streams . . . a symbol of diverse sentiments."[5] In him "peaceful folk saw order," said Maurice Barrès, "and those who were restless saw an adventure which would solve all their problems."[6] A Socialist deputy from the Isère, who, unlike Barrès, held Boulanger in the lowest regard, believed that "according to the circumstances, he will be a Monck for the Monarchists, Caesar for the *plebiscitaires*, General *Revanche* for the patriotic; he will double-cross the one, quibble with the others, and lie to them all. . . ."[7]

Boulanger's propaganda organization, like the General's bizarre succession of mentors and supporters, was complex, contradicatory and ideologically multifaceted. The movement started on the radical left in 1886, championed at different moments for different reasons by Georges Clemenceau, Henri Rochefort and Louise Michel. Then, clandestinely, royalists and Bonapartists took notice, and by 1889 Baron Mackau, Comte Dillon and the Duchesse d'Uzès had mobilized the General's image for reactionary ends. The ideological shift was never clear, however, and confusion worked to Boulanger's advantage. Discontented industrial workers in the Nord could be drawn to the quasi-socialist appeals of Boulangist agents, and Bonapartist peasants in the Dordogne or in mountain communes of the Isère could, at the same moment, rally to the General's variation on the Napoleonic myth.

This much is well known. Less familiar are the ways in which Boulangist organizers of all political stripes directed their campaigns from Paris and provincial centers and reached into peasant communities near and far. Boulanger as a symbol of the Left or Right is important, as are the immediate electoral successes or failures of contending factions. But the form, scope, and intensity of propagandizing in rural areas during the brief Boulangist years, and the impact campaigns had on the political acculturation of the peasantry, is, over the *longue durée*, even more instructive.

A well-choreographed rural ballet featuring legions of peasants rallying to the General never materialized. Instead, enclaves of support, hostility, and indifference coexisted in the same department, the same village, the same family. It would take more than a Bonapartist veneer or a socialist tint to attract rural Frenchmen; attitudes toward Boulanger proved as complex, self-interested, and localized as popular sentiments toward Louis Napoleon had been more than a generation before.

But, as we have seen, the countryside changed a great deal between Bonaparte and Boulanger. Old political networks were giving way to new modes of communication. One author maintains that the Boulangist crisis signaled the demise of the old-fashioned political style of personal influence and aristocratic prestige upon which the "notables" of rural France had relied throughout the century. . . . [It] represented a break with political methods of long standing . . . in the varieties of his popular image, [Boulanger] mirrored the vague and often conflicting aspirations of men for whom old loyalties were fading and new attachments not yet clear.[8]

This view, like that of Daniel Halévy, the chronicler of dying notables, is partly right: an "old-fashioned political style of . . . aristocratic prestige" was giving way in rural France. In Lorraine, for example, "la vie électorale" changed in the 1880s: "The notables' influence disappeared [and] a direct call to electors through meetings, posters, and political tracts became the rule."[9] But "notables" were not dead, just different. In rural communities increasingly dominated by peasants, personal influence and local interests remained crucial factors. In that sense, there were no abrupt changes. We know that industrial workers in the final decades of the century did not experience a clear break with the past—only gradual transformations and adaptations—and the same applies to those who worked the land.[10]

This large, well-organized, and, in many ways, unprecedented movement reached into the most remote rural communes. It came at a moment when economic crisis plagued peasants as much as city-dwellers, and, along with the practice of politics in the relatively new age of universal manhood suffrage, it contributed to a continuing awareness of new national political choices in rural communities. At the same time, however, the massive use of traditional popular imagery and peddlers shows that the movement was a case of old scenery, old props, on a changing, expanding stage. Never again would Epinal and its equivalents be pressed into political service on such a large scale. In the years following Boulangism many of the methods by which rural French men and women had been learning about politics—the sources from which they had been forming opinions—would be eclipsed by new methods indistinguishable from those found in the city. We shall see that in the workings of rural politics, Boulangism marked an end and a beginning.

To understand fully the impact of a national political movement like Boulangism, one must first chart the dissemination of news and information from the center, from Paris, to provincial cities; then step within a region, a village, sometimes even a family, to learn what local factors, if any, provided fertile ground for the national issue to take root. Patrick Hutton has argued that Boulangism divides into "two quite distinct phases:" an initial "populist" phase in which electoral campaigns and Boulanger himself played important roles; and a subsequent

> "political" phase in which the momentum generated by the movement was institutionalized. . . . During this period local political leaders with Boulangist sympathies played the larger role in most constituencies in building electoral coalitions of radicals and conservatives, politicians hitherto at odds over the question of commitment to the republican regime.[11]

Evidence from villages and hamlets supports Hutton's general observations and may be applied to those country folk uninterested or unversed in the formalities of national politics. Many peasants turned to this new movement, and in response built new coalitions using materials from within their community: politics homespun. These centrifugal and centripetal forces—the dissemination of the national message and the local responses—must be studied with equal thoroughness, unless, of course, one believes that the "metropole" deserves more attention than the "periphery."[12]

IMAGES: FROM PARIS TO THE PROVINCES

In 1889 five million Boulangist posters and seven million voting ballots were circulating throughout Paris. Millions more had reached the countryside. In addition, one hundred thousand photos and one million brochures entitled "La vie du général Boulanger" had been distributed. On a single day in 1887, twenty thousand portraits arrived in Le Mans (Sarthe) to be sold "in towns and in the countryside." Moreover, the General inspired hundreds of new songs, many of which were illustrated and dispatched in "scores of bundles" to the provinces.[13] "I found eight million [francs] to throw in the ocean," boasted Comte Dillon, Boulangist organizer and owner of a transatlantic cable company, "and I'll find five million more to wager on the popularity of the General." He found at least that and was joined by the Duchesse d'Uzès who contributed more than three million to the campaign. Much of it went for popular imagery.[14]

The private papers of Baron Mackau, royalist deputy from the Orne and one of Boulanger's most avid supporters, reveal a highly sophisticated national propaganda organization based largely on popular broadsheets, almanacs, imagery, and roving rural armies of political agents. Shortly after *La Cocarde* and Rochefort's *L'Intransigeant* had mounted their own Boulangist propaganda network, Mackau's Comité

Electoral des Droits began negotiations with Parisian and provincial printers for hundreds of thousands of posters, circulars, voting ballots, pictures and more. Five to ten francs would cover the cost of 1,000 short tracts entitled "Pourquoi nos campagnes souffrent" or "La République des paysans;" and Mackau's group would instruct local candidates and their agents on the best methods of disseminating popular propaganda.[15]

Henri Gautier, Parisian editor of *Les Veillées des chaumières* and *Gazette des campagnes*, offered his services, including his string of peddlers, to Boulangist candidates—and, one must assume, to any other candidate who would pay the price. Gautier knew the countryside well and recognized that posters, newspapers, and political meetings were not enough. He and other publishers suggested the use of almanacs which would interweave technical, agricultural information for peasants with the personalized propaganda of selected candidates (see fig. 2). The almanac's "apparent neutrality," said Gautier in a letter to Mackau, "imbues it with a power that no newspaper or brochure can match. It is the popular publication *par excellence*. Almanacs penetrate everywhere, especially where newspapers are not to be found, and they are always avidly read." Gautier could produce five million copies which, he reckoned, would reach 15-20 million readers. The cost, 600 francs per 15,000 copies (sold for 20-25 centimes per copy) was surely attractive and manageable for a movement backed by well-to-do barons, counts, duchesses, and highly successful Parisian newspaper publishers.[16]

Boulangists called on provincial as well as Parisian printers in a move which not only cut costs but enhanced the local character of the movement. For less than 75 francs, one company in Saint Etienne produced 15,000 *professions de foi* and voting ballots to be sent to rural communes in the hinterlands. In Puy-de-Dôme, they turned to a local printer for posters, ballots, and more. To the south in the Var, 20,000 biographies of a Boulangist candidate included photos of the General which agents carried into distant mountain communes during the 1889 elections.[17] In addition, we shall see that a profusion of Boulangist images in the tradition of Epinal complemented tracts, posters, almanacs and *professions de foi* in rural communities. This impressive array of popular propaganda, emanating from diverse, often antagonistic Boulangist organizations, flooded the countryside in the brief period between 1886 and 1889.

There had never been anything like it. Many compared the General's crusade to the successful campaign of Louis Napoleon four decades earlier; but propaganda, lithography, chromolithography, photogra-

2. Almanach Boulanger

phy, the postal system, political agents and the roads and railroads they traveled, had all improved in the interim. The liberal press law of 1881, moreover, had given greater freedom to peddlers. The deluge of Boulangist images made the campaigns of Bonapartists and Montagnards at mid-century, and the Comte de Paris and MacMahon in the 1870s, appear anemic in comparison. Impassable trails were giving way to new by-roads, and ideas and people had an easier time of it in Boulanger's day than they had had a generation earlier when Louis Napoleon sent his portrait, and Pierre Joigneaux sent his socialist paper *Feuille du village*, into rural communes. Propaganda in the 80s was not only unprecedented in bulk, but unequaled in distribution and potential impact.[18]

In Paris, long and tendentious newspaper editorials spiced with illustrations of Boulanger as republican hero or reactionary incompetent helped define the opinions of interested city dwellers. Publications of every political stripe took sides, and all the actors—Boulanger, Rochefort, Clemenceau, Ferry—were incessantly portrayed in print and picture, making the raw plot of the political play comprehensible to those close to the main arena—especially those in Paris. Others, relegated to cheap seats in the back (including, but not exclusively, peasants), often stood beyond earshot and had to depend on a simplified outline handed them by local enthusiasts and visiting agents. The form and content of propaganda in the countryside shows that rural people learned about the General through more traditional channels than did their urban counterparts.

In Paris, editorials in *La Cocarde, La Presse*, or *L'Intransigeant* were complemented by dozens of popular dailies and weeklies which portrayed the General in bold and varied front page illustrations. Political opinions, in prose and picture, were resoundingly clear. *La Bombe, La Diane*, the better-known *Le Pilori* with drawings by Blass and Alfred le Petit's *La Charge*, were all, in their distinct ways, Boulangist. On colorful front pages the General could be seen grabbing Jules Ferry by the ear while the detested Opportunist slapped back with his viper-like nose. Huge letters exclaimed "Down with Ferry!"[19] Meanwhile, anti-Boulangist illustrations adorned *La Griffe, La Silhouette, Le Grelot, Le Jeune Garde, Le Don Quichotte*, and *Le Troupier*. In one, the General was surrounded by a jar of cold cream and a bottle of hair dye (to preserve his youthful image and "blond" beard) and a hypodermic needle filled with morphine (for old battle wounds).[20] And this was tame. Scatological pictures of flatulence and defecation were not uncommon. One cover illustrates the worthlessness of the General's electoral support: feces are placed on a scale opposite Boulangist voting ballots, while nearby a figure wipes himself with a paper reading "Verdict of the People." Another, published shortly after the Nord victory, has Boulanger baring his backside to masses of adoring *cocardiers* while Rochefort, in priestly robes, blesses him with incense.[21] Then there were the curious "original sketches" with Boulanger and others striking pornographic poses. Commenting on the General's narcissism, the anonymous artist has him enjoying onanism while his benefactress, the Duchesses d'Uzès, looks on.[22] Such attacks might have titillated a Paris subculture, much as scurrilous *libelles* had done a century before, but it is unlikely that peasants shared the fun. Boulangist propaganda in Paris awaits its psychoanalytic historian.

It was also in the city that commercial and political publicity merged for the first time on a large scale in France. Comte Dillon, who studied politics while making his fortune in America, brought "Yankee publicity and *puffisme*" with him to France and to the Boulangist cause.[23] Through 1888-89 the front pages of Parisian and urban provincial newspapers reported news of the General while back pages carried his endorsement of products from aperitifs to throat lozenges:

> Le plus grand général
> Est le général Boulanger
>
> Le plus grand chanteur
> Est le chanteur Paulus
>
> Les meilleurs pastilles
> Sont les pastilles Géraudel.[24]

For the most part, soaps, pipes, watch chains, chocolates, cold medicines, and perfumes carrying Boulanger's name were confined to Paris, its suburbs, and provincial cities. This novel mélange of commercialism and propaganda was an important feature of political acculturation in the fin de siècle, and though it was largely an urban affair, the evidence suggests that trinkets arrived in a few rural villages.[25]

In the main, however, striking contrasts existed between Boulangist propaganda in Paris and that sent to rural communities. *L'Intransigeant* or *La Cocarde* may be found in some bourgs and market towns, but many country people learned about the General by way of hundreds of thousands of images which shared a common iconography very different from the front pages of *La Bombe* or *Le Jeune Garde*: most were simple, small compositions (because portable and inexpensive to manufacture and ship)[26] showing the General on horseback or in close-up posed against a neutral background. Only a few offered detailed illustrations which left little doubt about the intended message: in one engraving, two women dressed in the traditional costumes of Alsace and Lorraine plead with Marianne to rescue them while the General looks on steadfast and brave; in another, figures representing the French-Russian alliance are protected by Boulanger.[27] A large song sheet entitled "le Coup de balai" (fig. 3) had the General and Marianne sweeping frock-coated Opportunists from the Chamber and read in part:

> La vill' la campagne
> Ont soupé de vous
> Bourgogne et Champagne
> Normadi' Poitu
> Paris la province
> Demandent prompt'ment
> Que l'on vous evince
> Tous du parlement.[28]

This was unusual. Most images sent to the countryside contained no clear political message, republican or monarchist, Left or Right. An ex-deputy from the Landes, acting as a local Boulangist agent for Baron Mackau, complained that a manifesto sent to his department was "too weak, too dull, too parliamentary," and, he added, "it is not with those kinds of phrases that one stirs up the peasantry."[29] Instead, rural agents preferred simple, direct, uncaptioned images. "The Epinal industry . . . gives us the General standing against a gold background," reported *Le Petit Journal*, "his bust in a frame of flowers; the General on a white horse; the General on a black horse, the General reviewing the troops; a large portrait surrounded by laurel wreaths; and a portrait against a pink background. . . ."[30] Compared to Parisian propaganda, many details were missing; but as a recent scholar of popular imagery reminds us, one must study "blindness as much as vision. . . ."[31]

"L'image grave l'idée dans l'esprit," insisted an apologist for illustrated catechism manuals early in the twentieth century.[32] The insight was correct, but hardly original. From the wood engravings of the fifteenth century, through the popular *Bibliothèque bleue* to the mass production of *images d'Epinal* in the nineteenth, pictures had been the "readings" of the people, saints' images the "Bible of the poor."[33] Christ and the Apostles, the Virgin and the Holy Family, scenes of kings and queens, plants and animals, soldiers and emperors, of chivalry and romance, astrology and the apocalypse, were carried throughout France by peddlers—and never more often or with greater variety than in the nineteenth century when the Pellerin company of Epinal alone produced 1,112 different types of images copied thousands of times over. One historian reckons that "without exaggeration" up to the Great

3. Le Coup de Balai

War *images d'Epinal* had "inundated the entire world." Missionaries and others transported them to America, Africa, and Asia, but their first and richest market had been the remote regions of France.[34]

Yet, despite ongoing technological improvements crowned by the industrial methods of Epinal, the subject matter and style of popular imagery maintained an extraordinary sameness over the centuries. In the case of religious images (and most were religious) there was little reason for change. Christ's story was immutable. But even temporal subjects showed only slight deviations. When Restoration authorities reprimanded Jean Charles Pellerin for his immensely popular Napoleonic images, he recanted, swore an oath of allegiance to Louis XVIII, then ran off a series of engravings of the King and his family that seemed to have been traced from portraits of Napoleon and his clan.[35] In turn, depictions of Napoleon could have been traced from older cavalier prints of Jean de Paris or Louis XIV.[36]

The cavalier theme was an ancient one. In Dürer's *Death on Horseback* and earlier prints, horses played their traditional role of transporting souls from this life to the next. But, as André Varagnac has pointed out, "such a cult could not be tolerated by Christianity for very long. . . ."[37] Gradually, saints took to the saddle in place of allegorical figures and a new pictorial mode developed which, along with portraits of kings and noblemen on horseback dating from the seventeenth century, influenced the popular propaganda of modern army officers and ambitious political upstarts. (See figures 4 and 5.)

By the 1830s and 40s the Napoleonic legend was attracting the attention of provincial folk more humble (and less educated) than Stendhal's Julien Sorel. They had neither the time nor the equipment to read the *Mémorial de Sainte Hélène*, but they could (and did) collect colorful images of the Emperor. An early lithograph showed Napoleon surrounded by the Virgin and Saint Michael protecting the crucified Christ; and the cult continued to develop through images of Bonaparte at Austerlitz and Moscow—or simply alone, in profile, on horseback: a pose that would be struck by his nephew and repeated by Boulanger[38] (figures 6-9).

Sheets of images containing a repetition of identical units had long been a staple of Epinal (fig. 10). Small tricolor-rimmed portraits of Boulanger commissioned by *La Cocarde* grew out of this tradition (fig. 11). Mass-produced and easily disseminated, they were shipped to news vendors or political agents, cut out, pasted on any available surface, or simply scattered about in profusion. Similarly, country people often learned about heroic legends, religious and secular, through lithographs which portrayed basic events in a series of 16 or 20 vignettes.

4. La Mort se rend à la ville

These were the days before a thousand words were needed to understand a single picture, and though simple captions sometimes accompanied images, the pictures of Jeanne d'Arc or of General Boulanger
said it all (figs. 12 and 13). Police were on the look out for one lithograph sent to the countryside entitled "Aujourd'hui et demain." A strip
of images informed peasants and workers what their fate would be
after voting for Boulanger: penury and oppression "today," arcadia
and respect "tomorrow." On the one hand, the format was reminiscent
of the Epinal vignettes of Notre Dame de la Salette, Jeanne d'Arc, and
countless other religious and secular figures;[39] on the other, its relatively sophisticated modeling reflected the cartoons and caricatures of
the contemporary popular press. Of course, the "before and after"
technique was not born with Boulanger, nor was it limited to politics
or the nineteenth century. Religious or secular, the promise, if not the
outcome, was always clear: a correctly placed vote, like a religious
conversion, will achieve quick and miraculous results.

    The second half of the nineteenth century also marked the golden
age of the small devotional image. Peddlers sold thousands of inexpensive pictures of Jesus, the Virgin, and the Sacred Heart, and these
sujets de piété could still be found in peasant homes and pockets in the
twentieth century.[40] Their convenient size and simple compositions

5. Louis XIV

had much in common with Boulangist pictures. Indeed, they were sometimes delivered in the same bundle: enterprising peddlers in Belfort inserted Boulangist lithographs into stacks of saint imagery in order to avoid the questions of customs inspectors; and, perhaps, to fob their goods off on unsuspecting peasants. Finally, photographs of Boulanger—small and pocket-sized like devotional images—must have also intrigued country people who had had little access to this new and startling phenomenon.[41]

When a picture recalls old, familiar compositions, a deeper meaning is grafted to the subject. The evidence suggests that an element of "associative composition" was at work in the hundreds of thousands of Boulangist images, illustrated almanacs, posters, song sheets, and rosettes sent to rural France.[42] It might be an exaggeration to say that

6. Bonaparte, Premier Consul

images of Napoleon I secured the Tuileries for Napoleon III, remarks
Jean Mistler, "but it would be wrong to pretend that they did not
help."[43] Similarly, Boulangists complemented modern propaganda—
newspapers, political agents, manifestos—with traditional visual appeals destined for rural localities.[44] In August, 1889, police learned
that a manufacturer of religious articles in Paris had been contracted
to make 100,000 busts of Boulanger to be sent to the provinces. They
should not have been surprised. Peddlers who had carried platters
filled with plaster saints and Bonapartes to villages a half century before
were hired to do the same for Boulanger. The most blatant example
of traditional iconography pressed into modern service, one which
appeared in cafés throughout the Orne and elsewhere, showed the
General, uniformed and draped in the Tricolor, nailed to a massive
wooden cross. The secular Virgin, Marianne, is at his feet, and German
officers, like Roman centurions, rejoice in the shadows (fig. 14).[45]

Histories of Boulangism offer quaint descriptions of the peasant
cottage or village café where one found "glued to the wall . . . the
brilliantly colored portrait of General Boulanger on horseback."[46] They
had much in common with Napoleonic portraits worshipped by Zola's
miners in *Germinal* or pictures of Czar Nicholas which would be placed
near icons in Russian peasant huts a few years later. Boulanger's star

7. Napoléon I

8. Empereur Napoléon III

9. Général Boulanger

10. Notre Dame de la Salette

was never as bright, and it faded more quickly, but the way in which he and his agents appealed to country people fit neatly with proven forms of popular propaganda. In 1887 an official in the Sarthe warned that these methods were common in the countryside where political images had been hanging in farmhouses and inns for many years.[47] Another observer complained that "naive [Boulangist] posters, primitive images, foolish songs, mystical adulations" were nothing less than continuations of the "evil Napoleonic legend."[48] In fact, Boulanger's stunning electoral victory in the Dordogne in April, 1888, was attributed in part to his sagacious use of propaganda in cafés and in the countryside: memories of earlier *images d'Epinal* survived in this Bonapartist department, as they must have done in the Seine-et-Marne where crowds greeted the General with shouts of "Vive Boulanger!" interspersed with cries of "Vive l'Empereur!"[49]

Many believed that peasants were susceptible to "false slogans, repeated hundreds of times [which] sink into the unconscious by force

11. Général Boulanger, *La Cocarde*

of constant repetition."[50] A doctor in the Meurthe-et-Moselle reported that "naive people had their eyes filled with images of Boulanger and their ears ringing with his praises. And you know that no amount of reasoning could prevail against their folly."[51] Perhaps the doctor, intrigued by recent discoveries of the powers of hypnotism, was casting his net too widely. But he was not alone. Others, most notably the crowd psychologist Gustave Le Bon, insisted that the deluge of Boulangist propaganda aroused the "religious instincts" of the masses.[52] Agents in the Somme believed the General's success was assured in that department not only because other candidates were incompetent, but because the General's portrait on café walls was "the object of a pilgrimage. . . ."[53] Republicans in the Hérault feared that "there are so many naive voters that, with the help of fables and legends [Boulangists] could fool them and secure their support at the next elections."[54]

Histoire de Jeanne d'Arc, la Libératrice de la France

PELLERIN & Cᵉ, imp.-édt.

née à Domremy, petit village du département des Vosges

IMAGERIE D'ÉPINAL, N° 762

Jeanne d'Arc était une pauvre fille du village de Domremy, elle passait sa jeunesse à garder le troupeau de son père, et à prier Dieu et la Sᵗᵉ-Vierge.

Souvent elle offrait des fleurs à la Vierge Marie et brûlait des cierges devant son image.

Un jour l'archange Sᵗ-Michel, Sᵗᵉ-Catherine et Sᵗᵉ-Marguerite lui apparurent et lui ordonnèrent de chasser les Anglais du royaume de France.

Jeanne d'Arc alla trouver le chevalier de Baudricour, capitaine de Vaucouleurs, pour qu'il la fit conduire au roi de France Charles VII.

Jeanne d'Arc fut présentée au roi de France, par le chevalier Jean de Metz et le chevalier Bertrand de Poulengy le 25 février 1429.

Le roi ayant fait armer Jeanne d'Arc, elle partit avec une petite armée pour porter secours à la ville d'Orléans assiégée par les Anglais.

Jeanne d'Arc, en montant à l'assaut du fort des Tournelles, fut blessée à l'épaule d'un trait d'arbalète.

Ayant fait panser sa blessure à la hâte, elle retourna au combat et emporta le fort d'assaut. — Les Anglais furent surpris et faits prisonniers.

Effrayés des succès de Jeanne d'Arc, les Anglais levèrent le siège d'Orléans, en abandonnant leurs malades, leurs prisonniers et leurs provisions.

Quelques temps après, Jeanne d'Arc tailla en pièces l'armée anglaise à la bataille de Patay.

Jeanne d'Arc assistant au conseil du roi, lui promit que bientôt elle le ferait sacrer à Reims.

Quelques mois après, Jeanne accompagna le roi qui, entouré de toute la noblesse du royaume, fut sacré dans la cathédrale de Reims.

Pendant le siège de Compiègne, Jeanne d'Arc en voulant porter secours aux assiégés, tomba entre les mains des Anglais qui la firent prisonnière.

Elle fut mise en prison et reçut la visite des seigneurs Anglais qui l'accablèrent d'injures de toutes sortes.

Jeanne d'Arc fut jugée dans sa prison ; mais elle déconcerta ses bourraux par ses réponses héroïques et sa vertu.

Bien qu'innocente elle fut condamnée, à la honte éternelle de ses juges, et brûlée vive sur la place du vieux marché, à Rouen.

12. Histoire de Jeanne d'Arc

13. Une Biographie, Boulanger

14. Il Ressuscitera

It comes as no surprise that for many urban observers gullibility was synonymous with rural life. Naiveté—a word often applied to peasants by outsiders—indicates ingenuousness, lack of instruction or worldly experience; few would deny that peasants in varying degrees fit those definitions in the 1880s. But it may also mean lack of analysis, subtlety or depth, a tendency to accept without consideration. Rural people might have been more comfortable with posters and popular imagery than with the dense print of Paris or provincial newspapers, but their indifference to or isolation from the *Journal Officiel* or *L'Intransigeant* did not preclude the formation of subtle political opinions. City folk had different sources on which to base their political choices, but they had no monopoly on sober reflection.

Newspaper editorials and lengthy political treatises remained where they belonged (or so most Boulangist agents thought): in cities and towns. Almanacs, posters, and a few newspapers were available for those who wished to read about the General; but most of the propaganda destined for country people was visual and, in its iconography, traditional.[55]

"The important thing about popular heroes is not so much their own intentions," wrote Barrès, "but the picture of them that people create in their own minds."[56] Country people formed a picture of Boulanger and his movement from a composite of traditional and modern sources: familiar images of "popular heroes," politics discussed face-to-face, news brought by roaming bands of Parisian agents, and, on occasion, Boulangist newspapers. The issue is one of degree: in the late 1880s modern techniques had not yet eclipsed traditional methods in the countryside. In the Isère, for example, some peasants still believed that the Grotto of Balme provided an enchanted refuge for heroic bandits, most notably Mandrin, the popular eighteenth-century victim of old regime tax collectors. Legend had it that Mandrin held a meeting in the Grotto with his nineteenth-century equivalent, General Boulanger.[57]

Pictorial styles based on popular imagery, like old legends of enchanted local grottos, served to bring distant issues close to home. By mimicking Epinal, Boulangists avoided the appearance of a Paris-imposed, centralized campaign. As crafty religious and secular propagandists had done for centuries, Boulangists kept their message simple and traditional to give the impression, perhaps, that their propaganda (and, by extension, their movement) had been the grass-roots work of rural folk and not the calculated national campaign of distant urban administrators.

But the uses to which most rural people put their image of Boulanger

were neither atavistic nor naive: it is unlikely that they filed into cafés
to worship Boulangist icons with the same devotion or expectation they
brought to Lourdes or La Salette. Mysteries surrounding national politics died more quickly than those associated with saints and holy foun-
tains. Still, visual images and legends remained popular and useful
tools in the final decades of the century. To be sure, for urban observers
peasant politics included foolishness and mystical adulation, but whose
politics do not?

Popular imagery would never again play such an important role in
the dissemination of political propaganda in the countryside. As quickly
and decisively as television replaced radio in the mid-twentieth century,
newspapers eclipsed imagery at the end of the nineteenth. This, of
course, was part of a broader trend. Continuing improvements in every
aspect of mass communication—increased literacy, the spread of newspapers, journals, and much more—affected visual style. The simple
images that for centuries had been designed in the city for use in the
countryside gave way to illustrations and photographs for common
consumption in big towns and tiny hamlets; there is an iconography
of national acculturation. Now *images d'Epinal* have gone the way of
maypoles and Yule logs, serving a new purpose for a new clientele:
they still instruct and delight, but only the children of France, not their
parents, pay attention.[58]

PEDDLERS AND HAWKERS

Traveling through Brittany in 1840, Anthony Trollope met a peddler
laden with merchandise who informed him that "objects of fine art are
life's most noble attraction, and those who distribute them are the most
powerful agents of civilization."[59] If part of the "civilizing process"
includes an increasing awareness of another art, national politics, then
this peddler's successors were continuing the tradition half a century
later. Between 1888 and 1890 Comte Dillon, Baron Mackau, Henri
Rochefort, and other Boulangist leaders mobilized scores of Parisian
peddlers and camelots, paid them two to ten francs a day, plied them
with food and drink, provided train tickets and stacks of pictures and
posters, and sent them off to shout and sell the Boulangist cause.[60]

Images are imbued with more meaning when accompanied by words,
spoken words. Stained-glass depictions of religious scenes in churches
allow worshipers to ponder the visual while priests recite the written.
Only recently—in our century for the most part—have churchgoers
carried missals and bothered to read along. So it went for the prop-
agation of another faith: politics. If religious imagery and sermonizing

were tools "at the service of the faith,"[61] so, too, were secular pictures and the verbal messages carried by political agents, whose job it was to "heat up" the peasantry.[62] Outsiders from the city poured into villages and hamlets in the late 1880s; and when these professional agents are considered along with the thousands of images they and others sold or gave away, it is not difficult to understand why Boulanger was the first minister since Gambetta known to many French peasants.[63] The dramatic and pervasive campaigns waged by Boulangists—and, in response, by the official republican network—served to draw many country people into the national political process. The General's ragged army of propagandists aimed to enlist support (and votes), and no matter how they were received in remote localites—applauded or chucked out of the village—they succeeded in at least one regard: millions of French men and women, including, and most significantly, those who rarely bothered with newspapers and national politics, heard about the General and his attacks on the Opportunist Republic. Given the times and alternatives, not a few peasants paid attention.

An engraved song sheet entitled "La Carmagnole des camelots" had Boulanger (again on horseback) surrounded by young men selling copies of *La Cocarde* and *La Presse*:

> Camelots, crieurs de journaux (bis)
> Pour engraisser chaque jour nos
> Ventres, faut nous range
> Autour de Boulanger. . . .[64]

Hired to hawk newspapers and shout Boulangist slogans, these young men were not confined to the streets of Paris nor to the distribution of newsprint. The police archives hold remnants of contracts between the Boulangist National Committee and hawkers, and we know from these and other sources that agents were sent to the Marne, Somme, Pas-de-Calais, Nord, Orne, Indre-et-Loire, Charente, Ardèche, Haute-Garonne, Isère, even to Corsica.[65] The Amiens committee alone registered 100 Boulangist agents in August, 1888; most were peddlers or newspapers hawkers, and all came from Paris.[66] Perhaps much of the mass enthusiasm we associate with Boulangist demonstrations in Paris and the provinces should be reassessed in the light of reports that hired peddlers caused much of the fuss.[67] During Boulanger's visit to Nevers, hundreds of "squalling," brawling hawkers shocked local residents.[68] One historian agrees that agents in town and country "supplied vociferous support," and suggests that their contract included two extra francs for those who got into scuffles. Torn clothes would be replaced free of charge.[69]

Conservative Boulangists led by Mackau and Comte Dillon tried to revivify the beleaguered movement in the summer of 1889 by launching what one election worker called "propaganda voyages."[70] Reports from scores of departments show that agents carried tracts and images into rural communities and spent time cultivating local Boulangist "devotees." Mackau's ledgers list influential notables in each department who hired sympathetic villagers to hawk the Boulangist line. One agent in the Yonne summarized the organization well when, in a letter to Mackau, he advised against sending "Parisian" strangers into small communities; instead, one or two partisans in each village should be hired to distribute Boulangist propaganda.[71] Payments for these services ranged from two to ten francs for peddlers, and from 100 to 3,000 francs for experienced election workers who traveled extensively and often. One old soldier covered the lower Normandy countryside in search of Boulangist supporters among other retired army men; he lunched with rural guards and helped mount election campaigns in a number of western departments. Weighed down by nearly 100 pounds of prospectuses and constantly harrassed by police, he received the handsome monthly sum of 250 francs.[72]

The reception of Boulangist agents in the countryside was uneven and unpredictable. We shall study their impact in more detail in individual departments, but the experience of one équipe operating in the Orne was typical: carrying portraits, song sheets, and manifestos, the group was favorably received in a few communities, reviled in others, and met with indifference in still others. Boulangism enjoyed much success among wood-cutters in the Center, but not in one forest in the Orne where workers had a long-standing grudge against the local Boulangist representative and where new political appeals could not shake loose old personal grievances. On the other hand, in Alençon, peasants come to market showed more interest in copies of L'Intransigeant, La Presse and La Cocarde than did city folk who appeared "very indifferent" to the sale.[73] The number of newspapers carried to the countryside paled in comparison to posters, images, and song sheets, and it is likely that peasants visiting Alençon were taking advantage of those sources to which they had less frequent access than their urban counterparts.

In the early spring of 1888, peddlers marched through the streets of Cahors (Lot) singing "C'est Boulanger qu'il nous faut," "Il Reviendra," and other popular Parisian tunes, and selling song sheets engraved with heroic portraits of the General (figures 15 and 16). Local peasants bought most of the merchandise.[74] A few months before, country people visiting a fair in the Haute-Sâone had purchased Bou-

15. Mon P'tit Boulanger

16. Le Peché de la Cantinière

langist propaganda, but town-dwellers had passed by uninterested.[75] Conversely, in the Oise and Puy-de-Dôme hawkers had no success in peasant hamlets or in towns on market days: when they encountered resistance they were forced to give their stock away.[76] In Briançon (Hautes-Alpes) the local republican paper reported (with not a little relish and perhaps some distortion) that passersby were handed Boulangist rosettes but immediately tossed them away. Elsewhere, locals asked when "this charlatanism will finally come to an end."[77] Hawkers sent from Paris to the Ardèche were refused lodging at local inns, and one innkeeper, thinking Boulanger was among the group, shouted in patois "C'est Boulaingnejia déguijia. A l'ieau!"[78] Peasants in the Nord also threatened to throw visiting Boulangists in the lake. Miners in that department—strong Boulangist supporters—received reams of propaganda including bolts of fabric emblazoned with the General's portrait. But agents had less success in the hinterlands where rural folk were "bewildered by the strangers' gab" (le bagout ahurit les campagnards).[79]

Finally, impressionistic evidence suggests that some peasants visiting markets and fairs seized the opportunity to buy cheap and colorful pictures no matter what the subject: in the Loire-Inférieure in 1889, ribbons, rosettes, and military images sold to peasants were not, at first glance, Boulangist (fig. 17); only after close examination did they realize that the officer on horseback in one scene was Boulanger[80] (and not Bonaparte? the Comte de Paris? did it matter?).

In these examples and others the political and ideological are confounded with the customary, commercial, and aesthetic, and clear-cut interpretations become hazardous. This summary gives us a sense of the movement's national scope, but reveals little about how and why peasants took notice in individual localities. Alexandre Zévaès, a socialist deputy from the Isère, said that soldiers, thrilled with Boulanger's progressive reforms while Minister of War, sent letters praising him to families and friends in the "most remote hamlets [where] newspapers do not penetrate, or penetrate infrequently."[81] Paul Lafargue agreed that "soldiers returning home or writing to their families . . . have sown throughout France the seeds of this astonishing popularity. . . ."[82] In addition, provincial clergymen admired Boulanger and believed (or hoped their parishioners would believe) that "the General has been sent by God."[83] But these broad assessments apply to France as a whole, and though soldiers and priests surely had some influence in departments with large army garrisons and religious enclaves, such generalizations shed no light on specific rural communities.

What Henri Rochefort and the Boulangist entertainer Paulus could

17. General on Horseback

accomplish in a matter of days in Paris in 1886 took months in rural communities where national political issues had to make the journey and then be adapted to local realities and people: political labels were formed and attached more slowly in rural France than in Paris and provincial cities. Particular interpretations of Boulanger and his movement in the countryside would have to come from visiting agents and personalities within the community, and be shaped not only by propaganda and immediate needs, but by personal and political relationships of long standing. Boulangist organizers mounted extensive campaigns complete with pictures, print, and spokesmen; and peasants from the Marne to the Isère, from the Orne to the Gers, and beyond to Corsica, faced a new alternative to old political traditions.

Reports to Boulangist committees from traveling agents and their local contacts indicate that organizers tried to keep their fingers on the political pulses of rural communities. Agents in the Deux-Sèvres, for example, described the route they would take through that department, as well as through the Haute-Vienne, Corrèze, and Creuse, where they would interview locals on the spot and report back to the national committee.[84] Detailed descriptions of peasant discontent in the Drôme led agents to suggest that "a Boulangist candidate proclaiming himself straightforwardly [carrément] republican would have a good chance" in that department; and, indeed, a candidate emerged who spent long days traveling through the countryside.[85] In other areas, a Boulangist with a Bonapartist program might fare better; in still others, as in the Pas-de-Calais, exploitation of longstanding town rivalries might attract local support. From the Ardennes, Meurthe-et-Moselle, Aisne, Hautes-Alpes, Ain and other departments came more reports on the needs and desires of country people and the ways in which Boulangist could best tap local interests.[86] Agents did not always meet with success—their very presence often alienated suspicious peasants, and their analyses were frequently off the mark—but it is important to note that Boulangists made a concerted effort to probe the desires of French peasants. We shall see that government officials responded by turning their attention to politics in the countryside.

A battle was on between Boulangists and entrenched systems, and peasants, like miners in the Nord and petty bourgeois in Paris, were swept into the melée. Between 1887 and 1889 political methods born in Paris but familiar to country people reached out to the provinces to unravel traditional local ties. Successes were uneven, failures many, but the long-term effect on politics in diverse rural regions was great. A close study of four departments will show how the movement operated on the spot, and how Boulangists and their enemies drew significant numbers of country people into the national political process.

CHAPTER IV

THE RURAL LEGACY

La popularité. Ah! le beau mépris que j'ai pour elle! Pense-t-on que si Boulanger arrive à jouer en France le Bonaparte, il le devra en grande partie à la chanson de Paulus?

EDMOND DE GONCOURT, 1887

Goncourt was mistaken. General Boulanger's political fate, like that of his Bonapartist predecessors, would hinge on more than songs, imagery, and hired hawkers. The movement's sophisticated, well-financed organization could attract the attention of country people, but success or failure in villages and hamlets would depend on a variety of local conditions. We shall see that interest in Boulangism ranged from noteworthy in parts of the rural Isère, Savoie, and Orne, to marginal in much of the Gers, Marne, and Vendée. But peasants lived in concrete communities, not abstract administrative units, and only the "truffle hunter," as Emmanuel Le Roy Ladurie has put it, not the "parachutist" can unravel complex rural reactions. A close look at representative regions reveals that, win or lose, the General's campaign left a significant political legacy in much of rural France.

Paulus had been singing Boulanger's praises in Paris for a year before news of the General moved from accounts in Grenoble to political speeches and demonstrations in the Isère countryside. During a by-election in 1887 one candidate declared his support for "the project of General Boulanger," and lost. In fact none of the candidates excited voters; almost by default, M. Valentin, a republican and better-known than his rivals, became the new deputy in this department where personal and local questions played an important role. Widespread abstentions would provide a striking contrast to hotly fought elections a year later when Boulanger himself appeared on the ballot.[1]

On this election Sunday in May, 1887, rural communes remained especially aloof. Excellent weather, the first in weeks, sent peasants "off to gather fodder instead of voting." Work in the fields kept many voters far from the polls, while others held their distance no matter what the work or weather; the journey from outlying villages to communal *chefs-lieux* in the mountainous Bourg d'Oisans canton, for example, had to be worth one's while. Even an independent "agricultural candidate" failed to arouse peasant interest and finished last. None of the contestants wielded great influence in the department, and the rural voters' "indecision" in 1887 had as much to do with "the personal situation" as it did with "the political question."[2] Little had changed since the previous year when officials urged voters in the smallest communes to throw off their "lassitude and indifference" and extricate themselves from the "intrigues and influence of certain personalities," including priests who continued to apply pressure in villages.[3]

Rural indifference in 1886-87 had more to do with a paucity of relevant issues and persons than with peasant "lassitude." The agricultural crisis was severe, and a decent day's work in the fields more important, in May of 1887 at least, than participation in the electoral process. A rural almanac reporting on politics throughout France believed that recent elections "have proved that the political education [of rural voters] has made absolutely no progress."[4] Not surprisingly, the conservative and clerical almanac chastised peasants who turned to republican candidates, but it, too, misread peasant self-interest for political indifference. Hard work and political inaction marked 1887 in the rural Isère. General Boulanger, all the rage in Paris, was of marginal (and urban) interest.

But national politics had a place in peasant life beyond campaign weeks and election days. In July, 1887, a few Isère communes reported hearing references to Boulanger during modest *fêtes nationales*. The allusions were scattered and feeble indeed compared to those heard at the same celebration a year earlier in Paris when the new Minister of War—the hero wounded on battlefields in Italy and Indochina—made his triumphant Parisian debut.[5] Crowds greeted him, astride his black charger, Tunis, with shouts of "Long live Boulanger! Down with Ferry!" interspersed with choruses from the café song "En r'venant de la revue."[6]

The following July, in the small resort town of Uriage-les-Bains in the Isère, a traveling salesman "taken by drink" cried "Long live Boulanger." He was collared by police, reprimanded, and released.[7] Uriage might warm to the General a few years later, but for now he was the popular ally of Rochefort and Clemenceau, and conservative town officials wanted none of that. On the same day residents of Saint Marcellin applauded their mayor when he condemned Boulanger and proclaimed that France rejected all dictators.[8] In Grenoble three or four Boulangist shouts had "no echoes." A solitary peddler, hoping to match the brisk business of his counterparts in Paris, had little success selling song sheets and images on the Place Grenette.[9] A year later when, on the death of M. Valentin, another by-election was to take place, Boulangists made their move.

In February, 1888, a new "independent" daily newspaper appeared in the Isère. *Le Petit Grenoblois* was no more "independent" than its political partners in Paris—*La Cocarde, La Lanterne, L'Intransigeant*, Boulangist papers all. The broad and critical political message of *Le Petit Grenoblois* mimicked the standard Boulangist calls for "Revision of the Constitution and Dissolution of the Chamber." The title reflected its geographic boundaries, and articles geared to workers and petty bourgeois mirrored the Boulangist appeal to urban voters which was to be so successful in the Nord. The Isère peasantry received little attention.[10]

In Voiron, one official assured his superiors that the general population showed little interest in the forthcoming election, and added that he was convinced of Boulanger's defeat. A few days later, however, he expressed concern that "in light of the indifference which seems to reign regarding the elections, it would be good if a government spokesman could come to the area to stir up uninterested voters, because their intentions concerning the April 29 election are still unknown."[11] Boulangist rumblings in Grenoble, along with recent victories throughout France, were making republican officials in the countryside uneasy. Inscrutable peasants appeared uninterested (the subprefect of Saint Marcellin stressed "great indifference" in his region, too),[12] but one never knew.

Commenting on Boulanger's success in the Nord, *Le Petit Grenoblois* announced that the Isère (a department which "so loves to be boldly governed") would soon be blessed with a visit from the General.[13] He arrived, but on paper. In the next few weeks hundreds of thousands of voting ballots, thousands of pictures, posters, and brochures, and 30,000 free copies of *Le Petit Grenoblois* flooded the department, arriving in rural communities in the sacks and suitcases of nearly three score Boulangist agents.[14] The organized campaign began after the first ballot, which gave the General only 5000 votes. On May 9 *Le Petit Grenoblois* announced its commitment to the run-off election, and in the days that followed Boulangist agents concentrated on villages in the lower Isère from Grenoble toward Lyon, where they hoped to attract a massive rural turn-out on May 13.[15] How much could be achieved in four days? One official, describing the "incredible activity" of Boulangist propagandists, feared that the General might have a chance if "certain inhabitants of the countryside let themselves be duped by reactionary militants."[16]

Boulanger's opponents, the Radical Gaillard and the Opportunist Girerd, wasted no time getting the word to peasants that this upstart Caesar desired war and adventurism.[17] Girerd's agents tried to beat their Boulangist counterparts into villages, spreading tens of thousands of posters and bulletins in their wake. The extensive and well-entrenched republican network in the Isère, reaching from the prefect down to mayors in the smallest communes, mobilized to confront the Boulangist threat. Agents from all sides pushed and shoved their way into peasant villages; and only election results would reveal who campaigned more successfully. Republicans could not have been encouraged by reports like that from Saint Egrève: "We regret to say that in our community, there exists an insurmountable indifference."[18] Republicans hoped for widespread indignation and received more reports of popular lassitude. Nevertheless, lassitude would be eclipsed by lively interest in the days to come, and it is significant that in response to the Boulangist menace politicians and officials turned their attention to remote rural communes.

Country people old enough to remember must have compared the political storm around them with that of mid-century, when propagandists of every stripe had rushed to secure rural voters in that new, short-lived moment of universal manhood suffrage. Early in March, 1888, *Réveil du dauphiné* noted the comparison and reported that peasants and workers throughout France were coming to the urns shouting "Boulanger," just as they had done thirty-six years ago when they were clamoring for Louis Napoleon.[19] Two months later, in an article entitled "Au drapeau," *Réveil* described how, at this moment, a "shower of . . . circulars, voting ballots, and *feuilles soumises* are falling on our towns and hamlets." Bundles of *images d'Epinal* will spread the figure of "Saint Arnaud du café concert" everywhere.[20] Boulangist propaganda may have been frivolous for some, but government officials in the Isère worried about its impact on country people who had been addressed that way before. It was a distressing tradition. *Le Petit Grenoblois* had limited distribution, but pictures, posters and pamphlets with summaries of the General's program reached rural communities scattered across the plains of the Isère, and even appeared in barely accessible mountain villages deep in the Bourg d'Oisans.

On May 11, 40,000 Boulangist posters and brochures arrived at the Grenoble train station. Agents attached some to city walls, and sent

others to outlying rural communities—with only two days left before
the Sunday run-off. According to the subprefect of Saint Marcellin,
posters appeared in every commune in his region. In Vienne and
Voiron Boulangists were "not numerous," but agents tried to reverse
that trend in the hinterlands. The years 1848-51 had shown that communes around Vienne were less devoted to the Republic than the "red"
chef lieu. To the south, agents set out from Vizelle (that "cradle" of the
French Revolution"), Mens, and Corps for outlying villages. It is impossible to determine the number of posters seen by rural inhabitants;
the campaign was so heated that many were immediately torn down
or pasted over, as in Voiron where six Boulangist posters survived only
a few minutes. *Le Petit Grenoblois* reported that 6,600 *affiches* (of one
shipment totaling 9,000) had been lacerated. Republicans worked hard
to counter the Boulangist threat.[21]

On the eve of the run-off election, an unprecedented propaganda
campaign reached out to rural communities. Other factors would sway
peasant voters, but it is tempting to attribute the General's victory in
Corps, for example, to the fact that Boulangist agents followed Girerd's
men into the canton, saturating villages with propaganda at the last
minute. Local observers warned republican officials that Girerd might
not do well in Corps.[22] He did not; nor did the Radical Gaillard, who
would eventually prevail in the department.

Traditional organizations commonly associated with Boulangism had
little effect during the Isère by-election. Paul Déroulède's Ligue des
Patriotes had, by 1887-88, rallied to Boulanger's cause, fitting "General
Revanche" neatly into its program and greatly helping the movement
in Paris, Marseille, and other large cities.[23] It is perhaps obvious that
an organization founded as a gymnastic society for the physical and
moral regeneration of the French would be of little interest to peasants
toiling from dawn to dusk in rural fields. But calisthenics practiced by
vigorous youths, as well as by those whom in another context Robert
Paxton has called "liverish bourgeois,"[24] had given way to pure politics
by the late 1880s. One could be a member regardless of flab or physical
stamina.

In June, 1887, a League meeting in Grenoble attracted 600 spec-
tators, but Boulanger was not mentioned. A few months later, in Saint
Marcellin, two students came from Grenoble to form a League section,
but, says the subprefect, the conference was "literary," and politics not
part of the agenda. In February, 1888, with the by-election drawing
near, League members attracted an impressive 2,000 to a meeting in
Voiron, but the evening was devoted to patriotic speeches on the Lost
Provinces and, again, Boulanger was not discussed. The die was cast

in Grenoble, as it would be in other provincial centers, when the small local chapter ignored Déroulède's entreaties and decided not to support Boulanger in the election.[25] Shortly thereafter the section disbanded. When an attempt was made to resurrect interest in the League and Boulanger in September, police reported that inhabitants remained indifferent, except for one student in Grenoble who drew an audience of fourteen to a League meeting. Quite obviously, the young man enjoyed "no local influence."[26] Five years later, the prefect assured the Minister of the Interior that the League had still not been reconstituted and had never been important in the Isère.[27] There is no evidence of peasant support for, or interest in, the Ligue des Patriotes. The feeling, it seems, was mutual.

On March 18, 1888, L'Intransigeant in Paris published the first manifesto of the Comité républicain de protestation nationale. "The name Boulanger signifies: public liberties, democratic reforms at home, dignity abroad. . . ." Rambling pleas for more effective government and social justice were juxtaposed with condemnations of bungling Opportunists who had sullied the French image.[28] L'Intransigeant rarely reached beyond Paris. Even so, most peasants could hardly have been moved by articles devoted to students, dock workers, glass blowers, and miners; or to romanticized portraits of Blanqui and Louise Michel. This was the stuff which would make for victories in the industrial Nord and Paris, and for indifference in much of the countryside.[29] Another Paris paper, Le Petit Journal, with an enormous circulation of one million copies, had attained some popularity in the provinces; there is no evidence, however, that it appeared in significant numbers in the Isère.[30] One Boulangist militant said that the French peasant "only reads Le Petit Journal and only interests himself in agricultural, industrial and commercial news," not politics.[31] He was wrong on many counts. The paper had an occasional article on rural France, but urban workers and petty bourgeois were its principal clientele. In short, Paris newspapers, especially Boulangist newspapers, rarely addressed the peasantry.

Meanwhile, Le Petit Grenoblois continued to mimic its betters in Paris. Articles devoted to workers in Isère industries and town folk in Grenoble helped localize its appeal. From news on the front page to advertisements on the back, it was citified. Boulanger appeared as "General Dissolution" engaged in valiant battle against weak-kneed and traitorous republicans: the hero of the (urban) little man.[32]

More likely country people got their news from the Assumptionist Catholic paper, La Croix de l'Isère rather than Le Petit Journal or any other Paris source. La Croix would enjoy immense popularity in the final decade of the century, and be an important factor in the countryside during the Dreyfus Affair;[33] until the summer following the by-election, the General's Radicalism (read anti-clericalism, though Boulanger was vague on this issue too) and closeness to Alfred Naquet, the detested Jewish proponent of divorce, prompted only a few hostile comments. Indeed, until late 1888 *La Croix* concentrated almost exclusively on church issues.[34] Another Catholic organ in the provinces, *La Semaine religieuse*, important because read by rural priests, never mentioned Boulanger or his movement in the months surrounding the spring election. The Isère edition confined its rare political commentary to questions of church and state.[35]

The proliferation of local newspapers in the Isère would come in the final decade of the century. *Réveil agricole des alpes* and *Réveil des cultivateurs* focused on rural inhabitants, but they did not begin publication until 1893. In the early months of 1888, when Boulangism became an issue outside Grenoble, political news still arrived in peasant communities through traditional channels: travelers, soldiers, migrant laborers, peddlers, posters, and popular imagery.

Boulangist propaganda offered the Isère peasantry little concrete information beyond promising to "revitalize commerce, industry, and labor; [and] protect agriculture."[36] Specifics like those Jules Méline would present, for better or worse, a half-decade later were, for Boulanger, off the point and risky. Other propaganda shipped to the Isère in the early months of 1888 echoed the two-note theme of "Dissolution of the Chamber" and "Revenge." Military allusions and obsession with revenge must not have sat well with Isère peasants far removed from the blue line of the Vosges.[37] Rural people, like most sane Frenchmen, were not eager to leave their families and farms for the second time in less than a generation. Eugen Weber has it that until 1889 "the army was one of the countryman's bogeys," and not until the 1890s does one find "persuasive evidence that the army was no longer 'theirs' but 'ours.' "[38] Anti-militarism also persisted in areas where the army had been sent to crush local strikes. Although most country people did not share this particular grievance, they had sufficient reasons of their own to distrust an institution which took their sons and engaged in distant wars. Ironically, progressive reforms instituted by Boulanger while Minister of War helped popularize the military after generations of hostility; that took time, however, and did not mean that peasants approved of the General's *revanchisme*. Bellicose statements and threats to the long peace secured by the early Third Republic came not from peasants, but from the likes of Déroulède and Boulanger. Or so it appeared. One tract had advised supporters of the General to fire up peasants by convincing them that, without Boulanger, Prussians would be sticking their "dirty hands" and "chops" in our "soup bowls . . . and good French wine."[39] In the Isère the argument was turned on its head in an anti-Boulangist poster:

> To My Friends: The Peasants. If you want war vote for Boulanger. You are unhappy with your present plight and you are correct. But General Boulanger will not help you sell your wheat or live-stock at a higher price, nor will he destroy phylloxera . . . If you want your sons killed, your homes burned, your fields devastated by Prussians, Austrians, and Italians, vote for General Boulan-ger.[40]

If militarism and nationalism had been the only issues in the election of 1888 in the Isère, Boulanger's votes would have dwindled by half. They were not the only issues, however, and votes on the second round—rural votes—increased.

The General's image on engravings and lithographs; calls for revision and revenge carried by agents into the countryside; thousands of posters, pamphlets, and free copies of *Le Petit Grenoblois*; all these factors helped shaped rural perceptions of Boulanger. Not a few peasants were to come to the polls in the spring of 1888, and their votes for or against the General (or their abstentions) were based on a blend of recently formed opinions, long-standing political traditions, and a complex interplay of local pressure and influence.

The first round of the by-election took place on April 29. Boulanger, recently elected in the Nord, did not stand as an official candidate, and only *Le Petit Grenoblois* tried to arouse interest in the General. The deluge of propaganda was still to come. Nonetheless, he received almost 5,000 votes from widely scattered communes in nearly every canton. Voters cast 75,423 ballots (somewhat fewer than in the 1887 by-election), and the Opportunist Girerd edged out his Radical opponent Gaillard. Abstentions were over 60 percent.[41]

It was not the Nord, Dordogne, or Aisne where Boulanger had sailed to impressive victories, but it was not the Haute-Marne or Hautes-Alpes either, where defeat had been an embarrassment (126 votes in the latter). Boulangists found more than a flicker of interest in the Isère, and during the next two weeks aimed to increase the tally tenfold. They had to settle for threefold, but impressive strides were taken in a very short time, and rural communes played a principal role.[42]

On May 13 Gaillard prevailed with 40,488 votes. Girerd's tally fell to 37,923, Boulanger's rose to 14,374. A glance at the two ballots shows that the Radical did not win on Opportunist pickings; nor did Boulanger simply steal votes from his two rivals. Almost 20,000 new voters came to the polls, and the General's campaign was largely responsible. Abstentions had dropped by nearly 20 percent, an important indication that this election differed greatly from others in the Isère. Abstentions were almost always higher on the second round, but in May, 1888, that trend was momentarily reversed.[43] The aberration is significant and supports the view that the Boulangist campaign and the republican reaction it engendered served to politicize large numbers of rural voters who had sat out the first round, and, perhaps, every previous national contest.

The General's worst showing came in towns and industrial centers: Grenoble, Vienne, Voiron, La Tour du Pin, La Mure. In fact, on the second round he decisively won only four communes of more than 1,000 inhabitants, and carried only two *chefs-lieux*: Crémieu in the extreme north, and Clelles in the extreme south.[44] The geographic and economic bifurcation of the Isère played no part, it seems, in Boulanger's success (or failure). Traditionally, political conservatism marked isolated mountain villages, whereas republicanism thrived better on the plains where small-holding peasants were more often free from the pressure of local notables and priests.[45] But on the second round Boulanger received almost 9,000 votes in the approximate region of the lower Isère, almost 6,000 in the highlands. Given population distribution and the difficulty of voting in mountainous areas, these statistics reveal only that geography did not determine the General's popularity.

He carried two cantons: Bourg d'Oisans and Corps, both in the south and overwhelmingly agricultural. He lost their *chefs-lieux*, however: masons and workers in the town of Bourg d'Oisans did not flock to the General as they had in other semi-industrial centers of France. On the other hand, peasants in the small mountain communes of Huez, Clavans, Besse, and Venosc were almost unanimous in their support. On the first round the General received only 77 votes in the entire Bourg d'Oisans canton, a mere 64 in Corps; on the second his tally rose to 689 and 416 votes respectively. His opponents' support remained fairly constant, indicating that Boulanger brought almost 1,000 new voters to the polls in these two areas alone. Such was the case throughout the department, including those areas where the General was soundly trounced (Voiron, Touvet, Valbonnais). Again, many new votes came from small rural communes.[46]

What, if anything, did these dispersed peasant communities have in common—beyond agricultural activity—which might explain the election of 1888? Rural political traditions shaped the election in telling

ways. In the narrow region from Grenoble southwest toward the Ver-
cours, residents took little interest in Boulanger. He lost every commune in the Sassenage and Vif cantons, and received only a few dozen
votes in the cantons of Villard-de-Lans and Pont-en-Royans. The entire
area had been among the most consistently loyal to republicanism since
mid-century; in fact, Pont-en-Royans was the last Bonapartist canton
in a department with more than its share of "popular Bonapartism"
after 1850.[47] To the north, the General did very poorly in Vienne, one
of the historically radical industrial centers of the Alpine region, but
fared better in the hinterlands, which became Bonapartist strongholds
after 1850 (and General Boulanger's agents made a point of visiting
those hinterlands). In the countryside surrounding Saint Etienne-de-
Saint Geoirs and Roybon, Boulanger lost the bourgs but gathered a
few votes in communes which had earlier rallied to the Party of Order.[48]

Closer to the Rhône border, the General won the town of Crémieu
only a few kilometers from Lyon. A conservative region dominated by
large landowners up to 1848, Crémieu turned republican after 1849.
Montagnard propaganda from Lyon met with great success among
peasants.[49] Was 1888 an aberration? A return to the Right? Perhaps.
But personal influence remained a "decisive factor" in Crémieu politics,
and it is possible that election statistics hide the pressure that local
Boulangists applied on the rural population. The previous year a republican schoolteacher had placed ballots on a chair outside the town
hall because "the major part of the population, being illiterate, takes
the first thing they find."[50] Boulangist agents might have done the
teacher one better in 1888; they may have placed ballots on a chair in
the café or village square, then escorted voters to the town hall. We
shall see that they used these methods with some success in the neighboring Savoie.

Finally, Boulanger enjoyed modest victories in Corps, Clelles, and
Chartreuse, areas where religious influence was noteworthy. One observer believed that rural priests had been won over to Boulangism[51]
(less scared perhaps of his Radicalism than thrilled with his attacks on
the infidel Ferry); and it is possible that clergymen, propaganda agents
in situ, aided the movement in those regions.

A loose pattern develops, revealing modest Boulangist victories in
rural regions with conservative traditions, contrasted by overwhelming
defeats in consistently republican agricultural areas and in industrial
centers. The Nord, in other words, in reverse. The pattern is far from
rigid, however, and political traditions must be tossed in the mix along
with feuds, rivalries, and personal pressure.

A petition signed by voters from Bourg d'Oisans and sent to the

Isère prefect in May of 1888 affords a rare glimpse at electioneering in a rural community. Local *gardes-champêtres* had exerted "extraordinary pressure" on republican voters trying to exercise their "civil rights": ballots had been torn from voters' hands and replaced with those of other candidates; posters stripped from village walls and scurrilous anti-Government manifestos hung in their stead; contrary voters had been physically kept from the polls. An "unbridled and slanderous propaganda campaign" was mounted against local republicans. Finally, late at night, rural guards humiliated their opponents by staging a "charivari unworthy of civilized people."[52] Boulanger carried only two Isère cantons in 1888: one was the Bourg d'Oisans.

In Corps, his other stronghold, a complaint filed by residents of Monestier d'Ambel (pop. 152) a year after the election reveals that the aging mayor was a notorious Boulangist "à fond de coeur." The prefect had alloted fifteen francs for the commune's July 14 fête, but instead of purchasing decorations "our gallant Boulangist mayor sent his rural guard for pitchers of beer, most of which the mayor consumed with friends by 6 P.M. without informing the villagers." The mayor denied the charges, stressing that candles and flags had in fact been purchased along with "a few bottles of beer drunk in the village square by those who wanted to participate."[53] The true culprit in this minor village drama is of less significance than the power mayors could exercise over local and national political events. Monestier d'Ambel had rallied to Boulanger the year before,[54] and its mayor, with his hands on the purse-strings and beer bottles of the village, must have played an active role.

Indeed in the neighboring Savoie the Boulangist candidate, M. Masse, tried every old trick to entice rural voters. He promised bread, wine, *eau de vie*, tobacco, money, favors, and, perhaps most important, fishing rights on the local canal to Savoyards who cast Boulangist ballots. The Mayor of Ruffieux (pop. 881), in league with Masse, arranged for friends to form a physical barrier around the town hall to divert "doubtful" voters from the polls. Masse's opponents played the same game (though, it seems, less blatantly and with fewer resources). Fearing a close election, they fetched the village idiot, handed him a ballot, and guided him to the polls. Priests instructed parishioners to lacerate republican posters, families publicly insulted each other, and the village schoolteacher did not help his cause by arriving for the election drunk. Late in the afternoon, the Mayor quickly compiled a list of missing voters and set out to get them to the polls to vote for his Boulangist friend—an action, like most of the others described above, as illicit as it was common. Masse emerged victorious in Ruffieux, but only by 30 votes. Personal pressure, old alliances, and campaign money well (if illegally) spent made the difference.[55] The incident was reminiscent of politics in Emilie Carles' Haute Savoie village early in the twentieth century when the mayor secretly marked ballots before handing them to voters: a private code which enabled him to keep tabs on local residents and prepare for future contests.[56]

We shall recount similar incidents in rural communes in other departments. Of course, politicians bought drinks (and votes) and exerted pressure during election campaigns in cities as well. But urban politics, like urban living, was distinguished by the relatively rapid replacement of old local ties with new political alignments and organization. Meanwhile, long-standing personal and family alliances in small, circumscribed communities still greatly influenced the opinions and choices of rural people at the end of the last century; and served to set politics in the countryside apart from the politics of Paris and provincial cities.

Many factors contributed to the General's defeat in the Isère. Elected deputy to the Nord less than a month before, he had not bothered to visit the Southeast, and a vote for Boulanger was more a statement of protest, a sign of dissatisfaction with the alternatives, than an attempt to secure him as an official representative in the Chamber of Deputies. Many voters must have known that. In addition, the Isère, a solidly republican department, successfully mobilized its administrative network to defeat the General. Whether perceived as dangerously Radical or Bonapartist, he was the enemy of Opportunist officialdom. Political opponents responded to his massive propaganda crusade with an all-out effort of their own: Boulangist agents clearly won that round, but lost the main event. Furthermore, by-elections rarely engendered enthusiasm. The former deputy's death meant that Isère voters were called to the polls for the second time in a year (not including departmental and municipal elections); and Alain Lancelot has shown that few things insure political ennui more than a cluster of campaigns and elections.[57] This surely contributed to the high abstention rate in 1888, though it bears repeating that abstentions declined on the second ballot as a result of the Boulangist campaign. The General's support came largely from rural localities, from Isère peasants, but the final tally shows that republicans had not entirely lost this crucial constituency; the need for stability was still winning an uneasy battle with the desire for radical change. Finally, signs indicated that country people retained their penchant for lively interest in local politics over against half-hearted participation in the affairs of the nation. *Conseil général* elections had taken place in March, and, following a classic pattern, voter turn-out in rural regions was much higher than it would be in

May. In the Rousillon canton, for example, abstentions ran 15 percent in March and 43 percent in May.[58]

Yet thousands of votes from dozens of agricultural communes went to Boulanger. The evidence suggests that what had occurred two weeks earlier in northern industrial centers was repeated on a smaller scale in Isère villages. In the Nord, Boulangism provided a focus for discontented urban workers who lacked a party of their own. In other provincial cities, including Bordeaux and Nancy, the General attracted the support of disgruntled urban radicals and socialists.[59] Meanwhile, however, strong radical and socialist organizations in industrial centers of the Isère meant that workers had little use for Boulanger; in fact, his Bonapartist image posed a threat. But in rural communities immersed in agricultural crisis, a vote for Boulanger served as a protest as well as an attempt to support a new national movement which might take notice of the rural plight. Sometimes the commitment was deliberate and well-organized—as among wood-cutters in the Center who supported Boulanger and were to be in the vanguard of rural political organization in the 1890s[60]—more often, however, it was shapeless and far from premeditated, as among peasants in the Isère.

General histories of the movement describe the rapid rise and fall of Boulangism throughout France, and the Isère was no exception. In the months following the by-election, Boulangists tried to build on their modest successes: propaganda and agents continued to circulate throughout the department, and Boulangist candidates appeared on local and national ballots through 1889. However, by the time the General secured his victory in Paris in January, 1889, he had lost whatever momentum and appeal he had enjoyed in the Isère countryside.

Why? Republican subprefects, mayors, and councilmen in rural localities applied pressure on Boulangist enthusiasts long before Minister of the Interior Constans began his repressive anti-Boulangist campaign in Paris. Local politicians threatened by this new popular movement not only confiscated and lacerated posters and popular images but, more important, felt compelled to address rural needs in more concrete and meaningful ways than their doomsaying Boulangist opponents.[61] It worked, and in this context, the legacy of Boulangism in the Isère is impressive. Despite its failures, despite its inchoate character, its odd blend of the old and the new, Boulangism drew thousands of peasants into a brief but important national drama. The long prosperity of the Empire and early Republic had been broken by economic crisis, and rural demands increased. Some Isère peasants supported Boulanger, more rallied to republicanism or to socialism, but the nature of the conflict itself—the intense interest in national political alternatives that it generated—proved most significant.

We shall see that in the Gers, Boulangists found it impossible to penetrate existing political alignments dominated by local (largely Bonapartist) personalities. Meanwhile, in the Orne, similar personalities deftly grafted Boulangism to local conservative and royalist platforms. In the Marne, close to Paris, Boulangism took on the familiar features of fin de siècle politics, including anti-Semitism mixed with bellicose nationalism and militarism. Again, realities on the spot determined the destiny of the movement, and through it all peasants refused to behave like Engels' "mercenary soldiers."

In November, 1889, the weekly newspaper *La République des paysans* began publication in the Gers. It hoped to bring "republican ideas to the smallest hamlet" and asked readers to join it in thinking about more than "local politics."[62] Meanwhile, republicans in the Lombez canton organized subcommittees and tried desperately to secure electoral victories "in this region so pervaded by reaction."[63] A year earlier a police commissioner had lamented the economic malaise of country people, adding that it was especially "regrettable from the point of view of politics, because a few good harvests would be the best propaganda republicans could present to peasants."[64]

Republicans had a hard time of it in the agricultural Gers in the 1880s. The department, which had contributed 10,000 insurgents to the 1851 revolt against Louis Napoleon, had, a generation later, become one of the most Bonapartist regions of France. Repression stifled revolutionary action in the years immediately following the insurrection, but the economic prosperity of the Empire had drawn much of the Gers peasantry willingly to the Bonapartist camp.[65] Memories of political stability and abundant harvests died hard, especially in the difficult second decade of the Third Republic. Gers peasants, immersed in local affairs and the politics of self-interest—aware of, but unwedded to, national ideologies—embraced whatever regime addressed their needs most effectively, and in the 1880s republicans fared poorly. The overwhelming majority of Gersois had benefited from imperial prosperity (it had been called "the golden age"), and local Bonapartists led by Paul de Cassagnac aimed to keep that memory alive.[66] "Napoleon III was dead," writes D. W. Brogan, "but all the good that peasants thought he had done was not interred with his bones."[67] This is not a case of rural naiveté—blind devotion to mounted Caesars or Napoleonic myths—but of peasant realism, sagacity, and opportunism. Less than two generations later a similar story would unfold in another countryside. German peasants between the two World Wars recalled the years when imperial agrarian policies had fulfilled their needs; and it is likely that much rural interest in burgeoning National Socialism was an expression of support for a strong and stable protectionist regime reminiscent of the old Reich.[68] Events in the Gers countryside in the 1880s shared many of the same characteristics, with less tragic consequences.

In 1885, conservatives throughout France capitalized on the economic crisis, convincing a significant number of rural voters that republicans cared little about their plight.[69] Election results from the Gers confirm that conservatives (including Bonapartists) succeeded in putting the Republic *en cause*, and played on the *idée reçue* in this agricultural region that the regime was more favorable to urban workers than to country folk.[70] The year 1885 marked a gradual change in republican political organization in the Gers. Starting in 1887, and led by an influential prefect, Léonce Boudet, republicans began presenting country people with more relevant and concrete political alternatives. But this took time and would not bear clear results until the early 1890s. Meanwhile, Cassagnac and others held firm.

Ironically, the sophisticated Montagnard organization, so successful in the crucial years between 1848-51, was superseded in the following decades by an even more pervasive and effective Bonapartist network, controlled by Cassagnac: "I have done in the Gers . . . in a few years," he reflected in 1892, "what no other politician has done. . . . I have held a thousand public and private meetings."[71] And he had the votes to prove it. He should have added that his personal touch extended to mayors, councilmen, priests, rural guards, and postmen, who, in classic pork-barrel manner, applied Cassagnac's pressure on peasants in the hinterlands. By the 1870s and 80s Bonapartists had reaped the benefits of a patronage system started under the Empire and built "patiently and intelligently." A local historian adds that republicans were "still far from developing such an organization."[72]

In a department where the majority of peasants and sharecroppers lived in the commune of their birth, and where local ties remained strong, it is not difficult to understand why country folk greeted strangers carrying abstract political messages with hostility or indifference. Perhaps republicans enjoyed unexpected success in Gimont's local election in 1888 because, as one observer put it, conservatives could not field a suitable candidate "personally known" that year. Country people who had voted for an influential "reactionary" four years before, switched their allegiance to another familiar candidate, this time a republican.[73] Experience taught the Gers deputy in E. M. de Vogüé's novel *Les Morts qui parlent* that "the personal coefficient was everything in rural elections: the flock did not choose between two doctrines, but between two shepherds."[74] We must be wary of fictional accounts, but other evidence confirms that the "personal coefficient" assumed a central role in peasant politics in the Gers at the end of the century.[75] Boulangists would have to penetrate more than Cassagnac's umbrella organization; they would have to shake peasants loose from local political habits more deeply entrenched in the Gers than in most other French departments. They tried, but failed miserably.

In December, 1888, a lonely *colporteur* carrying Boulangist song sheets was accused of peddling without permission and detained by police in Cassagnac's principal fief, Mirande. A month later in the same town, a *musicien ambulant*, singing and selling copies of "Il Reviendra" and "La Revanche de Boulanger" had his merchandise seized by local authorities. At the same time, in the town of Nogaro, Boulangist manifestos posted on town walls during the night barely saw the light of day: by 7 A.M. an efficient and early-rising mayor had torn them down. It is not surprising that later in 1889 officials in Gimont could report that "The Boulangist manifesto has passed unnoticed here." It never had a chance.[76]

The Gers was not the Nord, Orne, Sarthe, or Isère, where peddlers laden with Boulangist propaganda surged into towns and villages. Their campaign in the Gers was half-hearted, and one suspects that organizers in Paris recognized that "General Boulanger, a Parisian stranger, distant and little-known," had very few supporters in the rural Southwest.[77]

Evidence from this remote region is sparse, but the fate of a few peddlers and the paucity of Boulangist sloganeering and skirmishing during elections or annual July 14 fêtes—common forums in other departments—reveal a lack of interest in the General's movement. One of the few references to a Boulangist incident in the Gers concerned two hairdressers. Passing by a café, one hairdresser heard his local competitor singing "C'est Boulanger qu'il nous faut." When he entered, a fight ensued and he was struck and cut by flying glass[78]—hardly a significant political *manifestation*, though undoubtedly important to those two fierce rivals. The more profound national issues surrounding Boulangism seem to have engendered little interest in the Gers. Boulanger never visited the department, and his appearance on the ballot in one local election in 1889 was a catastrophe: he garnered barely 5 percent of the vote and carried only one commune of 215 souls—by four votes.[79] A striking contrast to his performance in the Isère.

La République des paysans, the monarchist newspaper *Le Conservateur*, and Cassagnac's *Appel au peuple* all distrusted the General. For different reasons, of course. To monarchists and Bonapartists, Boulangism provided yet another sign of the Republic's ineptitude. Conservatives and reactionaries had their own ideas about "Revision" and "Dissolution"— Boulanger's two-note appeal—and there was no room (nor need) in the Gers for a third way.[80] Cassagnac used the Boulangist threat to the Republic for his own ends early in 1889, and even briefly heralded Boulanger's Paris victory as a welcome blow to parliamentary democracy.[81] But unlike his conservative counterpart in the Orne, Baron Mackau, Cassagnac never coopted the General's powerful image. Instead, Gers Bonapartists held to their earlier belief that Boulanger "is a national danger, with him we will have war, the final catastrophe, the death of our *pays*. . . ." He is, above all, a "*tartarin militaire*."[82] Themes of *revanche* failed in the Southwest where national politics were seen as too obsessed with "the big cities" at the expense of the countryside. The "true France," according to Cassagnac and, one suspects, most peasants, was "la France départementale."[83]

Bitter battles between town and country survived in the Gers where the "principal reactionaries" of the department maintained a strong hold on much of the rural population.[84] In September, 1889, thirty peasants armed with clubs and full of wine donated by conservative political agents, came to the town of Eauze from outlying hamlets for the legislative election. They passed the evening in their favorite café. At 10 P.M. a group of young men "marched through the streets . . . singing the *Marseillaise*" and celebrating a republican victory. They confronted the thirty peasants and a bloody battle ensued.[85] The conflict emerged in the context of a national election but was marked by local animosities, local politics; Boulangists, fighting for their political life throughout France late in 1889, played no part. A police agent reporting to Paris reckoned that Boulangism had not yet sufficiently penetrated the Gers to pose a threat to Cassagnac in the September election.[86] The life expectancy of the movement was short, as we have seen, and if inroads had not been made in the Gers by mid-1889, Boulangism was doomed.

The important political drama unfolding in the Gers at this time did not include Boulangists. Instead, the survival of entrenched Bonapartism, the gradual development of republicanism, and the slow implantation of moderate socialism distinguished Gers politics.[87] The few avenues open to Boulangists in other regions—a focal point for protest, quasi-socialist appeals, variations on Bonapartism, and so on—were all blocked in the Gers by indigenous organizations led by familiar local personalities.

Soon, those Gersois who had lamented the loss of imperial protection and stability would rally to the Republic: a Republic carefully building a thick network of local *meneurs*—notaries, lawyers, merchants, doctors, veterinarians—in an attempt to "seduce peasants" away from traditional alignments.[88] Departmental and national agrarian policies began to attract more and more country people in search of a decisive and responsive government. They began to appreciate the attention of local republican leaders like the deputy Boudet, and applauded the way they dealt with the Boulangist menace early in 1889. Rural reactions in the Gers were similar to those in other areas, from the Nord and Manche to the Saône-et-Loire and Aude early in 1889: peasants supported the government's "energetic" action against the General.[89] References to "energy" run throughout reports from this period: the "energy which the present minister [Constans] has exercised in this instance has produced a good impression among the rural populations. The public will renew the confidence it had lost and will prepare to combat the enemies of the Republic."[90] Confidence in the government had never been greater, echoed one official in the Saône-et-Loire; peasants were enthusiastic about both the increasingly favorable economic situation and the "energetic" action republicans had finally displayed. "That which saves a government," he concluded, "that which secures the devotion of the population, is the state of the economy and, at this moment, all is well . . . Boulangism is dead. . . ."[91]

The movement had barely lived in the Gers. But its quick demise at the hands of a decisive government helped breathe much-needed life and legitimacy into the republican cause in this Bonapartist stronghold. Boulangism failed locally, but it served a national purpose. In its end was a new beginning for republican politics in the rural Gers.

———————

Louis Napoleon's agents worked vigorously at mid-century to convince Orne peasants that the talent of the uncle had been visited upon the nephew. More important, they insisted that taxes would decrease, credit would expand, and livestock prices would rise with the ascension of a new Bonaparte. Their propaganda campaign—rivaled and surpassed four decades later by Boulangists—included imagery, popular biographies, and roaming bands of political *meneurs*. During the Empire and after, local Bonapartist notables made a point of associating agricultural prosperity with imperial stability, and as late as 1876 the majority of peasant mayors in lower Normandy remained professed Bonapartists. When in the 1870s and 80s the countryside suffered the disintegration of small industries and the impact of depopulation and exodus, many peasants turned not to radical republicans or legitimists, but to local conservatives who, in the Bonapartist tradition, promised order, prosperity and respect for property.[92]

Most influential of those conservatives was the Orne deputy Baron Mackau. Formerly Bonapartist, then royalist, but always pragmatically conservative, Mackau first met Boulanger late in 1887 when the General stood firmly in the radical camp. Boulanger had more ambition than firmness, however, and a secret meeting with Mackau helped set the stage for future conservative support. "Too open an identification of the Royal cause with that of the General was dangerous," notes D. W. Brogan, "and it was in the dark that the diverse elements of the attacking army advanced." If Mackau's group had its way, Boulanger, like it or not, would play Monck for the royalist pretender. Meanwhile, radicals who had given birth to Boulangism knew nothing about their man's right-wing intrigues—at least not until 1888. By then, organizations of the Left and Right were feverishly using the General for their own ends, and both factions tried to forget that Janus too had been bearded. "All pretended not to notice who their allies were," writes Brogan, "or, if that was impossible, to forget and forgive until the 'slut' [the Bonapartist term for the Republic] was strangled."[93]

But this takes us a long way from the Orne peasantry. Thanks to Mackau's clever tactics, country people associated Boulanger less with royalists (whom they feared) than with a new, revisionist alternative to an ineffectual Opportunist government. Unlike Cassagnac in the Gers, Mackau did not hesitate to exploit Boulanger's potential in the Orne. He developed an intricate organization in his own department, and played a key role in the direction of Boulangism throughout France. Had the General himself campaigned locally he might have met with defeat, as he had done in many other departments. But as a tool for local needs he fit perfectly. In April, 1888, a police commissioner reported that "there have been no demonstrations in favor of the General," but he added that "Mackau's political action and personal influence remain preponderant in this region . . . local republicans believe that their day will come only when Mackau's influence diminishes."[94] The Baron and his comrades called on Boulanger's image to attract popular support, to solidify their influence, and to secure electoral victories in town and country. The Orne provides an excellent example of a national movement tailored to local needs: of Boulangism without Boulanger.

In the Nord the General's agents focused on discontented urban workers, while peasants turned to moderate republicanism. In the Gers, still-powerful Bonapartists refused to make room for Boulanger and chased his agents from the Gascony countryside. The General's appearance on the Isère ballot in 1888 attracted substantial rural support, but the campaign lasted only a few days and success was therefore limited. In the Orne, however, Mackau worked long and hard to graft Boulangism to his far-reaching political network. Intimately aware of the problems confronting country people in his rural hinterlands, the Baron sent politicians and peddlers to markets and fairs and into rural cafés and village homes to tell peasants that local issues and personalities were part of a new and dynamic national movement: Boulangism.[95] Specially designed propaganda set pictures and stories of Mackau and other Orne politicians alongside images of the General striking Bonapartist poses. Boulanger needed more departments like the Orne, more talented supporters like Baron Mackau.

As early as 1887, prior to Mackau's involvement, Boulangist agents, directed from Paris, arrived in Orne communes to sell biographies of the General. By the spring of 1888 police estimated 6000 Boulangist followers in the department, adding that the figure was probably low.[96] Local vendors received copies of *La Lanterne*, *L'Intransigeant*, and other radical Boulangist newspapers to be sold, for the most part, in Orne cities and towns. In the countryside peddlers sold or gave away propaganda *par l'image*—pictures of Boulanger posed "on foot or on horseback"—and agents placed bundles of "lithochromatics in prominent spots in a great number of rural inns and cafés."[97]

During this period the Orne prefect received gloomy reports that the local population was unhappy with the "impotence" of the present government and desired an end to political divisiveness and a return to stability. We have seen that peasants could reject Boulanger as an irritating reminder of political chaos, or, if properly manipulated on the spot, could see him as a powerful symbol of stability, as a national focus for local grievances. Republican officials feared the latter and kept close watch on the increasing flow of Boulangist propaganda and people. In this early phase Parisian agents sent in to stir up locals helped introduce the General to the peasantry. Strangers attract attention. But if the campaign had remained in the hands of Rochefort and others in Paris, Boulangism would have had little success—and have been of little use—in the Orne. Peasants found Paris agents on day trips to the countryside more curious than relevant; after all, Rochefort's group aimed, first and foremost, to attract frustrated industrial workers.

Nor did Paul Déroulède's Ligue des Patriotes touch the rural Orne. Urban centers in the region had rallied to the gymnastic league early in the 1880s, but with its politicization after 1888 defections multiplied. League chapters in Flers and Laigle found a few Boulangist members among workers, but that group had also disbanded by 1888. Rural regions of the Orne, like those in the Isère, Gers, and most other departments did not, it seems, merit the League's attention. In Déroulède's view, only urban people needed regeneration.[98]

If Parisian radicals introduced Boulangist agents to Orne villages, Mackau and his allies spent the time and money needed to mold the movement to local campaigns. After the Baron committed his powerful group of conservatives and royalists to Boulangism, a second wave of popular propaganda swept the Orne. "We are on the eve of a new invasion of hawkers," reported one subprefect late in 1888.[99] Mackau and his fellow conservative, Lévis de Mirepoix, another Orne deputy, aimed to prepare the terrain for the 1889 legislative election. They enlisted the support of small, regional newspapers (*Bonhomme Percheron*, *L'Echo de Carrouges*, and others), and commissioned special editions of the Paris-based *Gazette des campagnes*. According to its editor, the *Gazette* would attract potential peasant voters who read the paper "from one end to the other" in search of "good agricultural information." The right political news could easily be inserted as well.[100]

To distribute this and other propaganda, Mackau, keenly aware that Orne peasants had a singular distrust of outsiders, hired familiar local personalities. Rural guards, postmen, and retired soldiers circulated posters, voting ballots, and pictures of the Baron, other right-thinking Orne politicians, and, of course, Boulanger. Agents "sold and sang" Boulangist propaganda at local fairs, and in one commune they enjoyed the accompaniment of the village drummer.[101] The spectacle, craftily conceived by outsiders, had the trappings of a spontaneous local exercise.[102]

The Baron's detailed notes on his agents reveal the scope and sophistication of the rural campaign: "M. Lebouq—knows the countryside well"; "M. Lecoufle—intelligent, use him to distribute propaganda in the countryside"; "M. Rivière—retired postman, very valuable"; "Femme Gatel—for hanging posters, though better to hire someone in each commune"; "M. Chauvière—very devoted, speaks often to the peasantry."[103] Encouraged to work markets and fairs, these and dozens of other agents came laden with propaganda printed locally, as well as with a wide variety of Parisian newspapers. Lévis de Mirepoix ("gets on well with the peasantry")[104] also visited markets "firmly shaking the hands" of country people and directing the distribution of Boulangist

photos and copies of Cassagnac's *L'Autorité*. This newspaper, said one
police agent, is distributed "in profusion" and is "beginning to have a
profound influence. . . ."[105] Along with *L'Autorité*, Lévis' agents sold or
gave away *L'Intransigeant* and *La Cocarde*. It was a bizarre ideological
blend which suggests that in the countryside Mackau's group tried to
dissolve the "reactionary" and "radical" boundaries of urban Boulangism. The propaganda of royalists, Bonapartists, and former *communards* came together in the rural Orne as a temporary political marriage
of convenience, an alliance against the Opportunist regime.

The Baron directed a shadow prefectoral system of sorts, with a
network of well situated "subprefects" and their assistants in towns and
rural communes. As the September elections drew near, Mackau received reports from regional contacts pressed into service to assess the
demands and desires of local populations. With Lévis de Mirepoix and
his group busy among peasants at markets and fairs, other agents
reported on the politics of workers in those small rural industries which
still survived in the Orne. From the forests in the center of the department came news of an "ardent Boulangism" among "workers"
(probably wood-cutters, sabot-makers and others in the area) who "detested" Marchand, the moderate republican candidate.[106] Marchand's
rival in the electoral contest, the ubiquitous Lévis, emerged victorious
in September. In the neighboring Mortagne arrondisement, where
Lévis owned a large factory in the Bellème forest, rural workers in
small competing industries might have found it more difficult to support their economic rival, no matter how attractive his Boulangism.
Mackau may have sensed this; in September another candidate, Duque
de la Fauconnerie, jumped on the Boulangist-revisionist platform in
the Mortagne (with, it is assumed, references to Lévis left out), and
defeated his republican rival.[107] In fact, three of the five candidates
who used Boulangist propaganda triumphed in September, 1889: Lévis
de Mirepoix, Duque de la Fauconnerie, and, in Argentan, Mackau,
who for years had either run unchallenged or had crushed whatever
feeble republican opposition could be mustered. Only in the two Domfront arrondisements in the extreme west of the department did moderate republicans succeed, largely because Boulangist and Bonapartist
candidates split the opposition vote.[108]

But more revealing for our purposes, republicans in Domfront responded to the Boulangist threat by mimicking Mackau's methods.
Orne republicans had long felt powerless in the face of popular Boulangism, with its wide and well financed network of propagandists.[109]
They aimed to change that. Candidate Christophe made a point of
visiting every commune in all the cantons of his region in an effort to

counter Boulangism and enlist the support of the local population.[110] This provincial campaign, along with Constans' repressive national measures directed from Paris, proved that Boulangism had not only mobilized local supporters, but had galvanized republican challengers, as well. Propagandists of every persuasion marched off to enlist the support of peasants in the most remote Orne communes.

Describing rural politics in lower Normandy during this period, one historian suggests that "the Boulangist wave, despite its active propaganda and its appeal to discontented peasants, did not succeed. . . . The rural world intuitively felt that the General did not have the qualities of a leader. . . . "[111] On the contrary, revisionist appeals and the General's image paraded by local candidates in the countryside worked to assure conservative victories and remind republicans of the political power of the peasantry in this age of universal manhood suffrage. Boulanger may have failed, but a local brand of Boulangism prevailed in the rural Orne.

In March of 1888 the army made its fateful decision to remove General Boulanger from military service. As a citizen, he could now stand in elections throughout France and, if victorious, enter the Chamber of Deputies he so maligned. The March incident "produced a certain emotion" in the Marne, where "friends of the General are numerous, especially among soldiers who disapprove of the army's decision and say that punishment will only increase Boulanger's popularity."[112] He had appeared on the ballot a month before in the department and, despite ineligibility, won 16,000 votes, placing second to the influential republican Léon Bourgeois. Government officials feared the future.[113]

The February campaign had been conducted in classic Boulangist style: his candidature was not announced until four days before the election when "a profusion of circulars and voting ballots" inundated the department and aimed to "awaken national political sentiment."[114] They described Bismarck gloating over French impotence, and reminded Marne voters that only strength could protect their borders and insure peace.[115] Northeastern departments, close to Paris and the Lost Provinces, seemed ideal targets for Boulanger's *revanchisme*: army garrisons and vivid memories of 1870, along with a large and fluid worker population in Reims and Epernay suffering from international competition, distinguished the Marne from the Gers and most of the Isère and Orne, and set a special stage for General Boulanger.

But Léon Bourgeois, a practical and influential Radical, countered the General's nationalism with a concrete local platform calling for

rural credit, tax relief, agriculture *chambres* on an equal footing with
those of commerce, reduction of military service, and much more.[116]
And Léon Bourgeois prevailed. Some conjectured that "reactionaries"
lacking a dynamic candidate of their own would cast Boulangist ballots
instead of abstaining; if they did, it was largely a negative response,
more an attempt to check the growing power of Bourgeois than an
enthusiastic backing of the General. Boulanger received votes from
numerous rural communes, but unlike his showing in the Isère three
months later, much of his support came from the large urban arrondisements of Reims and Epernay. Of 662 communes in the Marne,
Boulanger carried only 81. To succeed among cereal farmers, wine-
growers and their numerous field hands, the General would have to
provide more than vague rhetoric geared to distressed urban workers
and anxious patriots.[117]

Phylloxera and agricultural crisis arrived late in the Marne. During
the brief Boulangist epoch most peasants and wine-growers enjoyed
rich harvests and high prices. "Cultivators are generally content," reported one subprefect, "the harvests . . . have been abundant and prices
rewarding. . . . This happy circumstance has exercised considerable
influence on the political situation, which is excellent."[118] Republicans
fared well in the Marne countryside despite the Boulangist challenge.

Peddlers, *chanteurs ambulants*, and political agents visited Marne cities
through 1888 and 1889, and a few tried to sell their wares in the
countryside. Fifty-five-year-old Marguerite Perot, who shared a car-
riage and mule with her son, distributed Boulangist song sheets in the
hinterlands near Châlons-sur-Marne until authorities stopped her for
peddling without permission.[119] Young Leonard Couturon, armed with
images and song sheets, and arrested near Ay in February 1889, seems
to have been "among a number of hawkers sent from Paris. . . ."[120] In
the small town of Chatillon-sur-Marne officials confiscated 1,700 man-
ifestoes (double the population) and detained two peddlers. Boulangists formed a committee in Verzenay, and agents left the village for
"the countryside with free copies of the local Boulangist paper" (*Le
Réveil national de la Marne*) as well as engravings entitled "Vive la
France" and "Aujourd'hui et Demain."[121] Proximity to Paris and a
sophisticated network of roads, many of which dated back to the Champagne fairs of the Middle Ages, facilitated propaganda campaigns in
the Marne. Local residents could even enjoy an occasional look at
satirical Paris weeklies like *La Bombe*, a pleasure unavailable to the
majority of French peasants. Proximity to the capital also facilitated
government control, however, and vigilant republican officials quickly
suppressed agents and images.[122]

Boulangists desperately needed a victory in the September 1889 legislative election. One of their Marne surrogates, M. Abeille, launched a massive campaign to discredit the government. Three thousand people attending his rally in Reims heard him defend "the exploited worker." He assured skeptics that he was not an old Bonapartist but a republican of longstanding, and closed one appeal with "Workers! I cordially shake your loyal hands. Long live France! Long live the national Republic! Long live Boulanger!"[123] Parisian Boulangists sent emissaries to aid Abeille and others, and the subprefect of Reims reported that the principal roles in local Boulangist organizations are held by "strangers absolutely unknown. . . ."[124] Outsiders might blend into the urban environment of Reims, Epernay, or Châlons-sur-Marne, but they had problems in the countryside. "For fear of being booed by the hostile population," they hesitated to venture far from town.[125] Villagers in Mailly (population 885) not only booed a dozen Boulangists but showered them with rocks and threw them out of town. The same day in Vienne-le-Chateau, far from Mailly, a Parisian employee of *La Cocarde*, trying to stir up trouble during a republican meeting, was "jeered at and blackballed."[126] Marne agents did not possess the savoir-faire exhibited by Mackau's troops in the Orne.

Boulangist organizers focused on Marne workers, not peasants, but in the summer of 1889 agents in Paris launched an innovative (and illegal) attempt to get their message to rural inhabitants: they sent an insurance prospectus to communes throughout France with instructions that it be distributed "by all persons in frequent contact with the public";[127] news vendors, café owners, even barbers. In many communes it would be carried to hamlets and farmsteads by rural guards. On its last page the pamphlet contained a Boulangist manifesto under the heading "Our Goal." In Paris, the Sûreté immediately ordered prefects to stop all guards from circulating the clandestine propaganda. Disobedience would not be tolerated. In the Isère, republicans proved vigilant and efficient: most pamphlets were seized and burned before they reached rural communities.[128] Officials in the Marne destroyed a good number of packets, but others slipped past subprefects and mayors (how accidentally we shall never know) and arrived in rural communes.

In the winegrowing community of Courthiézy (population 383) the sole *garde-champêtre* was most definitely Boulangist. His enemies had been trying to catch him *in flagrante delicto* with a notorious village matron, but without success. In June, 1889, they caught him instead with the outlawed insurance prospectus and informed the subprefect.

His case provides an example of the byzantine nature of national politics in rural settings.

Few people were in more constant contact with the peasant population of Courthiézy than Pierre Gille, rural guard, and his son Eugène, town crier and bill-sticker, and few more involved in the spread of anti-government propaganda. The subprefect was not surprised that Pierre and Eugène had been caught with the Boulangist prospectus: it was only another in a series of incidents involving this village duo. For twenty years Pierre had been selectively arresting political adversaries for trumped up rural crimes major and minor.[129]

One festive night in June, local and national politics converged with a family feud at a village café when the Boulangist Gille exchanged insults with his cousin, the republican councilman Gérard. They had not spoken for eight years, ever since the guard had arrested his cousin for violating hunting laws, or (depending on the source) adhering to republican politics. This night they successfully ignored each other at neighboring tables until one accused the other of stealing a bottle of wine. A dozen peasants and winegrowers looked on, and eyewitness accounts compiled by gendarmes reveal a litany of political and personal alliances. The partisans of Gille and Gérard provided very different descriptions indeed. Gille's friends, including his immediate superior, the mayor, played down his rakish character and reactionary opinions and maintained that he was a "good fellow" who did not drink in excess and worked well for his pittance of 200 francs per year. "If he were better paid," proposed the mayor, "it is certain that we could demand more of him." Whether they could demand sobriety and republicanism is not clear. Others complained about the guard's immorality and penchant for mixing Boulangist politics with the policing of persons as well as property. The subprefect had to be called in from outside the village to mediate, and, for him, the guard's drinking, womanizing, and Boulangism warranted dismissal. Immoral behavior went with abnormal politics, and Pierre Gille fit the republican subprefect's definition of a dangerous rural type.

The guard's fate is unknown. We can assume that the political (and family) alignments of the next municipal council decided his future. Boulangist defeats after the fall of 1889 could not have helped. Parisian events had their modest village echoes, and Gérard might have been to Gille what Minister Constans was to Boulanger. In Courthiézy as in the capital, republicans stemmed the Boulangist tide.

The General's candidates in the Marne fared poorly in September 1889. In one of its few references to the peasantry, *Le Réveil national*, trying to save face, told of a rural commune where a Boulangist trounced an Opportunist candidate 400 votes to 10. "I don't know if all rurals are certain of what they want," reported the journalist, "but they all clearly know" that they want an end to that "blackguard Minister" (Constans).[130] This may have been true in *Réveil*'s unnamed commune, but the opposite was more often the case. Country people applauded the "virile" and "energetic" republican government for its handling of Boulanger; and, at the same time, peasants in the Marne were happy with the exceptionally good year (1889) just past.[131]

Prior to the 1889 elections, one of the General's local agents suggested that the *revanchisme* of Boulangist candidates might prove counterproductive among Marne residents who remembered 1870 and who feared another war. It appears that he was correct and that the fervent nationalism of easterners like the Boulangist Maurice Barrès, did not extend to peasants concerned more with local stability than with national renaissance and revenge.[132]

Yet, despite its electoral failures, Boulangism contributed an important legacy to the politics of the Marne, as it had in other departments. Unhappily, however, the movement did not simply provide a tool with which rural people might break old political ties and forge new ones with republicanism or socialism. Instead, it injected virulent anti-Semitism into its 1889 campaign and helped set the scene for what one author has called "the perversion of the populist mentality" which had marked early Boulangism.[133]

Five years before the Dreyfus Affair, and barely three years after the publication of Edouard Drumont's enormously popular anti-Semitic tract *La France juive*, Boulangists in the Marne excoriated republicans for their complicity with "la juiverie allemande."[134] In September 1889 *Le Réveil national de la Marne* echoed the racist hatred of *La Libre parole* in articles proclaiming "A bas les juifs!," "Vive Boulanger!" and "Mort aux Youts." Jews were "national vermin" who "starved workers," and Abeille, the local Boulangist, was the "prefect democratic candidate, anti-opportunist, anti-Prussian, anti-Jew. . . . We Boulangists have an abhorrence of Jews."[135] For now, most of this hate-mongering was limited to Marne cities where, as we shall see when discussing the Dreyfus Affair, a significant number of Jews lived and worked. But it also found its way into the countryside via broadsheets which railed against "the Jewish conquest" and promised future reports from Drumont.[136]

Boulanger's political history is black enough. It should be noted that he seems to have personally abhorred anti-Semitism; his letters to the Duchesse d'Uzès and his close friend Alfred Naquet reveal his detestation of Drumont and his refusal to graft anti-Semitism to his cause.[137]

But one thing is certain: he lacked control, especially over those followers who used anti-Semitism to stir emotions and garner votes. In the Marne, Boulangists, in a final attempt to save the moribund movement, dropped the pretense of civilized politics and mounted a savage campaign aimed at the department's significant Jewish population and at local fears of a "foreign" menace. It was unsuccessful, but in an article entitled "Toujours les Juifs," *Le Réveil national* looked to the future: "soon the Jewish question will pose itself in a manner so pressing, so categorical, that it will demand an immediate and radical solution. . . . Will I say it?" queried the journalist, "It does not displease me to see the Jew abused."[138]

Friedrich Engels spoke for others when he described peasants as "mercenary soldiers" eager to follow a strong-willed leader.[139] Like the two Napoleons (the story goes), Boulanger wielded an almost mystical power over naive country folk steeped in superstition, untutored in the political ways of the modern world, and predisposed to men on horseback. According to most contemporaries and many historians, the General would succeed or fail in cities and industrial centers. Urban politics meant important politics.

A closer look at the countryside, however, confirms that peasants played a significant part in the movement, and that Boulangism greatly influenced rural politics at a critical moment in the early Third Republic. Out to attract peasant support, Boulangists grafted old but still powerful political customs to a new national movement. This, in turn, provoked republican officials who tried to persuade country people that generals, plebiscites, and popular imagery were things of the past. Success or failure depended not only on the scope and sophistication of the movement, but also on the uses to which peasants on the spot could put Boulanger. Long-standing rural traditions remained strong in villages and hamlets increasingly dominated by working farmers, and, contrary to conventional wisdom, these rural people set their own political agenda from within their communities. They decided when and how an issue, or a new leader, might strike a relevant local chord. Boulangists who recognized this—agents versed in the rural political cultures of their areas—enjoyed striking success in 1888-89. Baron Mackau's organization in the Orne provides the best example of effective Boulangist tactics, and agents in communes of the Isère and Savoie also deftly played on local customs and Bonapartist traditions. In other regions, country people greeted Boulangism with hostility or indifference. Radical republicans in the Marne and parts of the Isère, and Bonapartists in the Gers, had rallied strong rural support; Boulangism could not penetrate entrenched political and personal alignments in those areas. Variations could be found throughout rural France.

The General's ideological vagueness often worked to his advantage. Nearly a century after the fact, he played out Tallyrand's long career in the space of a few months. Radical or socialist in tone, imperial or conservative in style, he could stress one or the other depending on local circumstances, political memories, and prejudices. Sometimes, however, studied confusion led to catastrophic failure, as in the Vendée, where Legitimists supported by priests with a strong hold over country folk preferred the Pretender, and where republicans wanted a candidate less tainted by Bonapartism or royalism. In his brief Vendée campaign, the General ignored peasants. Convinced (though wrongly) that they were lost to Legitimists, he focused instead on railroad employees and workers in small industries near the Charente-Inférieure border. Boulanger had garnered many votes in the latter department, but Vendée republicans refused to sanction this Emperor in new clothes, this "sous-Badinguet." Boulangism in the Vendée, said one trenchant observer, is "too clerical for the 'Blues' and not clerical enough for the 'Whites.' "[140]

The General's name appeared on scores of ballots in legislative and local elections throughout France in 1888-89. But electoral victories or defeats are less revealing than campaign methods, the voting process itself, and the total number of electors mobilized by those Boulangist and government agents who flooded into rural communes. Evidence from diverse and widely scattered villages suggests that nearly two decades after the founding of the Third Republic, the workings of rural politics remained greatly influenced by personalities, family ties, local interests and local intimidation. In the Vosges, for example, the 1889 campaign became a political carnival featuring votes exchanged for wine, money, and promises that peasant sons (in short supply) would not be conscripted. Boulangists used psychological pressure (threats that the village priest would excommunicate republican supporters) and physical force (the rural guard would "drub" indifferent locals and push them to the polls).[141] Similar tactics emerged during Boulangist campaigns in the Savoie, and far to the west in the Landes, thousands of francs shipped to the area went to pay off prospective voters. Republicans triumphed, said one frustrated Boulangist, because they bought more votes and harrassed more electors with greater diligence. An exaggeration, perhaps, but pressure must have been strong enough to warrant the comment.[142]

Such methods remained integral features of rural politics in the late

1880s, and serve to illustrate the differences between country and town. Politics in Paris and provincial centers shared many of these characteristics, but the decreasing importance of family alliances, of personal feuds and rivalries, combined with the abstraction of issues and the relative orderliness associated with modern political behavior, became the rule in cities while it remained the exception in small face-to-face communities. In the countryside, Boulangists used traditional methods in an attempt to break through local allegiances and present peasants with a new national political alternative; it worked in rural communes where old alignments proved weak or nonexistent, it failed where still powerful organizations made no room for novelty.[143]

But through it all, in victory or defeat, more and more peasants came to realize that local issues, rural demands, could attract the attention of national movements in search of agrarian support. This important step in the political acculturation of the peasantry can be traced to the contributions made by a brief but pervasive movement mounted in the name of a mediocre army officer with little genuine interest in the plight of country people. Boulangism, commonly seen as a comic-opera phase in the evolution of the Third Republic, went a long way in preparing the rural politics of the twentieth century.

PART THREE

THE DREYFUS AFFAIR

CHAPTER V

OLD LEGENDS AND
NEW MYTHS

*En un mot, à partir de 1394, époque à laquelle
elle chasse les Juifs, la France montera toujours; à partir de 1789, époque à laquelle elle
les reprend, elle descendra sans cesse . . .*

EDOUARD DRUMONT, 1886

*Nous vivons dans un temps où, suivant le mot
de l'Ecriture, le jour est appelé la nuit et la
nuit le jour.*

L'UNIVERS ISRAÉLITE, 1898

Boulangists contributed to the architecture of modern European anti-
Semitism. Constructed early in the Third Republic, it reached its height
in France during the Dreyfus Affair. Anti-Semitic attacks may have
been peripheral to Boulangism outside the Marne and a few other
regions, and largely centered in cities, but those supporters of the
General who chose to revivify the dying movement by politicizing anti-
Semitism must take their place alongside Edouard Drumont, his contemporary Karl Lueger in Austria, and their twentieth century descendants.

Political anti-Semites did not let their cause die with the General.
They had just begun. In the half-decade preceding the arrest of Captain Dreyfus, they used the Panama scandal to attack what they perceived to be a corrupt, flaccid and Jew-ridden parliamentary Republic.
Hundreds of thousands of Frenchmen lost millions of francs in Fer-
dinand de Lesseps' Central American boondoggle, and though no Jews
were among the politicians or company officials accused of bribes, anti-
Semites characteristically ignored the evidence and pinned blame on
traitorous Jews controlling events in the shadows. The campaign created sensational headlines, ruined a few politicians, and sold news-

papers (the circulation of *La Libre parole* reached 300,000 at the height of the scandal);[1] but most country people, with little incentive and less capital to invest in a distant tropical canal, seemed uninterested. "A great lassitude" existed regarding Panama-inspired anti-Semitic propaganda; it "stirred little emotion."[2]

The fate of the Republic in rural areas would hinge less on revelations of political corruption exposed by professional anti-Semites in Paris than on specific government policies and the continuing attempt by peasants to extricate themselves from agricultural crisis. In the 1890s not a few country people behaved like a "reactionary" peasant in the Gers who changed his politics (and his vote) because he attributed good prices and rich harvests "to the benefits of the republican regime."[3] If republicans failed to respond he might change his vote again. Anti-Semites set out to convince peasants that republicans were impotent and that their curse should be laid at the doorstep of Jewish conspirators.

Critics of the Third Republic found significant enclaves of support in rural areas in the final decades of the century. However, it is well to contrast the gradual economic improvements throughout much of the countryside following the Boulangist years with the continuing struggle of industrial workers, with the *mal du siècle* which obsessed Parisian intellectuals, and with the doomsaying rhetoric of virulent anti-Semites. Hardships remained in the countryside in the late 1890s, but now along with increased prosperity and rising expectations. The important question asks what relevance did the issues surrounding the main national event of the epoch, the Dreyfus Affair, have for country people far from the central "arena." The historical reservoir of anti-Semitism and nationalism proved deep in a few rural areas, shallow in most others—Boulangists had focused their early anti-Semitic attacks on the northeast for a reason—and the Dreyfus Affair would provide yet another litmus test for national politics in the French countryside.

The army placed Captain Alfred Dreyfus under arrest in 1894, precisely five centuries after Charles VI expelled Jews from France. The symmetry must have pleased anti-Semites who delighted in cultivating (and corrupting) history and myth in order to drape their propaganda campaigns in a cloak of legitimacy. But their selective rhetoric reflected more than a perversion of the truth for political purposes; it also mirrored inconsistencies inherent in historic French attitudes toward Jews. Banished from France in the fourteenth century, they were invited back in the spirit of Enlightenment and the Declaration of Rights of Man and granted citizenship in 1791. France was the first continental power fully and irrevocably to extend civil liberties to Jews. But official policy had an uneven effect on unofficial opinion, and the nineteenth century brought a new, virulent strain of anti-Semitism to France.

By the time of Dreyfus's arrest, anti-Semites had armed themselves with an impressive array of modern scientific evidence "proving" the racial inferiority of Jews, as well as their penchant for the calculated economic exploitation of unsuspecting Aryans. Racism was not invented in the nineteenth century, but refined: dissected, analyzed, reasserted, and couched in positivistic vocabulary. The absurdity of such pseudo-scientific posturing is, for our purposes, irrelevant: anti-Semites sold books and newspapers and won influential followers.

Mostly urban followers. The anti-Semitic works of Proudhon, Alphonse de Toussenel, Auguste Chirac and others did not shape the opinions of country people. They had other sources of information. In the new age of mass politics, anti-Semitism became vulgarized in every way, and on the eve of the Dreyfus Affair Parisian "popularizers" reached out to graft old myths to modern science and mobilize all Frenchmen against the Jew. "Indeed, during the last decades of the nineteenth century," writes George Mosse, "when racism forged ahead everywhere, it was France that seemed destined to be the country within which racism might determine national politics."[4]

What did country people know and read (or hear read) about Jews? How was that image transmitted by peddlers, journalists, village priests, local politicians, and other personalities in different regions? And finally, what form did Dreyfus-related demonstrations take outside Paris and provincial cities? This chapter will examine how anti-Semites and others sent their message to the countryside; it will investigate traditional rural perceptions of the Jew and show how Parisians often misread, oversimplified, distorted, or ignored those perceptions. The next chapter will present specific examples of the impact of the Dreyfus Affair in rural France.

"Anti-Semitism, a secular nineteenth-century ideology . . . and religious Jew-hatred," wrote Hannah Arendt, "are obviously not the same."[5] What was obvious to Arendt was unclear a century ago, when many country people considered the Jew an amalgam of Christ-killer, usurer, politician, capitalist, and urbanite. In a rural world where face-to-face communities were tightly knit, the Jew—urban and "foreign"—could be the quintessential outsider. For sociologist Georg Simmel, the European Jew was the classic "stranger"; forbidden from owning land, he embodied "that synthesis of nearness and distance which constitutes the formal position of the stranger."[6] In the final decades of the nineteenth century anti-Semites tried to exploit this traditional distrust and present the Jews as the "relevant other"[7]—the source of all ills, from the breakdown of Christian order to corruption in government, immorality in the cities, and economic ruin in the countryside.

"If the Jew did not exist," goes Jean-Paul Sartre's famous remark, "the anti-Semite would invent him."[8] In most rural areas, where Jews were unseen and unknown, anti-Semites tried to do just that. New campaigns waged by the popular press fed old legends, and the image of the outsider, the usurious deicide, was encouraged in communities where "the figure of the Jew was unknown in the flesh."[9] In 1907 an observer could still remark that outside the cities the Jew is known only through lingering *images d'Epinal*[10]—and, he should have added, through the pages of anti-Semitic tracts, newly arrived in the countryside. Often those tracts had to inject new elements of hatred and fear into popular perceptions of the Jew. In many parts of France the best-known image remained that of the Wandering Jew, who, refusing Christ shelter on the road to Calvary, had been condemned to roam eternally through a hostile world, never living, never dying (fig. 18). But this story, also, could be read two ways: Ahasuerus, the Wandering Jew of medieval legend, could represent a merciless and cursed figure, or he could be "turned into a hero" as he had been in Eugène Sue's popular *Le Juif errant* (1844-45).[11] Much would depend on what local priests and others on the spot made of traditional myth and imagery.

Of the myriad anti-Semitic pamphlets, periodicals, and newspapers which inundated Paris, the evidence suggests that only two had a major impact in rural areas: Edouard Drumont's massive tome *La France juive* (1886), which sold over a million copies and reached 200 printings in twenty-five years;[12] and the Catholic Assumptionist daily newspaper *La Croix*, which first appeared in 1883 and descended into anti-Semitic polemics after 1890.[13] None of the similar books and newspapers reaching rural communities enjoyed the success of Drumont and *La Croix*, and none could match the vitriol designed to attract rural readers to the urban-centured cause.

The Dreyfus Affair came at a time when literacy was widespread but newly arrived in many rural areas. In 1900 one priest insisted that peasants rarely read "long and serious articles" in newspapers; in his village the projection of illuminated images attracted country people more than news print.[14] Still, the printed word, sacred in its origins, had joined the image in its power to inform, fascinate, and influence. There is little doubt that the ten years between Boulanger and Dreyfus were among the most crucial for the development of agencies of change—including education and literacy—in the countryside.[15] It has been

18. Le Juif-Errant

estimated that between 1894 and 1899 *La Croix*, Drumont's newspaper *La Libre parole*, and a few other anti-Semitic sheets attracted one million readers a day.[16]

In 1892 *Le Petit Journal* advertised an illustrated version of *La France juive*, and arranged to distribute copies free of charge.[17] Four years earlier, a "popular edition" of Drumont's work, which aimed to attract workers and peasants, had been sent into the countryside.[18] When Daniel Halévy visited a small village home in the Center shortly after the turn of the century, he found *La France juive* sharing the sparse bookshelf with the Bible.[19]

Without benefit of sales or distribution records, one must turn to contemporary accounts, as well as advertisements in regional newspapers and special periodicals to determine the widespread popularity of Drumont's dense and notorious opus. *La France juive* might not have been widely *read* (a formidable, even masochistic task), but it was highly visible and its message well-known.[20] In *La France juive devant l'opinion*, published shortly after the major work, Drumont was delighted that his treatise

> had been a brilliant success. These two copious volumes . . . have aroused, awakened, and comforted souls throughout France. Its free voice has . . . finally proclaimed the truth and told what has become of the Fatherland since it fell into the hands of the Jews.[21]

What, exactly, in that "free voice" was relevant in rural communities?

Nestled between swollen passages on the decadence and conspiratorial nature of Jews in Paris are references to the countryside and Jewish "manipulation" of French agriculture. Rural France is dying, laments Drumont, ravaged by "la bande juive."[22] The Semite knows nothing about the land and everything about exploiting peasants through usurious rents. He is merchant by instinct, while "the Aryan is farmer, poet, monk, and above all, soldier."[23] Drumont propagates the ancient myth of the Jewish usurer and extends it to the Rothschilds and others who "control" France. They are responsible for a new, more oppressive form of usury: exorbitant land taxes and wrongheaded government policy.[24]

Drumont's work appeared at a moment when economic conditions in the countryside were desperate and scapegoats popular: Opportunist republicans, freemasons, Protestants, and Jews. This, of course, paralleled the rise and spirit of Boulangism—and the ineffectual Republic was their common target. But as we have seen, Drumont's disciples, for a variety of reasons, were unable to graft their program to the General's.[25] Rabidly anti-Semitic Boulangists like the notorious and unbalanced Marquis de Morès, won few friends and influenced fewer still. It would take later events to revivify Drumont's appeal and breathe new relevance into old stereotypes.

Usury, a favorite sterotype for anti-Semites, was, in reality, an age-old, nation-wide, and largely Christian practice. Madame Bovary's moneylender, Lheureux, enjoyed a sophisticated clientele in his Norman market town in 1857, and told Emma that she might repay him when she wished. After all, he added, "We are not Jews!"[26] With few exceptions, Jewish moneylending in rural areas had been limited geographically and chronologically to the East in the years leading up to and including 1848 when Alsatian peasants attacked local Jews, "victims of their reputation as usurers."[27] By the end of the Second Empire, however, intense and overt peasant anti-Semitism had all but disappeared in the East where most Jews had abandoned traditional rural activities and moved in great numbers to the cities, especially Paris. These active Alsatian moneylenders had not been alone. Christian usurers in the area were no less the objects of peasant "hatred and contempt."[28]

Eugen Weber, in his thorough study of a dozen departments, found no reference to Jewish usury outside cities and Alsace and Lorraine.[29] Throughout France, small landowners turned to local moneylenders who were sometimes beneficent, often ruthless, and always eager to set rates approaching 30 percent. Philippe Vigier tells of peasant indebtedness in the Alpine region, growing through the July Monarchy and culminating at mid-century. In the Drôme and Isère, "Black bands" of moneylenders charged outrageous fees and held entire communities hostage. A contributing factor to the 1851 insurrection in the area was the peasants' desire to "teach a severe lesson to the rich bourgeois of the plains who traditionally had exploited them"; one of the principal Montagnard demands had been the abolition of all usury. Nominally, at least, most local moneylenders were as Christian as their victims.[30]

At the time of the Dreyfus Affair in the Isère, peasants were still forced to borrow from local sources to survive until the next harvest or market fair. In the Var, they turned not to Jewish usurers, but to local café owners, their "informal bankers."[31] Popular legends in Gascony contained familiar allusions to Jewish avarice ("close-fisted like a Jew"), but they had little relevance in the rural Southwest, where no Jews lived. Although anti-Semitic mythology had long equated Jews with usury—Christian usurers were called "Christian Jews"—peasants, like those in the Southwest who had become victims of "unscrupulous usurers," knew their moneylenders firsthand and knew that they were rarely, if ever, Jewish.[32]

Yet the myth persisted that Jews had ruined France. Drumont claimed that 150,000 Jews lived in Paris and another 400,000 in the provinces[33]—outlandishly inflated figures that peasants had no way to verify beyond their locality, and no reason to disbelieve. In reality, the total Jewish population of France numbered approximately 80,000. Because of traditional restrictions dating from the middle ages, Jews rarely lived in rural areas; they remained "the most urbanized people in the world." Over half lived in Paris, others settled in towns of the East, and small concentrations could be found in other provincial cities. Old, established communities, like those in Provence, lost population at the fin de siècle as many Jews moved to Paris. By the time of the Dreyfus Affair, the great majority of French and foreign Jews resided in or near the capital. Meanwhile, the countryside was, for the most part, a countryside without Jews.[34]

Peasants were familiar with indebtedness, usury, and local economic tyranny. They also knew that the republican regime had promised meaningful rural credit and had not yet delivered. Many sought explanations and relief at a moment when anti-Semites sought an audience. The link had to be forged. Spokesmen were needed to graft Drumont's message to local realities; to indict Jews (whom most peasants did not know) as founders and perpetuators of usury (which peasants knew and feared); and, finally, to present Drumont's convoluted thesis to rural folk too busy, poor, and, often, illiterate to struggle through the 500-page "popular edition."

It appears that the Ligue nationale antisémitique, started by Drumont and revived by Jules Guérin, shared the same fate as Déroulède's Ligue des Patriotes: both had little effect on country people. Often in tandem with Catholic groups like the Union Nationale, the anti-Semitic leagues appealed to a wide range of city folk, from a disaffected "intellectual proletariat," to unemployed or underpaid petty bourgeois and workers who attributed their economic plight to "rapacious" Jews.[35] The combined membership of the two organizations probably did not exceed 25,000 in all of France at the height of the Dreyfus Affair, and though the riots of 1898 are proof of their effectiveness, their influence did not reach beyond small, active branches in major cities.[36] The new wave of anti-Jewish rhetoric coming from Paris reached peasants through familiar channels which, circumstances permitting, gave concreteness to otherwise irrelevant abstractions.

Rural priests proved willing and articulate disciples. Friend or foe, as village residents they were in the thick of local life. While their pastoral influence waned in different regions at different times, their position as (comparatively) learned and informed neighbors survived after church attendance declined; and they could play a potentially powerful role in the dissemination of anti-Jewish propaganda. Indeed, the secular Republic's threat to the Church, along with the flock's growing indifference, encouraged priests to search beyond the liturgy for issues which might infuse their mission with modern meaning.[37]

Variations on the Clochemerle theme persisted in many villages: priests locked in personal and ideological battles with mayors and schoolteachers, each side dragging its supporters into the fray, dividing communities and causing administrative headaches. Coded maps of French religiosity—strong in Brittany and parts of the North, weak in the Paris basin, mixed in the Southeast—mask complex and contradictory nuances of village life. Religious participation or lack of it need not reflect the immediate, personal influence of the local priest.

One report on the Gers, for example, tells how the department's inhabitants rejected the clergy's politics and remained indifferent to their reactionary pleas.[38] A closer look, however, reveals small communes in the Mirande, Eauze, Lombez, and Condom cantons wracked by internal rivalries heated enough to alarm subprefects. The vicar of Cazeneuve (pop. 368 in 1888) never stopped preaching anti-government politics from the pulpit and in the streets, and his counterparts in the communes of Roquepine and Montlaur seized every opportunity "in sermons, confessions, and daily reports to parishioners [to] arouse and perpetuate" anti-government hatred.[39] Commenting on the Montlaur situation, one official was concerned about the "pernicious influence" of the fanatical priest over his "gullible parishioners." When the priest succeeded in having the republican schoolteacher transferred, he attributed his victory to the "miraculous" intervention of Paul de Cassagnac.[40] In this rural department where Cassagnac's influence was strong and widespread until the end of the century, and where personalities remained important in dispersed, isolated villages, some politicians considered priests useful spokesmen. Here, as elsewhere in France, the Ralliement and the Republic would eventually take hold. But not well enough or soon enough to prevent three anti-Semitic deputies—supported by local priests and notables—from being elected in the rural Gers at the height of the Dreyfus Affair.[41]

In the Isère, the entrenched anti-clericalism and developing socialism found in some regions was challenged by the dynamic Monsignor Fava, by provincial branches of Abbé Garnier's Union Nationale, and by the popularity of religious enclaves like Chartreuse and Notre Dame de la Salette.[42] In 1888, the prefect informed Paris that the Chartreux, while not politically active, wielded great influence in surrounding communes. It would not be wise, he cautioned, to move against them.[43] Priests had some success as Boulangist agents in parts of the Isère, and we shall see that *La Croix* enjoyed unparalleled popularity in that department until the end of the century, penetrating the smallest communes and disseminating anti-Semitic propaganda through, among others, rural priests who often served as the paper's peddlers.

Evidence from rural Calvados, Finistère, and the Vendée confirms that through the final decades of the century priests continued to preach politics from the pulpit. They threatened wayward (read republican) peasants with excommunication and insisted that parishioner's wives, devout if not political, should pressure their husbands to vote for "the good cause." Some evidence and much imagination suggests that the pressure took many forms.[44]

In the Marne, priests and Catholic organizations were most active among workers in Reims, Epernay, Vitry-le-François and Châlons-sur-Marne. Jewish inhabitants in the area presented convenient targets (the Marne had nearly 1,500 Jews in 1898).[45] Anti-Semites found larger constituencies in Marne cities than in most other towns of France where there were few, if any, Jewish residents and where anti-Semitic traditions were less developed.

In 1898, the Paris-based *L'Univers israélite* published a long editorial on the dangers of anti-Semitism and the role of priests in the countryside:

> The great mass of the population, influenced by wicked books and legends, sees the Jew as something deviant, constructed differently than other men. . . . God knows that . . . peasants in the most remote provinces . . . have heard *curés* describe us as creatures of the devil and sorcerers.[46]

Clergymen drew on a rich repertorie of propaganda, ancient and modern. Myths of avarice and ritual murder were now complemented by nationalist diatribes.[47] "Our priests have a mission . . . to fulfill," wrote the author of *La France juive*; they must "clearly show that our fate is in the hands of a few German Jews." Drumont was pleased with provincial response. "Talking with rural *curés*, and reading their letters, I have understood how useful my book has been."[48]

In December, 1898, when Drumont's newspaper *La Libre parole* solicited donations to a monument for Colonel Henry (the recent suicide responsible for forged documents in the Dreyfus case), rural priests sent their few francs and joined the chorus of hate. "Long live Christ! Long live France! Long live the Army!" wrote one from a "small and very anti-Semitic village." Three Maurennais priests from the mountains of Savoie called themselves "Frenchmen of France" and sent a franc each. They wanted to lay their hands "on the filthy Jew Reinach."[49] In the years leading up to the Dreyfus Affair, village priests wed the historic plight of Christ to the modern plight of rural France, presented the Jew as the common source of all ills, and, in some areas, tried to bring distant anti-Semitic diatribes closer to local realities.

These *curés* were themselves rural inhabitants, and that reveals something about the mood in the countryside on the eve of the Dreyfus Affair. But we are left at the church door of a silent rural world, unsure of what country people thought, uncertain about how they reacted to village priests who were respected by some, despised by others, and ignored by not a few.

A close look at the distribution of "the most anti-Jewish newspaper in France," *La Croix*,[50] brings us nearer still to the elusive peasantry. Pierre Sorlin has examined the paper's provenance, circulation, and impact on the provinces, but his rich study is limited to major cities. Sorlin and others recognize the success of *La Croix* in the countryside, but offer no information on rural sales.[51]

Department-wide statistics of newspaper circulation tell little or nothing about readership. We assume that large cities and bourgs provided the major audience, though a handful of copies destined for notaries, mayors, priests, and the like reached geographically and culturally isolated rural areas.[52] In the case of *La Croix*, however, the evidence indicates that peasants in many regions received the paper regularly. Departmental archives—with collections often destroyed by fire, flood, or an archivist's fancy—leave impressionistic accounts. For example, *La Croix* sent departmental editions to the Gers and the Orne in great numbers in the 1880s and 1890s, but how they reached rural communities is hard to divine from sketchy documentation.[53] On the other hand, we can follow *La Croix* into small communes in other departments and learn who sold it, where, and, on occasion, how many copies.[54] It was not the only newspaper in rural France, but it dominated peddlers' reports in the decade leading up to the Dreyfus Affair, and reached not only village priests but peasants as well. When placed in the context of oral anti-Semitic propaganda from Drumont-inspired priests, lingering myths of avaricious "Juifs," and a general distrust of outsiders, it becomes clear that many country people were being presented with a false and malicious image of the Jew—and, *mutatis mutandis*, of Captain Alfred Dreyfus.

During the winter of 1897-98, *La Croix de l'Isère* more than doubled its daily circulation, from 3,000 to 7,000, and the popular Sunday edition reached 20,000 copies.[55] A year later, after the tumultuous anti-Semitic riots, but before the Dreyfus retrial at Rennes, an Isère police commissioner put the "present circulation" of all *La Croix* editions at 22,000.[56] If each issue had been passed along to a dozen people in cafés and elsewhere, total readership could have reached an extraordinary 250,000, almost half the Isère population.

There is no clear breakdown of circulation statistics, but Isère administrative reports and peddlers' applications attest to *La Croix*'s popularity. In the small commune of Sardieu midway between Grenoble and Lyon, a woman hoping to supplement her meager *journalière* income sold *La Croix* to local inhabitants. It was the only source of printed news. Another woman had great success in the village of Beaufort selling an extraordinary 35-40 copies on Sundays after working six long days in the commune's traditional silk industry.[57]

La Croix reached exclusively agricultural communes, as well. Rencurel, whose census list is a litany of "cultivators," did not have the benefit of a news vendor. The postman delivered papers to local residents, including stacks of *La Croix* to the vicar who, in turn, distributed them each Sunday. In La Murette, the village priest was officially registered as the peddler of *La Croix*; and in Chormanche, near the Drôme border, copies were distributed after Sunday Mass. In the Vendée, in the militantly Catholic West, every *curé* in every canton received copies of *La Croix* directly from Paris on Fridays. They then took to the countryside and gave the paper to "isolated" peasants living "far from intellectual centers." It "confounded political and religious questions," said one republican official, and had an "evil influence on the countryside."[58]

Every Sunday in many rural communes priests and peddlers stood by church doors selling *La Croix* to passersby. Some clergymen hoped to lure peasants from the church steps to the communion rail with gift copies,[59] but five-centime-per-paper sales of *La Croix* had as much to do with the business of journalism as it did with the business of God. Sunday was a day of rest for the indifferent and the religious alike, and many peasants, especially in dispersed hamlets and farmsteads, must have enjoyed visiting the village center for conversation, commerce, church-going, or all three. The popularity of *La Croix* in communes like Varaciuex in the Isère, where no other newspapers were available, need not be linked to levels of church attendance or religiosity. In nearby Têches, peasants could avoid the church steps altogether and spend Sunday afternoons reading and discussing *La Croix* over absinthe. The tavern owner doubled as the newspaper's local vendor.[60]

Village feuds would often erupt between the paper's supporters and critics. When a stranger arrived in Séchilienne (Isère) with copies of

La Croix, the mayor asked the prefect to send republican newspapers to surrounding hamlets in order to counteract *La Croix*'s "reactionary" propaganda, a sign that the paper wielded significant influence. Local governments would normally provide funds for such mundane matters, but Séchilienne's municipal council included two reactionaries who found *La Croix* and its philosophy more to their liking than either republicanism or their old nemesis, the mayor.[61]

In the neighboring Savoie, where *La Croix* "could only fulfill its mission by becoming, more and more, the newspaper of the rural population,"[62] the ex-mayor of Saint Paul-sur-Yenne took over as the local vendor in 1892. He kept his municipal council seat, but devoted his time to selling *La Croix* at the church door and along roads linking isolated hamlets to the tiny village center. He was, it seems, also devoted to irritating the new republican mayor who warned the prefect that his predecessor was in cahoots with the vicar to influence inhabitants.[63] The winners and losers of these local battles are of less significance than the fact that *La Croix* and its politics became intertwined with rural feuds. It would be through these personalities and this paper that peasants in many communities would receive news and commentary on the Dreyfus Affair.

A decade later, the mayor of Héry-sur-Ugine denied a peddler permission to sell *La Croix* because it "injures the government and everything that is republican and honest . . . this filthy sheet is only good for sowing the seeds of division in the region."[64] The prefect, bound by the 1881 press law, overruled the mayor and issued a license. The Dreyfus Affair was recent history, the separation of Church and State about to be formalized, and *La Croix* continued localizing divisive issues.

In the Ain it was done on wheels. Young members of local Catholic groups mounted bicycles and delivered *La Croix* to the department's more remote (and flat) communes. What percentage of the extraordinary 13,000 copies reached peasants in the Ain is unknown, but rural response must have been sufficient to make the exercise worthwhile. And in the Vendée, we shall never know how peasants in Saint Philbert de Bouaine reacted to a notorious priest who found time not only to distribute an extraordinary 300 copies of *La Croix du Dimanche* each week, but to impregnate his domestic—twice.[65]

Sorlin stresses the popularity of *La Croix* among the artisans and weavers of Epinal, Remiremont, and Reims in the Vosges and the Marne.[66] Most copies were destined for workers in these and smaller towns like Vitry le François, but a significant minority went to rural communes. Most of the ten score peddlers' requests available for the

Marne in the 1880s and 90s do not specify newspaper titles. When they do, however, *La Croix* predominates. *Le Petit Parisien* and an un-named Boulangist paper are cited a half-dozen times, while *La Croix* and its sister publications *Le Pèlerin* and *Le Laboureur et le vigneron* appear in 34 requests. The titles and the size and location of the ped-dlers' communes suggest a rural audience.[67] Here, too, *La Croix* was injected into local politics. In 1900, the commune of Songy was in search of a new rural guard; of the two nominees, both "reactionaries," a quiet day laborer was chosen over the "depraved scoundrel" who peddled *La Croix*, publicly insulted the President of the Republic, and greatly annoyed the subprefect.[68]

Far to the southwest, regional newspapers did well in the Gers, where stories of lively local politics figure often in reports from police called to the scene of café conflicts. Maurice Bordes describes intense interest in "la vie locale" in this rural department, and reckons that the four or five newspapers dealing with immediate issues were more popular than those analyzing "les grands problèmes."[69] *La Croix du Gers*, with extensive coverage of local and agricultural news, as well as information on national politics, was among the more attractive papers. Rural priests provided its best audience in the Southwest,[70] and undoubtedly intro-duced parishioners to its pages. Things were not much different in Emile Guillaumin's Allier. Both departments had a sharecropper pop-ulation, and the influence of local notables remained important through the end of the century. Guillaumin tells how free copies of *La Croix* were distributed to peasants on Sundays at election time with instruc-tions on how to vote. It was the only available paper.[71] In the Gers, however, Cassagnac's *Appel au peuple*, like his Paris-based *Autorité*, had an anti-Semitic bias, and it is possible that *La Croix*'s impact on the Gers at the time of the Dreyfus Affair was less strong, because less monop-olistic, than in other French departments.[72]

This "easily accessible newspaper," notes Sorlin, "agreeable to read, attracted a new public that the press had not yet conquered."[73] Popular among workers and petty bourgeois in the North and Northeast (in-cluding the Marne), *La Croix* was no less successful in many rural communities throughout France. Sent to the provinces in individual packets, it enjoyed a great advantage by arriving in the countryside ahead of other Paris-based newspapers.[74]

It was indeed easily accessible, and its new peasant readership must have appreciated the paper's efforts to address rural life in editorials and articles. On December 22, 1897, a month before the explosion of the Dreyfus Affair, *La Croix de l'Isère* issued a typical warning: a Parisian fertilizer salesman was in the region exploiting peasants and hawking

overpriced, inferior products. He "smelled like a Jew" to the "Peasants'
Friend" who signed the article.[75] Countless similar anecdotes—usually
false, always dramatic, and impossible for peasants to confirm—simplified and localized *La Croix*'s broad anti-Semitism. The Gers edition
carried small, captioned illustrations on the rigors of rural life. One,
entitled "Au village," showed a cadavorous peasant grooming his ema-
ciated cow, and read: "If they only paid as much attention to us as
they do to Dreyfus! . . ." Illustrations appear in other departmental
editions, but with less frequency than in the Gers; a sign, perhaps, of
the paper's attempt to attract semiliterate peasants in this remote area.[76]

Unlike most regional newspapers, *La Croix* struck a balance between
national news and local (including agricultural) concerns. Its tone was
far from balanced, however, and the vivid front-page image of the
crucified Christ, followed by impassioned anti-Semitic editorials, signaled its bias. But in the context of provincial journalism, *La Croix*,
more than any other large paper, gave the peasant reader both detailed
agricultural information and a survey of Parisian events.

In the Isère, *Le Petit dauphinois* (republican) and *Le Droit du peuple*
(socialist) are examples of popular provincial papers aimed at an urban
clientele. Meanwhile, *Réveil agricole des alpes* and *Réveil des cultivateurs*
concentrated on agricultural news with only a rare nod to national
politics.[77] In the Gers, newspapers from *l'Avenir républicain* to Cassagnac's *Appel au peuple* were more cognizant of local interests, but, in the
main, focused on Parisian and world events with a perfuctory "Chronique locale."[78] The situation in the Marne was complicated by the fact
that local papers competed with dailies easily delivered from nearby
Paris. The Marne had regional papers, but they, too, presented warmed-
over urban news.[79] Finally, there were scores of special newspapers
and periodicals in provincial France at the end of the century—Catholic
and secular, political and agricultural—but few had the variety of *La
Croix*, and fewer still rivaled its circulation in rural communes.[80]

"Politics," said André Siegfried, "like nature, has its seasons."[81] So
do newspapers. Readers might find Parisian political news of interest
one day, local advertisements, floods, fairs, or infanticides the next.
Peasants were interested in agricultural news most days, however, and
the popular Sunday edition of *La Croix* contained an important supplement, "Le laboureur," devoted to technical advice, fertilizer and
phylloxera information, and rural anecdotes. It usually appeared on
page three between national and local news. Throughout the 1890s,
departmental editions presented these handy tips alongside scathing
indictments of strange Jews, "fouling" the pure air of rural France.[82]
At the height of the Dreyfus Affair, "Le laboureur" was surrounded

by anti-Jewish editorials, articles, letters, and illustrations. In one January, 1898, edition of *La Croix Vendéenne*, articles on weather conditions and harvest news shared space with violent attacks on Zola's "insult" to the army and the intrigues of "cosmopolitan Jewry." The peasant had his news and anti-Semitism too. [83] We shall see in the next chapter that the important question asks why and how country people responded to those anti-Semitic appeals. If they responded at all.

Lingering images of the *Juif errant*; ancient fables and legends of avaricious Jews; Sunday sermons spiced with tales of ritual murders and, at Easter, symbolic beatings of Jewish Christ killers; inflammatory tracts by Edouard Drumont and departmental editions of *La Croix*: this was the panoply of anti-Semitic propaganda available to French country people in various areas in varying degrees at the end of the century. In some regions peasants responded in ways that would delight Drumont; in others the persecution of Jews rekindled memories of past injustices and country people rallied to the Captain's side; in still others complete indifference reigned. In the end, the extent to which Dreyfusards and anti-Dreyfusards attracted rural interest depended on the strength of old prejudices and the degree of local discontent.

In his recent, massive study of French anti-Semitism at the time of the Dreyfus Affair, Stephen Wilson agrees that more work is needed on the local level. He suggests, however, that country people in many places, "geographically remote, poorly educated, preoccupied with their work . . . simply did not or could not understand what the Affair was all about." We shall see that most country people found the Affair no more "complicated and confusing" than did city folk,[84] but their reactions unfolded in the context of distinct local rituals far from the view, far from the understanding, of government officials and other, largely urban, observers. For good reason, most peasants remained uninterested in the Affair, while others articulated their interest through an ancient, particularistic vocabulary.

In the late fall of 1897, *La Croix de l'Isère* described a "charming talk" given by a "peasant orator" at a local agricultural syndicate. In patois he covered everything from the benefits of fertilizers to the horrors of rural migration. When, in his peroration, he professed love "de la petite et de la grande patrie" he was, unwittingly, describing the setting in which diverse reactions to the Dreyfus Affair might take place a few weeks hence.[85] In the early months of 1898, the burning issues which rocked "la grande patrie" and drew the rapt attention of Europe, might or might not intertwine with the people and politics of "la petite"—in the villages and hamlets of rural France. A constellation of traditions, customs, prejudices, even conceptions of time and space, could adapt the Dreyfus Affair to immediate needs. In a few regions it fit like Cinderella's slipper to local interests; in most others, the Affair was never more than a distant irritant, irrelevant and abstract.

CHAPTER VI

DIFFERENCE
AND INDIFFERENCE

*Rien de particulier à signaler au point de vue
de la politique générale qui est plutôt traitée avec
indifférence par la majorité de la population.*

ISÈRE POLICE REPORT, 1898

Late on the night of January 24, 1898, a handful of homemade posters
were attached to walls in the town of Vitry le François (Marne). "Down
with the Jews," they read, "Worker, your sole enemy is the Jew; hang
him to the lamppost; down with Zola; long live the Army!" The police
commissioner in this large *chef-lieu* was not alarmed: "Simply youthful
roguery," he informed the subprefect, with no echo, no menace to the
general population. He detained six men and arrested one: twenty-
five-year-old Ernest Lirman—a drunk.[1]

The local republican newspaper called the display a cowardly act,
the work of a few youngsters overexcited by *La Libre parole* and encouraged by certain Catholic organizations.[2] Two weeks later, after
Lirman had been fined five francs, *La Libre parole* accused the subprefect of being too hard on "our friend" and knuckling under to pressure
from "the numerous hook-nosed tribes who have installed themselves
in Vitry le François."[3]

The police commissioner was mistaken. The incident was repeated
dozens of times in January and February throughout France, ignited
by Zola's article "J'Accuse" which had stunned Paris on January 13 and
had spread to provincial cities a few days later. The Vitry case—in-
consequential compared to massive riots in Paris, Lyon, Marseille, Rouen,
and other large towns—possessed most of the elements common to
urban anti-Semitic demonstrations: student or worker involvement;
written propaganda (often well-written or professionally printed); links
with anti-Semitic leagues and Catholic organizations; ammunition from

the pages of *La Libre parole* and other Paris-based papers; and immediate and visible urban targets, Jewish merchants.[4]

Ernest Lirman and his gang penned their diatribes on the backs of popular broadsheets—crime stories and cheap illustrated periodicals like the *Dramatique roman militaire*, glorifying the army and Fatherland. The Marne, like the East in general, was sensitive to *revanchiste* appeals; the strident patriotism laced through popular novels, taught in schools, and preached from pulpits, produced youngsters acutely aware of the German menace. The bogus but believed threat of "la juiverie allemande," standard fare in fin de siècle literature, was nowhere more effective, more relevant, than in those departments between Paris and the lost provinces of Alsace and Lorraine—the two centers of French Jewry.[5] In Bar-le-Duc (Meuse), next to the Marne and closer still to Alsace, a brave but defenseless rabbi challenged peddlers selling anti-Dreyfus songsheets in March 1898. Police intervened before the peddlers could toss the rabbi into the Marne river. Twelve days later, demonstrators attacked Jewish shops and chased the rabbi from town.[6] In Epernay one hundred young men shouted "Down with Zola and the Jews!" and in nearby Reims students did the same.[7] On the morning of January 26 visitors to the covered market in Châlons-sur-Marne were greeted with a portrait of Zola, defaced and inscribed "Down with the Jews' Man!"[8]

Proximity to Paris and the Eastern frontier intensified nationalist, xenophobic sentiments, but other urban areas throughout the hexagon were also shaken by anti-Semitic riots in the early months of 1898. Medical students in Marseille and Tours, unspecified "students" and "young people" in Grenoble, Nantes, Caen, and dozens of other provincial towns, took to the streets attacking Jewish shops, homes, and synagogues (where they existed), and shouting identical slogans. Whatever the age, sex, or profession of the participants, a strikingly similar leitmotif, an unchanging litany of hate, accompanied these demonstrations.[9]

The political calendar of the Dreyfus Affair reflects an urban agenda. Robert Byrnes describes student members of the Paris anti-Semitic league who lived in the provinces and "devoted their summer vacations to promoting anti-Semitism there."[10] "There" meant the provincial cities, not the rural fields of France where, for working peasants, summer vacations were unknown and anti-Semitic disturbances, where they existed, took a different form. National politics—including the Dreyfus Affair and attendant anti-Semitism—reached the countryside, but filtered through local avenues of transmission, adhering to timetables and issues relevant to rural France.

According to accounts from most government officials and local witnesses, a significant part of the rural population was unmoved by the Affair. From Mazières-en-Gâtine in the west to communities surrounding Saint-Etienne in the Loire and Narbonne in the Aude to dozens of villages and hamlets in the Isère, reports stress mass "indifference."[11] The tone and language of police and prefects are reminiscent of the earlier Panama scandal: "As for the populace, the Dreyfus Affair leaves it absolutely indifferent" (Saint Brieuc, Côtes-du-Nord); ". . . campaigns by *L'Aurore* and other papers have produced no impression on the population" (La Tour du Pin, Isère); ". . . no impression on the public . . . indifferent and skeptical except for twenty individuals, always the same" (Montereau faut Yonne, Seine-et-Marne); "the situation is absolutely different in the city and the countryside. . . . [The Dreyfus Affair] had barely touched those who lived isolated and occupy themselves with calm work in the fields" (Limoges, Haute Vienne); "Nothing to report regarding the political situation which is, above all, treated with indifference by the majority of the population" (Vienne, Isère); "The Dreyfus Affair has left the public . . . completely uninterested" (Bourgoin, Isère).[12]

Richard Cobb has warned us about the prejudices of prefects and police—the legerdemain of fearful or ambitious officials[13]—and it is possible that some reports of tranquility in rural regions in 1898-89 were concocted to impress superiors. But on close examination the evidence suggests that, this time around, it was less a case of intentional deception than accurate reportage in most instances and a misunderstanding of how and why peasants reacted to the Affair in a few others. Standard definitions of "indifference" fit neatly into official (urban) presuppositions about remote peasants more concerned with fêtes and harvests than national and international politics. In an 1899 article entitled "Qu'est-ce que le public?" one observer condemned the "inertia," the "slothfulness" of the masses. "Indifference . . . routine, fear, and hatred of novelty" make them "morally and intellectually flawed." Significantly, the author implied that peasants were by definition indifferent because they were too "absorbed from sun-up to sunset by work in the fields."[14] Like naiveté and hero-worship during the Boulangist epoch, indifference during the Dreyfus Affair was *a priori* perceived as a peasant trait. If, as was often the case, rural reactions to grand events took place in the context of local habits and customs—directed inward to regional concerns instead of outward to national targets—officials tended to discount them as irrelevant, define them as examples of political indifference, or ignore them altogether.

In fact, much of the peasantry seems to have been genuinely unmoved by the Affair and the anti-Semitism which surrounded it. *L'Univers israélite* overstated its case in January 1898 when it maintained that "anti-Semitism has overrun the entire country and penetrated all levels of the population."[15] It failed to strike a chord in most rural regions, though in some communes local circumstances prepared fertile soil for the Parisian event to take root and Dreyfus and Zola captured the attention of isolated, allegedly "indifferent" peasants.

We have seen that there was no clear break between city and country in political awareness, no octrois wall of national consciousness. Yet the events of 1898-99 suggest a mix of "reactive" and "proactive" forms of political behavior.[16] Urban anti-Semitism was brutal, unreasoned, and in its way, primitive. It was also loosely organized in development and transmission and, in that sense, modern. The concerns of urban rioters were, because of their setting and structure, closely linked to the panoply of social and political issues surrounding the Dreyfus Affair in Paris. Similar elements often existed in rural communities but in embryonic form and alongside established avenues of communication and influence. The few Dreyfus-related demonstrations in rural France reveal that entrenched myths and the immediate politics and people of the locality were of greater importance than distant events. Peasants "halfway between revolt and ceremony"[17] show that though life in the countryside changed in the late nineteenth century much remained the same.

In a Var village at mid-century local residents ceremoniously slaughtered and hanged a rooster. Was it a traditional folkloric act with little significance beyond the locality? Or a symbolic condemnation of the new government, an important political statement? An intermingling of both, says Maurice Agulhon, a "contamination" of the ancient by the modern, the local by the national: a demonstration of a society in transition.[18] Two hundred kilometers northwest in the Puy-de-Dôme ancient rituals also served as vehicles for political expression. Celebrating the third anniversary of February, 1848, young men clad in traditional costumes planted a Liberty Tree then parodied the assault, burning, and drowning of a villager "dressed in white from head to foot." The incident took place during the Carnival-Lent cycle "at a time when village youths were preparing their traditional Mardi Gras and Ash Wednesday masquerades."[19] Again, it was a rural society in the penumbra, in transition.

The politicizing experience of 1848-51, along with structural changes in the countryside in the closing decades of the century, are said to

have drawn most peasants out of archaic local political habits and into
the national picture. Grain riots disappeared in the 1850s, the "proactive" slowly eclipsed the "reactive," and by the 1880s and 90s, if not
before, local festivities had been stripped of meaning. Peasants turned
their attention to the complexities of political organization, and folklorists turned theirs to moribund rural customs. Rural France had
"modernized."

Not entirely. Structural transformations in the countryside helped
maintain, not destroy, many aspects of rural political culture, and Dreyfusard and anti-Dreyfusard demonstrations, where they occured, followed not only national political agendas but private calendars as well,
shaped by ancient festivities, village traditions, and work routines. Long-
standing members of small face-to-face peasant communities shared a
unique rural timetable which, in 1898, allowed village demonstrations
to parallel, but not duplicate, events unfolding in Paris.

In a 1907 article on the genesis of anti-Semitism under the Third
Republic, M. Levaillant described popular response to the Dreyfus
Affair:

> In reality, the actual defendant was not Captain Dreyfus, or even
> Dreyfus the Jew; it was the legendary Jew in general, the Jew of
> the Middle Ages who had supposedly died with the Revolution,
> but whom anti-Semitism had revived in the popular imagination:
> the Christ-killer, the profaner of the Eucharist, the poisoner of
> fountains. . . . Dreyfus was a symbol and therein lies the expla-
> nation for his bewildering experience.[20]

To country people who were aware of him, Dreyfus could symbolize
a modern deicide and more. He, Zola, and others could become focal
points for ancient fears and prejudices, but also for political and personal rivalries. Symbolic roosters (or their equivalents) and ritualistic
parodies survived the century and provided the framework for rural
reactions to the Affair. Paris, no longer a remote story-book land of
castles and kings, was the premier city of a centralized state worthy of
the peasants' attention, and byzantine national politics were nothing
new to those weaned on the 1851 insurrection or on Boulangism. Yet
communes throughout France still focused on *la politique du clocher*,
and scattered cries of "Down with the Jews, Dreyfus, and Zola!" were
often political implosions directed at regional, not Parisian, realities.

The early months of 1898, the most tumultuous period of the Affair
in Paris and provincial cities, was a time when peasants worked least
and celebrated most. The Carnival-Lent cycle, so important to rural
demonstrations half a century earlier, had not lost its appeal. The weeks

leading to Easter marked the gradual "return to active life" after a long winter of scarcity, "the beginning of a new year in the calendar of the fields".[21] At this moment rural habits came together in a bizarre mix of pagan ritual, secular leisure, and Christian penance. If the season was essential to an understanding of rural politics in 1848-51, it was no less important in the early months of 1898 when anti-Semitic disturbances occured *pari passu* with observances of Christ's birth, death, and resurrection. Each Sunday in the pages of *La Croix* and *Le Semaine religieuse*, and in the sermons and conversations of village priests, the Christian drama was played out, reminding everyone of the Savior's death at the hands of the Jews. With few variations it was the same every year, but in 1898, news of Dreyfus and Zola imbued some local rituals with national meaning. We shall see that peasants who expressed interest in the Affair reacted in the context of, among other things, the season in which the urban-centered event took place.

At the same time, a secular ceremony—more recent in its origins, but no less important to peasant families—occurred on designated mornings in late January or early February. The annual drawing of lots for military service (*tirage au sort*) took place in the *chef-lieu* of every French canton. Peasant youths accompanied by sweethearts and parents marched from villages, hamlets, and farmsteads laden with bouquets, ribbons, talismans, and charms. The day began with official pledges of allegiance to the Fatherland and ended with young men from enemy communes locked in traditional yearly battles.[22] The mélange of anti-Semitism, nationalism, and militarism which surrounded the Dreyfus Affair in the cities was expressed in some rural areas through these long-established religious and secular rites—observances which reflected the interior concerns of communities as well as the penetration of national politics. The conscript who shouted "Down with Dreyfus! Long live the Army!" and the peasant who burned a Zola mannequin in a purification ceremony grafted the national to the local. On their terms.

On Sunday, February 27, 1898, during the traditional "firebrand" feast in the rural Isère commune of Chapareillan near the Savoie border, inhabitants incinerated a mannequin representing Zola "the impudent defender of the traitor" Dreyfus. *La Croix* found it a sign of "true patriotism," "a significant anti-Semitic act."[23] *Les Brandons*, the first Sunday of Lent, was celebrated in different ways for different reasons throughout France. Torches were paraded through fields to destroy insects and insure rich harvests, cats and other animals were sacrificed in fertility rituals, straw mannequins were burned and then thrown in rivers to mark the end of extravagance as the austere weeks of Lent began. In the Dauphiné, recurrent themes ran through communal variations: yet, invariably, young men danced and sang while a mannequin burned.[24]

But why Zola? How had a distant Parisian novelist become the principal element in Chapareillan's ancient peasant rite? Is it enough to assume that the village priest and other personalities helped along by *La France juive, La Croix,* and *Le Semaine religieuse* had excited the population with anti-Semitic harangues and incessant horror stories of Parisian decadence? It is possible, but similar campaigns were being waged throughout rural France and most areas reported widespread indifference. There is another—secular, political and local—explanation for the Chapareillan incident. An Isère deputy, M. Rivet, lived nearby. During the Boulangist years, an Isère agent informed Baron Mackau that Rivet "does not concern himself with rural interests; he is the son of a schoolteacher and understands nothing about agriculture."[25] Reports filed after the 1898 fête confirm that constituents remained dissatisfied with Rivet's inability to defend the interests of local farmers. Tobacco planters and other peasants ridiculed Rivet's lack of influence, and inhabitants of Chapareillan criticized his handling of local transportation problems. He was ineffectual, unpopular, and, most important for our story, a Dreyfusard. At the annual "fireband" fête, traditional ceremony became the vehicle for local grievances, and the national politics of an unpopular deputy provided the vocabulary. The Dreyfus Affair had arrived in Chapareillan.[26]

In the mountain bourg of Saint Jean de Maurienne in neighboring Savoie, the Mardi Gras procession "was replaced by an anti-Semitic demonstration complete with a Zola-Judas mannequin." *La Croix de Savoie* had encouraged its readers to participate.[27] The three Maurennais priests who sent money and anti-Semitic epithets to *La Libre Parole* a year later must have done their share to stir up the local population, and tension was probably heightened by an internal feud between anti-Semites and a schoolteacher who had the pluck to shout "Down with the Army! Long Live Zola!" Here, too, a mannequin was burned in a ceremony which wed prophylactic ritual to modern politics.[28]

To the north, in the Marne, rural communities reported no manifest reaction to the Dreyfus Affair, except for an incident in the small commune of Pogny, ten kilometers southeast of the department's capital Châlons-sur-Marne. Shortly after anti-Semitic demonstrations had occurred in Reims, Epernay, Vitry le François, and Châlons, Pogny responded to the Dreyfus Affair in a manner more reminiscent of peasant communes in the Isère and Savoie than nearby urban centers. The geographic and socio-economic structure of the Marne differed greatly from that of the Southeast, but rural reactions to the Affair in these diverse regions confirm Robert Redfield's belief that peasant society "is a kind of arrangement of humanity with some similarities all over the world."[29] In Pogny, a community of 589 souls, the Dreyfus Affair emerged in the context of a bitter local feud which began on Tuesday, February 22: Mardi Gras.

Adhering to local custom, the young men of Pogny staged a Mardi Gras cavalcade through neighboring communes, followed by a traditional village festival. When a twenty-four-year-old day laborer, Charles Jules Ménonville, was asked for his customary share to cover (mostly liquid) expenses, he refused, saying he would rather "throw the collection box in the canal." Two young *cultivateurs* reported him to the mayor. Five days later an enraged Ménonville entered the local café where his accusers had gathered for an afternoon card game. In front of a half dozen witnesses he called one young man a "lying, slothful pig, a big ass," then added: "You squealed to the mayor . . . if I had a knife I'd plant it in your belly." Turning to the next victim he repeated the obscenities and ended with "You're a no-good bastard, a liar, a Zola, a Dreyfus!" He "grumbled for another half hour," then left. In his testimony to police, Ménonville denied the Zola/Dreyfus reference (was it more shameful or dangerous than pig, ass, sloth, liar, or bastard?), and explained that he refused to contribute to the festivities because the cavalcade driver failed to wait for him when they stopped at a nearby commune. According to officials, Ménonville was probably lingering in that commune in the company of "two or three absinthes" he was in the habit of imbibing. He was a "dangerous sort" indeed, and the commune would do well to "rid itself of this good-for-nothing rotter."[30]

Surely Dreyfus and Zola were discussed in other communities in the Marne (in more delicate fashion), but police, prefectoral, and newspaper reports are silent on rural reaction outside Ménonville's locality. How had Dreyfus and Zola made their way into murderous threats shouted in a peasant café? On the surface there was nothing extraordinary about Pogny. Most inhabitants were listed as *propriétaires exploitants*, with a few bricklayers and fifteen day laborers, including Ménonville.[31] A closer look, however, reveals that Pogny was the birthplace of Colonel Henry, the notorious forger and anti-Dreyfusard who was to commit suicide later in 1898. When the Mardri Gras incident occurred, Henry's father was one of the few dozen farmers residing in Pogny.[32] In a small rural community where neighbors were well-

known and rivalries acute, this personal link must have helped introduce at least the rough outlines of the Dreyfus Affair to local residents.

The Mardi Gras cavalcades and communal fêtes which provided the
setting for Pogny's little battle were not unique to the Marne. In the
Dauphiné, young men collected money at the end of the traditional
ceremony for food, drink, and festivities. Late in the evening they
gathered round a burning effigy and shouted "Poor, poor Mardi Gras
you are leaving us. . . ."[33] These fêtes, or "vogues," occurred frequently
in the Dauphiné, and provided a setting for demonstrations aimed at
national figures and, as Van Gennep maintains, "local personalities
whom the community wanted to mock," much as they did at periodic
charivaris.[34] On the eve of Lent, 1898, the Marne village of Pogny was,
in a sense, closer to the communes of Chapareillan and Saint Jean de
Maurienne 300 kilometers to the south than it was to nearby cities like
Reims or Epernay where anti-Semitic demonstrations were taking a
different form.

In her engaging study of the "Rites of Violence" in sixteenth-century
France, Natalie Zemon Davis describes how Catholics and Protestants
used accusations of "pollution" and "contamination" against each other.[35]
Three centuries later a similar obsession with "purification" marked
anti-Semitic demonstrations. Dreyfus and Zola were presented as in-
fectious creatures contaminating France. In Paris, grotesque songs and
illustrations covered the pages of popular anti-Dreyfus propaganda,
and virulent editorials in *La Libre parole* and other publications continued the imagery:

> Si l'on veut purger l' pays
> Et disinfecter Paris
> A la porte il faut qu'on foute
> Le sale Youte![36]

In the countryside, priests, *La Croix*, and others applied the purification theme to prophylactic rituals. Peasants often shouted the same
slogans as crowds parading through city streets, but in rural communities flaming effigies still possessed a meaning no longer part of
urban demonstrations. Mannequins acted as *boucs emissaires* and more
for rural inhabitants; they were inextricably linked to long-standing
beliefs that the incineration of an effigy, the inflammatory act itself,
somehow influenced the fate of local crops and communities.[37] Customs born in rural fields take on new meaning when transplanted to
city streets. From long before 1789 through the 1871 Commune, the
burning of mannequins and guillotines held a strong exorcistic meaning for Paris crowds. By the end of the century, however, such acts

were becoming purely symbolic.[38] But to those living on the land, this familiar purgative ritual represented something more than an emblematic political gesture. Not all peasants had access to, or complete faith in, scientific and technological changes which were, at that moment, filtering into rural communes via agricultural syndicates and new publications.[39] It took time for chemical fertilizers, insecticides, organized demonstrations, and Parlimentary politics to replace talismans, torches, festivals, and flaming straw-men.

On January 21, 1898, the police commissioner of Montmorillon in the traditionally conservative Vienne department described a peculiar incident which took place during the annual *tirage au sort* in that *cheflieu*:

> . . . the young conscripts danced and sang as they always do, but this year another activity was added; one which, unfortunately, is popular in many localities. Immediately following the drawing of lots, the young men made a mannequin on which they wrote 'Death to Dreyfus! Long Live France! Long live the Army!'[40]

Following the dancing and singing came the burning of the Dreyfus effigy.

Just as the Christian calendar provided a perfect moment for anti-Jewish demonstrations, the secular schedule prepared the scene for exhibitions of nationalism during the annual drawing of lots. To young men stirred up by military festivities, Dreyfus, the convicted traitor in league with the Germans, and Zola, his "Italian" accomplice, were ideal targets, no matter how distant. In fact, in the East, where the German threat was greatest, and in the Southeast with Italians just across the Alps, these two Parisian personalities could fit neatly with local fears.

An almost ritualistic preparation for the *tirage* began for young Frenchmen with the patriotic teachings of Third Republic schoolteachers; continued through the Boulangist and *revanchiste* years, when local government officials worked with village priests to incite in young conscripts a fervent desire to serve the Fatherland. On Sundays in November, preceding the January or February *tirage*, many rural communes held elaborate "departure masses." Choirs sang, tricolor and Church flags waved side by side, and colorful processions wound through village streets: by the late 1890s it had become a Ralliement *à la mode*.[41]

In the Isère, Abbé Garnier, the anti-Semitic, anti-Dreyfusard leader of Union Nationale, delivered a "heated and apostolic speech" to conscripts at Saint-Etienne-de-Geoirs.[42] Meanwhile, in villages throughout the department, lesser-known priests echoed Garnier. By the following January, the subprefect of Crémieu—where Boulanger had triumphed a decade before—was worried; he posted extra police at the *tirage*, and demanded that all references to Dreyfus be deleted from speeches and all shouts be prohibited.[43] These extraordinary measures insured a quiet *tirage* in Crémieu, but nationalist and anti-Semitic demonstrations marred festivities in a few other communities near and far. In the Haute Savoie sixteen mayors from the Douvaine canton near the Swiss border signed a protest condemning Zola and announced it at the *tirage*, as did their distant counterparts in the Mortagne-sur-Sèvres canton of the Vendée.[44] In the Gers in early February, 300 young men marched through Auch shouting "Long live the Army! Down with the Jews and Zola!" and throwing stones at the few Jewish-owned or -run shops in the vicinity.[45] Conscripts from Puteaux, Suresnes, and Nanterre, near Paris, organized a cavalcade with a Zola mannequin. A large sign placed in its arms read "Down with Zola!" and young demonstrators rode alongside crying "Down with the traitors! Long live the Army!"[46]

Set in relatively large *chef-lieux* throughout France, the *tirage* was a special day when peasant conscripts from outlying regions accompanied by family and friends invaded cities and bourgs. Much has been written about the importance of market days, labor migration, peddling, and the *tour de france*, as avenues of political acculturation—ways in which the isolated made contact with the informed. The annual *tirage au sort* provided an equally important moment for rural inhabitants who otherwise might not have ventured far from their communities.

The behavior of young conscripts in La Roche-sur-Yon (Vendée) provides another illustration of the localized nature of Dreyfus-related demonstrations in the provinces. On the night of January 24, 1898, fifteen young men from town and from the countryside sang the *Marseillaise* and shouted "Long live the Army! Down with the Jews!" There was little trouble that night, but three days later conscripts turned on a member of their group who, like Ménonville in the Marne, refused to contribute his share to the annual festivities. M. Normand thought it "ridiculous to march through the streets carrying flags," and his infuriated peers responded by posting handwritten placards reading "A bas les Juifs! Conspuez Zola, Conspuez Normand!" (see fig. 19). The prominence of Normand's name, and the relative insignificance of Zola's, suggests that these Vendée troublemakers were employing national epithets for local consumption, and that burning issues surrounding the Affair paled in comparison to heated regional rivalries.[47]

Of course the Dreyfus Affair was not the first extra-regional political

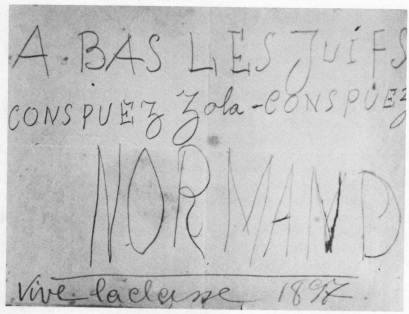

19. Conspuez Zola, Conspuez Normand

theme to impinge upon local military festivities. Peasant conscripts from the communes of Genes and Antigny in the Vendée carried a Boulangist flag to their ceremony in 1889 (local police believed they had been "unconsciously provoked by the vicar);[48] and four years later in the Marne, anarchists nailed signs to village posts calling for conscripts to boycott the *tirage*.[49] Throughout France it had long been a day when an army of conscripts, many from the rural hinterlands, met political propagandists hoping to enlist new recruits.

References to Dreyfus and Zola, exhibitions of anti-Semitism and nationalism in the context of the *tirage*, are less evidence of a new national political consciousness among rural people—that had already been raised in most regions, while it lay in wait in others—than examples of Richard Hofstadter's "marginally related issues" unfolding in a familiar "arena."[50] The *tirage au sort*, like Mardis Gras and *Les Brandons*, was an annual event permeated with local meaning and surrounded by ancient superstitions, many of which were moribund at the end of the century, some of which persisted. National politics often marked these ceremonies, expressed by way of a traditional and particularistic cultural vocabulary.

In the Northeast legend had it that a conscript would draw a *bon numéro* if, on the day of the *tirage*, he got out of bed left foot first, departed from the house the same way (the right foot in Lorraine!), and, en route to the ceremony came across a white horse, a hunchback, and a magpie. He was doomed to a bad number if he met an old woman, a barking dog, or a priest.[51] Such fantastic tales (and if the hunchback were an old woman?) might have been apocryphal, but at the turn of the century they were still discussed and occasionally practiced, and that fact tells something about lingering habits and persistent superstitions. In 1909 in the wine-growing region of the Côte-d'Or and Nièvre, one witness described conscripts who, in order to draw a good number, carried a small morsel of their own afterbirth, which anxious mothers had saved for the special occasion.[52] Customary prayers, chants, and music also marked the festivities: "We shall carry the blue, white, and red/We shall carry the flag of liberty"; "Conscripts are jolly fellows/They will always drink."[53] And cause trouble too.

The Dreyfus Affair became intertwined with seasonal rituals, personal rivalries, and, in the Cevennes, with Protestant/Catholic tensions. Almost a century had passed since the White Terror had rocked the region dividing Protestants and Catholics and adapting national events to immediate religious and socio-economic issues.[54] Reactions to the Dreyfus Affair show that the nineteenth century had done little to change such local habits. Dreyfus was among the subjects illustrated in kaleidoscopes sold at a local fair for two *sous*. Passersby could view pictures of the Captain (perhaps for the first time) through these colorful and accessible contraptions. When asked why so many inhabitants had been Dreyfusards, a local witness responded: ". . . because [Dreyfus] was a Jew and . . . because he had suffered like the Protestants; there was a similarity of suffering."[55]

There is no evidence of similar responses in, for example, the Protestant canton of Mens in the Isère;[56] but the silence of the sources need not indicate indifference. One observer noted that in certain towns in the Midi where "there are no Jews . . . anti-Protestantism replaces anti-Semitism."[57] Nor were there any Jews in the fictional village described by Anatole France; there, the "anti-Jewish crusade consisted principally in attacks upon the Protestants, who formed a small, austere, and exclusive community of their own."[58] In parts of Germany at this time, Protestantism was "infected with anti-Semitism and racism, especially where it was in the majority";[59] but in Protestant enclaves of France the opposite was the case. Reports of virulent anti-Jewishness rekindled memories of another kind of prejudice, prompting some Protestant villagers to take the side of a distant army officer.

Nor were Protestant peasants the only Dreyfusards in rural France.

Police, prefectoral, and newspaper reports focus only on disruptive demonstrations—and most were anti-Dreyfusard and anti-Semitic. But in many areas country people refused to be drawn to the anti-Semites' cause. Sources which concentrate on the inflammatory may conceal numerous enclaves of rural philo-Semitism, as well as support which had little or nothing to do with the religious question.

Whatever the case, feuds, fêtes, and Sunday sermons persisted in the countryside, complemented, not entirely eclipsed, by modern political organization and propaganda launched from the cities. Posters, bulletins, broadsheets, confetti, politicians, and peddlers made their special tours of France during the Dreyfus Affair, though the campaign could not compare in scope or impact with that waged by Boulangists a decade earlier. The General's agents penetrated the most remote regions, while Dreyfusards and anti-Dreyfusards only skimmed the urban provincial surface. Their propaganda campaigns were neither timely nor pervasive, and they rarely attracted rural interest. In fact, it appears that much of the popular imagery dealing with the Affair surfaced months after the crisis had passed. For example, two images— one commissioned by anti-Semites, the other by Dreyfusards—recounted the high points of the Affair in the traditional serial style of Epinal. "History of a Traitor" and "History of an Innocent" illustrate, after the fact, the political legacy of the Dreyfus years, and serve as popular documentation of Charles Péguy's belief that everything begins as a *mystique* and ends as a *politique* (see figs. 20 and 21). But these and other images did not emerge soon enough, nor were they widely enough distributed, to prompt peasant interest. Other posters presented a photographic rogues' gallery of the Affair's principal actors and reached scores of provincial centers late in 1898 (see figs. 22 and 23). One observer spoke for others when he said that they attracted a few curious passersby, but were read "with a certain indifference."[60] A decade before, Boulangist propaganda had been designed to strike early, to anticipate and exploit rural needs; Dreyfusard and anti-Dreyfusard imagery in the countryside for the most part chronicled events *ex post facto*.

One exception, a poster, is worth noting. Throughout 1898-99 Jules Guérin organized a series of anti-Jewish demonstrations in the provinces. He published an appeal to the peasantry in his paper *l'Antijuif*, and distributed posters condemning Jews who were "pillaging France."[61] Examples of peasant reaction to Guérin's appeals are rare, but on a September 1898 market day in Laval (Mayenne) the Groupe antisémitique hung a poster entitled "La Patrie en danger," and the local police commissioner described how this led to "great panic among

20. Histoire d'un Traitre

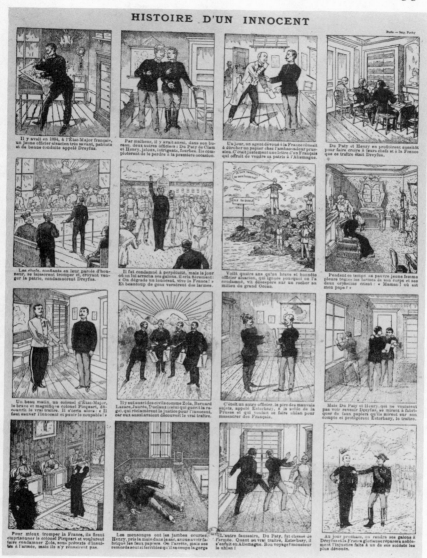

21. Histoire d'un Innocent

22. Dreyfus est un traitre

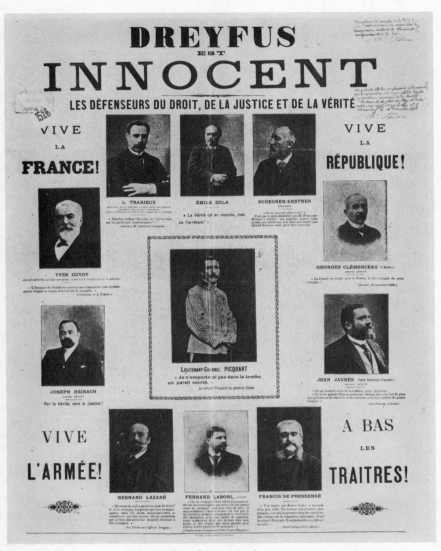

23. Dreyfus est un innocent

LA PATRIE
EN DANGER !

Des Patriotes comme **Drumont** et **Morès**, depuis plus de dix ans nous dénonçaient

LE PÉRIL JUIF

Ils démasquaient les agissements, les accaparements, les coups de Bourse d'une vile poignée d'Hébreux vomis sur la France par tous les ghettos d'Allemagne.

On n'a pas voulu comprendre Drumont et Morès.
On a traité les antisémites de prophètes de malheur.
Les Français ont fermé les yeux sur le péril qu'on leur signalait.

Pendant que les CUISTRES DE LA LITTÉRATURE PORNOGRAPHIQUE, plus ou moins à la solde d'Israël, endormaient le peuple en l'amusant et en le corrompant ;

Pendant que les ÉCUMEURS DE LA POLITIQUE, valets ou prisonniers des Juifs, déchiraient la Patrie et attisaient le feu de nos luttes politiques ;

Le JUIF continuait la ruine de la France !

Et nous avons vu les BARONS et les CHEVALIERS D'INDUSTRIE, faire le coup de l'UNION GÉNÉRALE.
Et nous avons eu l'ACCAPAREMENT DES BLÉS.
Et nous avons eu l'ACCAPAREMENT DES CUIVRES.
Et nous avons eu le **PANAMA.**
Il ne manquait plus que de vendre la France après l'avoir ruinée et déshonorée.

C'EST FAIT !

NOUS AVONS MAINTENANT LE COUP DE LA TRAHISON. Judas Dreyfus a vendu la France un peu plus de trente deniers. Il n'y aura désormais que les aveugles pour ne pas voir le Péril Juif.

PAUVRE FRANCE !

A quoi lui sert d'être le plus beau et le plus riche pays du monde !
Les Juifs, qui ne sont même pas le 1/300e de la population, ont accaparé à eux seuls 1/4 de sa fortune totale.
Les Juifs, en France ont tout accaparé, tout sali, tout détruit.

Seule, notre Armée restait debout !

Et voilà que pour *SAUVER UN TRAITRE*, un Syndicat de Juifs à la solde de l'Étranger tente de ruiner l'honneur de cette Armée. Pour souffleter des *Officiers* qui ont versé leur sang sur le champ *de bataille*, les Juifs ont cherché des mains plus sales que les leurs et ils ont confiés cette détestable besogne à des égoutiers qui ont gagné de l'or en remuant la boue, *à des gens qui*, en 1870, *étaient on ne sait où.*

FRANÇAIS,

C'est à la faveur de nos discordes, que LES JUIFS et leurs COMPLICES font leur ŒUVRE NÉFASTE.
Trève de divisions ! Assez de Déchirements....

LA PATRIE EST EN DANGER !

LES JUIFS, après nous avoir ruinés, divisés, déshonorés, sont en train de chambarder la France, pour le plus grand profit de la

YOUTRERIE UNIVERSELLE.

Eh bien ! unissons-nous pour chambarder l'omnipotence Juive.
Et en attendant de **bouter hors de France les Juifs**, ces parasites dangereux, détruisons par tous les moyens leur influence politique, commerciale ou financière.

Il commence à être temps de rendre la FRANCE aux FRANÇAIS!

A bas le Syndicat ! A bas les Juifs et les vendus ! !

VIVE L'ARMÉE

Un Groupe d'Antisémites.

Nancy, imp. Vagner, 3, Rue du Manège.

AVIS IMPORTANT. — Ce tract pourra être affiché après avoir été timbré à 5 cent.

24. La Patrie en danger

peasants who had come to the fair" (see fig. 24). Many farmers "took back the wheat they had brought, saying that we are on the brink of war . . . more than a thousand hectoliters . . . went unsold." Significantly, the poster included a condemnation of the Jewish "wheat monopoly."[62] The same poster appeared in twenty-five French towns causing "considerable alarm"; as in Delle on the Eastern frontier, where the mayor reported that local peasants were asking if Paris was in the midst of revolution.[63] But most of this propaganda—like the pro-Dreyfus speeches and campaigns of Jaurès, Pressensé, and Zévaès—was confined to major cities.[64] In Grenoble, for example, the 1899 trial of Max Régis—a maniacal anti-Semite accused of fomenting riots in Algeria—threw the city into chaos. Members of Catholic and anti-Semitic groups, along with soldiers from the local garrison, battled young workers on the Place Victor Hugo and Place Grenette, much as they had done in January, 1898.[65] The action was heated, bloody, and urban. Again, Isère villages did not share Grenoble's interest.

Of course, country people throughout France could share with city-dwellers a traditional distrust of the state and a concern over the growth and impact of large-scale industrial capitalism; and anti-Semites could hope to exploit that distrust. In rural regions, however, we must follow Maurice Agulhon and realize that to "talk of struggle 'against the state' is to abandon the description of peasant struggle for a retrospective interpretation which runs the risk of anachronism. . . ."[66] In the Hautes-Alpes, for example, Emilie Carles, a rural schoolteacher, described how her peasant father had cultivated an old habit of "revolt against the state." The state was "the first among thieves," but Emilie's father was a peasant "of olden times" who felt no comradeship with urban proletarians. Quite the contrary, he confined his revolt to intransigence, to a stubborn distrust of change, and to local targets.[67] His strong but involuted reactions, like heated but particularistic villages responses to national events, would continue to be the rule rather than the exception in much of rural France; and, for some peasants, such reactions would be grafted to issues surrounding the Dreyfus Affair. Anti-Semites hoped to depict the Captain and his supporters as modern personifications of a state controlled and manipulated by Jewish capitalists, descendants of rapacious usurers; this was the link they set out to forge in the countryside.

"Each class of society which came into contact with the state as such," observed Hannah Arendt, "became anti-Semitic because the only social group which seemed to represent the state were the Jews."[68] Departmental editions of *La Croix* destined for rural readers did their best to convince French peasants that the economic upheavals of the 1880s and 90s could be laid at the door of Jewish capitalists. "Two monopolies are overruning the world," said the director of *La Croix*, "the state and the Jew. But the state will always be the servant of the Jew."[69] Drumont and his disciples embellished the theme in pamphlets and popular tracts. One, which purported to analyze the history of Jewish "treason from Judas to Dreyfus," stressed that

> ... our farmers, victims of Jewish speculators who monopolize and manipulate the market, are abandoning a countryside which can no longer support them ... the true cause of this evil is the introduction into France of a new [sic] element; the Jew. ... We no longer want to be governed, plundered, deceived by the Jews. ... We want to be our own masters. ... Long live France! Long live the Army! Down with the Jews and their friends.[70]

Drumont and an anti-Semitic deputy from the rural Landes had composed the passage. In the neighboring Gers, where rural constituencies sent three anti-Semites to the Chamber in 1898, local notables pressured small landowners, sharecroppers and day laborers. M. Lasies, a newly elected deputy from Condom, appealed to peasants in June 1898 and promised

> to be successful with our agricultural demands and to make speculators and monopolists give way to rural workers who, through their daily labor, shape the grandeur and prosperity of the nation. ... I shall have no other goal than to purge France ... of pillaging Jews. ...[71]

The number of Jewish inhabitants in the Gers could be counted on Lasie's two hands. They clearly had nothing to do with an ancient and inequitable agricultural system, with problems caused by a paucity of rural credit. Jews could, however, be made into something they were not by the likes of Lasies, Cassagnac, Drumont, the local priest, and others who disseminated national news. Anti-Semites (not alone, of course, and not always) offered peasants elaborate explanations of their economic troubles and adjusted Parisian politics to fit rural needs.

The appeal was not limited to the Gers. In 1897, anti-Semites told Isère farmers that Jews, after monopolizing money, would do the same with the "soil of France, through the purchase of vineyards, forests and prairies. ... Peasants ... have become slaves, serfs. ..."[72] A year later *La Croix* advised peasants that if they wanted to "escape total ruin" they must open their eyes and vote for men committed to "rural democracy. ... No more Jews, freemasons, politicians."[73] In the spring of 1898, between the demonstrations of January and February and the May legislative elections, newspapers and politicians addressed the peasantry as directly (better put, as passionately or simplistically) as anti-Semites and *La Croix*, and were helped along by publications like *Chronique du Sud-est* and *La Démocratie rurale* (the latter, calling for lower taxes, collected a petition with one million signatures in the 1890s).[74]

George Dupeux reckons that the "passions of the Dreyfus Affair became entangled with the discontent born of the economic crisis. . . ."[75] The few rural contributors to Colonel Henry's monument confirmed that economic issues fueled some peasant anti-Semitism. References to phylloxera and other allusions, says Stephen Wilson, indicate a general "hostility to capitalism." One subscription came from a *petit vigneron*, angered by the fact that the "yids" could drink the excellent wine of Montreuil Bellay which he harvests.[76] It bears repeating, however, that the Northeast battled phylloxera into the 1890s, while conditions in most other regions gradually improved. The discontent described by Dupeux, acute during the Boulangist years, had waned in most villages and hamlets by the time of the Dreyfus Affair.

The rhetoric of Drumont, *La Croix*, and others was populist, impassioned, and radical. Like early Boulangism it hoped to attract small landowners and agricultural workers suffering from falling prices and excessive taxes. Anti-Semites (again, like Boulangists) avoided traditional political labels by being fervently negative—anti-state, anti-foreign, anti-politics—thereby trying to find a home among the frustrated and fear-ridden. As with most political movements, however, they concentrated on the growing cauldron of urban discontent. Rural exodus provided fodder for political appeals, but anti-Semites focused on peasants' sons in Paris rather than on aging farmers tied to their land and customs.

Throughout France, political appeals from the Left and Right often proved ineffective "because they were not accompanied by concrete action."[77] Anti-Semites presented scapegoats, cited (fallacious) reasons for the rural plight, and stirred up a few communes in their quest to link traditional anti-Jewish fears to modern political action. Anti-Judaism, which had been religious at first, had become economic—or rather, "the religious causes which had once been dominant . . . were subordinated to economic and social causes"[78]—but modern anti-Semites in the French countryside suffered from an inability to concretize and to act. They never organized in rural France as they had done in Germany in the 1880s and 90s. The Peasant League of Hesse, for example, "unfolded an active propaganda campaign by means of newspapers, but also through some twenty speakers who went from village to village and town to town exhorting, explaining, and condemning

Jews and capital."[79] To be sure, Drumont, *La Croix*, rural priests and others exhorted, condemned and tried to explain, but they never mounted a significant and efficient anti-Semitic organization outside French cities.

At the height of the Dreyfus Affair a coalition of forces sometimes worked in their favor—acute xenophobia in some areas, lingering economic crisis, new mass literacy, a liberal press law, rapid social change, the convenient arrest of a Jew for treason—and anti-Semites seized their chance. But on the whole, agitators in rural France could not crystallize peasant fears of deicides, usurers, foreigners, or the state and direct them toward large-scale involvement in the Dreyfus Affair comparable to that found in the cities. The countryside never reached the pitch of Paris, Marseille, Rouen, or those dozens of other urban centers torn by riots in the early months of 1898. Nationalists and anti-Semites and their Dreyfusard foes met with pockets of interest in rural areas where there was an immediate reason to rally for or against the cause; but they found greater spaces of true indifference where, this time around, the national event in question had little to offer.

What prevented much of rural France from rallying to this extraordinary *affaire* which, for two years at least, had captured the attention of the urban nation? Why did legions of French men and women of the Left and Right—workers and shopkeepers, priests and university professors—react with such fervor while masses of country people remained only marginally interested or indifferent? A contemporary observer, discussing Drumont's brand of anti-Semitism, touched on a possible explanation:

> What characterized *La France juive* above all . . . was less its accusations against *Israël*, than its stream of reproaches against the Republican regime. . . . M. Drumont strove to create a strong link between Opportunism and the Jews.[80]

Peasants had not given up on the Republic. Discontent and anger still marked parts of rural France—and Drumont's appeals worked in a few communes—but responses were momentary, the peasantry skeptical. Four major factors, among others, helped offset extreme nationalist and anti-Semitic entreaties in the 1890s: effective republican, and, increasingly, socialist responses to immediate rural needs; the lack of pervasive hostility toward Jews outside cities and the East; the inability of anti-Semites to organize in the countryside, partly because of their misreading of rural realities; and perhaps most important, the slow but steady improvement of the agricultural situation throughout most of France after two decades of trauma.

The Republic had been attacked from every corner, its economic policies condemned (often correctly) as ineffective and unjust. But throughout the 1890s, thanks to issues raised by the Boulangist threat, and thanks to Minister of Agriculture Jules Méline, republicans attempted to ameliorate the rural plight. The extent of Méline's commitment, and the undeniable inadequacy of his agricultural programs, should not obscure the significance of his rural appeals. By the time of the Dreyfus Affair, the ravages of phylloxera had abated in much of France, broad-based agricultural syndicates were gradually recruiting members from remote communes, threshing machines and chemical fertilizers were reaching hitherto untouched regions, and hope, if not prosperity, was returning.[81] After the crisis-ridden 80s, the agricultural situation was undergoing a relative improvement;[82] and although Méline might have had little to do with the recovery, he stood as the preeminent spokesman for rural France in the republican government. On January 27, 1898, while the Affair raged in Paris, the government announced a long-awaited Law on the Reduction of Land Taxes. Much still needed to be done, but Méline and other republicans enjoyed a "legitimate popularity" in the countryside which anti-Semites could not undermine.[83] Drumont's anti-government harangues did not always fall on deaf ears in rural France, but peasants who remained committed to the Republic paid little attention.

The historical anti-Jewishness of many socialists changed with the Dreyfus Affair. Eugen Weber suggests that before that, into the 1890s, the "Left probably remained the most audible source of attacks on Jews . . . with frequent articles in official publications like the *Revue socialiste*, where the use of terms like 'parasites' and 'microbes' was nothing exceptional. . . . The popular rebellion against the hardships of the modern world found in the Jew a convenient symbol."[84] References to Jewish capitalists had continued through the 1890s, but by 1899 the Isère deputy, Zevaès, advised a meeting of the Parti ouvrier in Grenoble that all capitalists, not just Jews, should be their targets. He condemned the anti-Semitism of rabid nationalists, and, like Jean Jaurès before him, declared his support for Dreyfus. (This particular audience shared Zévaès's ideology but not his enlightened views on Dreyfus's civil liberties, and a melée broke out ending the meeting.)[85] Although urban workers remained primary targets, socialists had done well in recent rural elections, making inroads into departments like the Cher, Nièvre, Var, and Isère[86]—though real successes would come with the new century.[87] In 1898 neither anti-Semitism—still a lingering ingredient in their political recipe—nor the Affair itself seems to have played a major role in socialist appeals to the countryside. Like many republicans, they aimed for "concrete action" in rural areas,[88] whereas anti-Semites offered scapegoats, facile explanations, and little else.

Rural priests and propagandists tried to revivify lingering myths of foreign Jews, and a few areas responded with anti-Jewish demonstrations. But much of rural France was like André Siegfried's West where anti-Semitism, if it existed, was not heated and "popular" as it had been in Alsace.[89] In fact, historians point to the militantly Catholic West for examples of "theoretical anti-Semitism," a prejudice "divorced from any acquaintanceship with Jews and often linked with Catholicism."[90] Priests continued to wield significant power in some rural regions of the West at the end of the century, but in most of the countryside "sympathy for men of the cloth," writes Eugen Weber, "was either lukewarm or downright bitter."[91] Throughout France, and for many reasons, peasants paid less attention to clergymen, and the potency of sorcerers and devils (and Jews as devils) declined with the decline of magic. Indifference, or, perhaps, popular French depictions of the repentant Wandering Jew—a benighted but benign traveler—weighed more heavily than threats of usury, ritual murder, and Christ-killing. Moreover, a significant minority of peasants—often Protestant peasants—rallied to Dreyfus, exhibiting a philo-Semitism which would continue into the twentieth century, most notably during the Vichy years, when Protestant villagers sheltered Jews fleeing French and German fascists.[92]

Georges Dupeux maintains that economic crisis sometimes acts as an "electro-shock" on citizens, and prosperity an "anesthetic." The short but devastating crisis and political conjuncture of the Second Republic, says Dupeux, contributed to widespread upheaval at mid-century, whereas the long, insidious crisis of the 1880s produced different reactions in the countryside. Rural victims, undergoing pervasive economic malaise for almost two decades, adjusted gradually to gradual solutions. On the other hand, agrarian depression—long- or short-term—is not the sole factor leading to popular upheaval. Carefully constructed political networks in rural areas, serving to organize and mobilize country people, are of crucial importance.[93] Agricultural crisis may provide an issue, but without political organization rural struggles will remain unfocused and ineffective. As we have seen, anti-Semites lost on both counts: their rural appeals were haphazard, and the economic situation, a powerful issue to exploit, improved in the late 1890s. Most country people preferred, a stable Republic searching for concrete agricultural policies to the radical, random, and exclusively negative appeals of anti-Semites.

Moreover, the slow but steady amelioration of conditions in rural France tended to encourage tolerance, not tension; as one author puts it, "while slow upward mobility is closely associated with tolerance, rapid mobility either upward or downward, is positively related to interethnic hostility."[94] If, for example, Boulanger had grafted Drumont's propaganda to his political appeals at the height of the agricultural crisis, rural anti-Semitism might have proved more of a factor than it was a decade later during the Dreyfus Affair. But unlike their counterparts in Germany and Austria, French anti-Semites in the 1890s were unable to mobilize peasants and create an agrarian base for a new mass movement. No less virulent than their central European neighbors, their vision and their organizational skills were limited, and their peasant audience, where it existed, less willing.[95]

Scores of cities and towns throughout France experienced some form of Dreyfusard or anti-Dreyfusard demonstration in 1898. Those which did not were exceptions. On the other hand, the evidence suggests that only a handful of rural communities—during Mardis Gras, Carnival or the *tirage au sort*—expressed any interest in the Affair. They, in turn, were exceptions in a countryside where local issues shaped village agendas. During the most tumultuous months of the Affair, periodic reports on public spirit submitted by close, well-informed observers confirm that the overwhelming majority of residents in small rural communes had little in common with "politicians" and others who "bother themselves with the Dreyfus Affair . . . the major part of the public is indifferent."[96]

On February mornings in 1898, Marcel Proust's Jean Santeuil "started early from home so as to arrive in good time for the Zola trial . . . and there he stayed, fasting, excited, emotionally on edge." At night, Santeuil and others like him wondered "happily to themselves whether there would be anything thrilling in the *Figaro* when it was brought up on the morning tray." It was "one of the most exciting cases," and what observers "had to say was just as comforting, just as salutary, as the steaming bowl of *café au lait* which must be sipped in leisurely fashion while the day's news was being absorbed."[97] Santeuil's dizzying interest in the details of the case was as unlike rural reactions to the Affair as leisurely mornings spent over *Figaro* and breakfast trays were unlike the daily habits of working farmers. Politics could be a leisure activity for peasant and bourgeois both, but during the fin de siècle their methods and schedules had little in common.

A month after Jean Santeuil's exhilarating plunge into the politics of Paris, while rural communes were recovering from Mardis Gras and *Brandons* festivities, Edouard Manet's niece, Julie, described a party at her Paris apartment:

> We put on costumes to receive Monsieur Mallarmé and Monsieur Renoir, who did not have the carnival spirit and started all over again on the eternal discussion of the Dreyfus case. . . . It must have been grotesque, the two men having a serious talk—with Monsieur Renoir very excited—and three people in bizarre costumes sitting and listening without opening their mouths.[98]

The real Carnival, the traditional Carnival—a centuries-old celebration determined and circumscribed by the calendar of the Church and attendant seasonal rituals—had taken place a month before in rural France. In the cities, where the traditional meaning of Carnival had become irrelevant, it had lost not only its original meaning and purpose; it had become unmoored from its integral slot of time within any given year. The word "carnival" to Julie Manet and her peers, had become synonymous with masked and costumed revelry. An ancient custom was shaped to new needs and personal timetables. Costumes were "bizarre," or playful, or seductive, and determined more by fashion than by a symbolism which no longer applied. The one regret that participants in this sort of Carnival might voice was that such a gala event might turn sour: the carnival spirit at Julie Manet's gathering was ruined by the seriousness of politics.

Most peasants did not share the intense interest of Renoir or Proust's Santeuil in the Dreyfus Affair.[99] When they did, however, their involvement was no less profound. Proust, again, believed that "absolute calm" reigned in the countryside during the Affair.[100] Not entirely. Rural reactions unfolded in diverse and desultory ways in scattered regions, and very often proved indecipherable to officials (and novelists) reporting on village politics and public spirit. Most peasants in communes near and far ignored the Affair for good cause; others responded, but very differently than their urban countrymen. That their politics were misjudged had much to do with the preconceptions of those who were doing the judging. Rural differences continued to be confounded with political indifference.

CONCLUSION

*Notre unité politique et notre centralisation ad-
ministrative nous portent à exagérer infiniment
l'uniformité de la nation, l'homogénéité des
populations. Volontiers on se figure les communes comme des pierres concassées pour l'en-
tretien des routes, différentes de forme et de
volume; mais identiques comme composition,
simples fragments d'une même roche. Rien de
plus contraire à la verité.*

ARSÈNE DUMONT, 1897

In the decades between mid-century and the Boulanger and Dreyfus
Affairs striking changes occurred in the French countryside. With the
demise of small local industries and the exodus of many young artisans,
day laborers and rural bourgeois, thousands of hitherto economically
and socially complex communes became the domain of seasoned peasants. The process had begun early in the century, but after 1850 the
number of communes with fewer than 500 inhabitants increased dramatically, and rural *listes nominatives* in the 1880s and 90s show that
farmers now predominated in villages and hamlets. Moreover, the
expansion of the national market economy, along with advances in
education, communications, and the military system, also helped make
for a new and different rural world in the second half of the century.
Much of this fits neatly with the contention that deindustrialization
and exodus had created a "traditional" (agricultural) countryside by
the fin de siècle; at the same time, it confirms the belief that urban-
based agencies of change reached out to peasants during these decades,
drawing them into a more homogeneous national culture.[1]

But what of rural politics? Did they, too, develop along a linear
progression, with peasants forever politicized after 1851 or Frenchified
after 1900? Did politics in the countryside "modernize" *pari passu* with
new roads and railroads, with rising rates of literacy or proletariani-
zation? Rural reactions to Boulangism and the Dreyfus Affair have
shown that the reality was more complicated than that, the politics of

country people more desultory, and more deeply rooted in established customs.

In the 1880s and 90s peasants were, depending on the locality, descendants of *nu-pieds*, Revolutionary brigands, Bonapartists, mid-century Montagnards, or rural folk who had never bothered with politics, local or national: and traditional alignments (or customary indifference) played crucial roles in shaping peasant opinions. But new generations must learn for themselves the political ways of the near and distant world, and form their own definitions from constantly changing social and economic realities. While memories of, say, 1851 may have survived, additional factors were shaping peasants' opinions and choices. For example, we have seen how the political complexion of the rural Gers changed dramatically in just over one generation: Bonapartist repression in the 1850s, rich harvests in the 60s and 70s, then economic catastrophe in the 80s, led to a new conjuncture for a new generation of peasants in the Gers and elsewhere in France. In short, rural political traditions must be examined along with different types of alliances, familial and personal, and they must be carefully placed in the context of geography, generational change, and immediate local interests. "Each 'current event,' " Fernand Braudel reminds us, "brings together movements of different origins, of a different rhythm: today's time dates from yesterday, the day before yesterday, and all former times."[2] All these factors make politicization (to borrow from E. P. Thompson), like class, "not a thing but a happening."[3]

In Part Two we examined the brief but widespread Boulangist threat to the Republic. In the Isère, the General's agents grafted national appeals to old political traditions in formerly Bonapartist strongholds (or in areas without noteworthy political alignments) and drew many new rural voters to the polls in 1888. On the other hand, in the Gers, an intricate Bonapartist patronage network dominated by local personalities and influential families acted as a barrier to political challenges. By the early 1890s republicans offering concrete agricultural policies loosened the ties that bound Gers peasants to Bonapartists, while socialists also began to receive modest support in a few rural areas. Boulangists found no room and no reason to mount a comprehensive campaign in the Gers. Meanwhile, in the Vendée, their attempt was only halfhearted. In some rural enclaves, Legitimists, supported by village priests, rejected the new movement as suspiciously radical, while in industrial areas of the department Boulanger smacked of Bonapartism. As in the Gers, far to the south, the General's supporters found no room to maneuver. They found much room in the rural Orne, however, where an elaborate political network, manipulated by royalists and Bonapartists, used the General's popularity (and his massive propaganda) to attract rural support. Boulanger never won an Orne election, but local agents capitalized on Boulangism and won many. Finally, in the Marne, the movement failed to engage the interest of peasants and wine-growers who prospered through the 1880s. Other factors, including the local relevance of *revanche* and the early stirrings of political anti-Semitism might attract some country people, but, in the end, workers in depressed urban industries, not peasants in agricultural villages, rallied to the General in the Marne.

Still, throughout France in varying degrees, Boulangism provided a new national alternative to old political alignments at a critical moment; even more significantly, it forced entrenched organizations to take more careful note of rural voters. Boulanger did not always mobilize the peasantry, but he did incite republicans, socialists, and conservatives to address the interests of country people more clearly and concretely. Whether Boulangists won or lost in rural communities was of less significance than how, quite literally, they played the political game.

On the one hand, the movement deserves its burlesque image; personalized soaps, candies, and liquors, colorful *images d'Epinal*, and the General's highly publicized suicide created a bizarre, circus-like atmosphere. On the other hand, the calculated exploitation of those same elements made Boulangism the first large-scale national movement— as contemporaries put it—to "Americanize" political campaigning in France. Three decades earlier, during an Illinois senatorial campaign, Lincoln and Douglas appealed to farmers in a series of festive debates which were a "perfect exemplification of nineteenth-century American democratic practice at its best";[4] barely a decade before Boulangism, Gladstone's enormously successful Midlothian campaigns "recast the nature of the conduct of politics in England."[5] General Boulanger did the same in France: peasants in dozens of departments learned about national politics from traveling agents, peddlers, and, in some instances, from Boulanger himself, surrounded by hired bands of vociferous hawkers. Old devices, including popular imagery and *colporteurs*, had been put to political use in the French countryside before; but given nearly two decades of universal manhood suffrage, liberalized peddling laws, new roads and railways and easier access to remote rural communes, the scope of the General's campaigns surpassed the propagandizing of mid-century and of the 1870s. Proposals for electoral reform submitted to the Chamber of Deputies after 1900 still referred to the "Boulangist period" and to the industry of "Barnums politiques" which had "Americanized" election campaigns. Beyond doubt,

Boulangist methods and organization heralded a new age of popular politics in France.[6]

But, in one of its aspects, Boulangism also marked a finale: never again would popular imagery in the tradition of Epinal be used on such a scale. It had been sent to the countryside to attract rural support, and in those years before Ferry's education reforms had a decisive impact on villages and hamlets, popular images, peddlers, sympathetic rural guards and town criers helped spread the Boulangist message to areas where oral traditions and visual imagery still played meaningful roles. In the years to come, however, more and more peasants would turn to the same news sources as their urban countrymen. One might argue that the power of newsprint eclipsed the power of visual imagery in mass politics in France for only a few decades—from the demise of Boulangism to the advent of televised campaigns. If so, the period fits neatly with Geoffrey Barraclough's engaging discussion of technological advances and the chronological boundaries of "contemporary history": 1890-1960.[7]

Country people who rallied to Boulanger or supported his rivals did so because new conditions, including a pervasive and sophisticated propaganda organization and immediate economic turmoil, prepared fertile soil for the national movement to take root, to have an effect. Historians of Boulangism stress its importance among wood-cutters and other rural proletarians in, for example, the Cher department.[8] We have seen that the movement succeeded in tapping rural interests in many other parts of France as well, and that the political attitudes of country people described by a provincial newspaper in 1889 were changing: "When one asks a rural voter if he cast a ballot for the General . . . he invariably responds, 'Does he [Boulanger] have property in the area? Does he own land? When the reply is 'no,' the peasant shrugs and says, 'Then why would I vote for him?' "[9] They would vote for him, or for his surrogates, because they increasingly realized that local agricultural crises were linked to the world beyond and demanded a national remedy. Other peasants rejected the General and supported government candidates who, significantly, had been mobilized by the Boulangist threat to address rural interests. During these crucial years, more and more peasants began to look beyond their village boundaries for national solutions to local dilemmas.

A decade later, however, rural responses to the Dreyfus Affair would show that politics in the countryside continued to function on its own terms, with its own priorities, and that not all national issues had a national following. Reactions to the Affair illustrate the relative importance of important events; they shed more light on the persistence of rural particularisms and point out the uneven nature of national politics in fin de siècle France.

Neither political anti-Semites nor their Dreyfusard foes ever mounted an effective organization in the countryside. Anti-Semitic leagues and Catholic groups which mobilized thousands of students, workers, and others in Paris and provincial cities, and fueled the riots of 1898—like pro-Dreyfus campaigns in the provinces waged by Clemenceau's *L'Aurore*—either ignored country people or failed to strike a relevant chord in rural regions. The situation was not as it had been a half-century earlier when local political networks helped draw country people to national events and new ideologies, nor as it had been a decade before when Boulangists met with some success among peasants searching for economic relief and alternative political choices. Other factors might attract peasants to the Affair—fervent nationalism, militarism, old traditions of philo- or anti-Semitism—but infrequently and in desultory ways which had more to do with local political or personal implosions than extra-local (national) issues. Anti-Semites had little success with old and ongoing attempts to convince peasants that "Jew" was synonymous with "usurer," as Marx and others had believed that "Judaism" was synonymous with "commerce."[10] Consciously or not, anti-Semites hoped to transfer peasant hatred and distrust of moneylenders (who were evil) to Jews (who they insisted monopolized moneylending) and thereby equate Jews in the popular mentality with evil and with economic injustice. It rarely worked. Peasants, as we have seen, knew their (mostly Christian) moneylenders at first hand, and refused to make the connection that anti-Semites desired. Unlike the political anti-Semites of central Europe who, during these years, exploited the prejudices of peasant leagues in Germany and Austria, French anti-Semites never developed the essential agrarian base needed for a broad-gauged national movement. The shock-troops of Guérin's Ligue antisémitique and similar groups in 1898, like the crowds who shouted "Better Hitler than Blum!" four decades later, were, to an overwhelming degree, urban: rural people, still a majority of the French nation during the Dreyfus years, had little to do with the hateful violence which surrounded the Affair.

In the end, some villagers might adapt the broad outlines of the Dreyfus Affair to feuds and rivalries, or engage in demonstrations which paralleled Carnival-Lent rituals; more often, it seems, they remained indifferent. The few instances in which a constellation of traditions, personalities, and entrenched local battles adapted the Affair to immediate needs, show that peasants were less concerned with the Dreyfus case itself than with the epithets and invectives it provided for unrelated rural altercations. These were the rare exceptions which prove a rule.

Contemporary accounts and traditional histories often contrast the pervasive malaise, the deep uncertainty, anxiety, and anomie of the fin de siècle, with an arcadian vision of a simpler, healthier rural world. In the minds of many politicians and urban observers, the peasantry was the "reservoir of French society," writes Stanley Hoffmann, "while the "working class was its swamp.""[11] Rural folk were held up as symbols of strength and stability: Maurice Barrès, for example, felt that Parisians had become enfeebled (débiles), whereas peasants and provincials remained a vital source of national energy.[12] These dramatic and simplistic contrasts were offered by urban intellectuals and politicians for whom rural exodus, like the growing demands of industrial workers, had become "a neurotic worry."[13] But, Virgilian myths aside, crucial distinctions between rural and urban France persisted at the end of the century.

We have seen that the agricultural crisis had abated throughout much of the countryside by the time of the Dreyfus Affair. After more than a decade of economic trauma, peasants were beginning to attract the attention of government officials who, for benevolent or nefarious reasons, wished to curry the favor of rural interests. Work on the land remained hard, rising expectations exceeded real benefits, and Roger Thabault's religion of "Progress" overstates the case.[14] But the decade between Boulangism and the Dreyfus Affair did mark a turning-point. By the late 1890s peasants were enjoying more abundant harvests, and the plight of those country people who stayed on the land was clearly improving. "Above all, at the very end of the century," writes Roger Brunet, peasants felt an "undeniable relief (soulagement)." Higher wages for rural workers, combined with an "augmentation of peasant holdings," meant a rising standard of living for most country folk in the final decade of the century: the Dreyfus decade.[15] Anxieties, uncertainties or anomie could touch peasants as profoundly as city dwellers, but the mal du siècle so dear to historians of modern France was not a feature of rural life.

Le Petit Journal reported in 1888 that troubles in France are "on the surface," they had not reached "the depths of the nation."[16] On the contrary, the crisis of the 80s was profound and had much to do with rural responses to national issues, including Boulangism. Troubles surrounding Dreyfus a decade later, however, were of limited and urban interest. This, along with other factors—including the uneven nature of anti-Semitism in rural areas and the ineffectiveness of pro- and anti-Dreyfusard organizations in the countryside—alters our traditional view of the Affair without denying the lasting political and social importance of that dramatic event.

In 1899 Captain Dreyfus returned to France after more than four years on Devil's Island. As his special train sped through the Breton countryside, one bystander asked, and was told, who was on board. His response would have shocked the hundreds of reporters, demonstrators, and government officials awaiting the prisoner's train, and it surely contradicts those histories of the Affair which, for so long, have insisted that the "whole country" was consumed by blind hatred and intolerance.[17] Evidence from rural regions suggests that this fellow was less well-informed than most country folk, but his reply captures the spirit of the Affair throughout much of rural France. Still watching the train move toward Rennes, where the "eyes of the civilized world" were focused, he turned to a neighbor and asked, "Qui ça, Dreyfus?"[18]

History often "proceeds in jumps and zigzags," wrote Friedrich Engels, "and if it were followed in this way, not only would much material of minor importance have to be included, but there would be much interruption of the chain of thought. . . ."[19] The historian's task is a forbidding one: to deduce which jumps are irrelevant interruptions, which zigzags telling detours. The private calendar of the individual often strays from the public calendar of the collective: vagrants, ragpickers, even the less marginal Restif de la Bretonne, paid little attention to grand French Revolutionary events, concentrating instead on satisfying their immediate, non-political desires.[20] Similarly, particularistic local movements have frequently stood apart from broad-gauge national events: French peasants during the Great Fear, like English Diggers during the Civil War, expressed desires and demands which sometimes paralleled but often diverged from the better-known (because far better-recorded) march of events. And, as we have seen above, rural politics at the end of the nineteenth century still proceeded, as one historian has put it in another context, "dialectically and in concentrated bursts."[21] Such detours offer important correctives to historical accounts which, for too long, have represented entire nations as acting in concert during major political upheavals. They do not divert us from the larger picture (Engels *dixit*), but attract us to different, less familiar, but no less telling, scenes.

In many rural areas Boulangism marked a pivotal moment in the political evolution of the peasantry, whereas the Dreyfus Affair, despite conventional wisdom, attracted only marginal interest. The varied responses of country people to those two political "watersheds" show that in late-nineteenth-century France critical moments of political linkage still came in waves which swept over the nation when local circumstances were right, but remained limited to specific harbors of political action when circumstances were uneven. More significant than a quest for pivotal moments of political acculturation, however, is an attempt to understand how urban-based national events were adapted to the workings of rural politics, and why peasants responded in the ways they did.

I have stressed that life in the countryside at the end of the century was still marked by age-old work routines, local rituals and ceremonies, intricate, intimate kinship networks and other personal relations in small agricultural communities. But what do these distinctions reveal, and why did they endure so long? Why did officials still have to insist in the final decades of the century that "personal local rivalries must be sacrificed for the common good?"[22]

The survival of "rough music" and charivaris in nineteenth-century England and France, says E. P. Thompson, indicates the persistence of a strong "local *dialect*"; the continuation of that dialect reveals a "traditional consciousness" which endures despite "erosion brought by emigration."[23] Moreover, it is a consciousness sustained by, among other things, "extremely narrow kinship ties." Gradually and unevenly, charivaris were replaced by more organized and consciously political movements less beholden, concludes Thompson, to "traditional forms of popular violence."[24] But as long as these activities or others like them survived, communities maintained distinctive customs, including political customs, which shaped their reactions to outside (and inside) demands and pressures.

The stories I have recounted in these chapters—of old feuds and village rivalries, of popular images and oral cultures, of *Brandons* fêtes, Mardis Gras and charivaris merging with national events—have not been included solely to add anecdotal spice to the historical narrative; nor are they meant to imply that primitive peasants clung to atavistic ways out of ignorance or isolation. Instead, they are offered as examples to suggest that strong local "dialects" persisted in the countryside at the time of the Boulanger and Dreyfus Affairs, and that they survived, ironically, as a result of the sweeping structural transformations which marked the second half of the nineteenth century.

Modern agencies of change at once upset and solidified rural cultures. Large numbers of artisans, laborers, and rural bourgeois left the countryside in response to the shifting demands and loci of French industry: they left wine-growing villages in the Marne for Reims or Paris, sharecroppers' hamlets in the Gers for Toulouse or Bordeaux, isolated mountain villages in the Isère for Vienne or Lyon. For the most part, and for obvious reasons, the travelers were young. Some departed reluctantly, others with eagerness, but whatever the case, throughout the final years of the nineteenth century, they departed. Those peasants who remained on the land witnessed the development of new rail lines, by-roads and other improvements offered by republicans anxious to ameliorate rural conditons, and, perhaps, stem the exodus.

Yet, for the overwhelming majority of peasants who lived far from the modernizing, mechanizing large farms of the Paris basin, life on the land maintained a pace, a rhythm, determined not by new agricultural hardware—which most farmers could not afford and did not possess until well into the twentieth century[25]—but by scythes and pitchforks and human and animal power. One economic historian has called the final decades of the nineteenth century in France a "transitory resting place" when small peasant holdings marked by ancient agricultural routines coexisted with, and still outnumbered, the mechanized farm-factories of the future. At this moment of "technological dualism . . . the old showed no tendency to be pushed aside by the new." Nor, as we have seen, did old political habits.[26]

The way the structure of everyday life on the land shaped the structure of rural politics—the culture in agriculture—has been part of this story. Peasant villages changed dramatically in the final decades of the century: the life of the simple man, Père Tiennon, gave way to the life of his creator, Emile Guillaumin. But country people, many of them living in the rural communes of their birth, continued to work at politics much as they worked at sowing and harvesting—with their own tools.

NOTES

INTRODUCTION

1. APP Ba 1052, August, 1899.

2. Richard Cobb, *Paris and Its Provinces, 1792-1802* (London, 1975), p. 117.

3. T. E. Lawrence, *Seven Pillars of Wisdom: A Triumph* (Garden City, 1935), p. 6.

4. For mid-century, see Maurice Agulhon, *1848 ou l'apprentissage de la République, 1848-1852* (Paris, 1973); Ted W. Margadant, *French Peasants in Revolt: The Insurrection of 1851* (Princeton, 1979); John M. Merriman, *The Agony of the Republic: Repression of the Left in Revolutionary France, 1848-1851* (New Haven, 1978); Roger Price, ed., *Revolution and Reaction: 1848 and the Second French Republic* (London, 1975); Charles Tilly, "The Changing Place of Collective Violence," in Melvin Richter, ed., *Essays in Theory and History: An Approach to the Social Sciences* (Cambridge, Mass., 1970) and "How Protest Modernized in France, 1845-1855," in W. Aydelotte et al., *The Dimensions of Quantitative Research in History* (Princeton, 1971). For regional accounts of rural politics and culture at mid-century, see Maurice Agulhon, *La République au village* (Paris, 1970); Jean Dagnan, *Le Gers sous la Seconde République*, 2 vols. (Auch, 1928-29); Peter McPhee, *The Seed-Time of the Republic: Society and Politics in the Pyrénées-Orientales* (Unpub. diss., University of Melbourne, 1977); Philippe Vigier, *La Seconde République dans la région alpine*, 2 vols. (Paris, 1967); and Alain Corbin, *Archaïsme et modernité en Limousin au XIXe siècle* (Paris, 1975).

5. See, for example, Roger Thabault, *Education and Change in a Village Community: Mazières-en-Gâtine, 1848-1914*, trans. Peter Tregear (New York, 1971); Georges Dupeux, *Histoire sociale et politique du Loir-et-Cher, 1848-1914* (Paris, 1962); Tony Judt, *Socialism in Provence* (New York, 1979). On winegrowing communities, see, for example, Leo Loubère, *Radicalism in Mediterranean France: Its Rise and Decline* (Albany, 1974); and J. Harvey Smith, "Agricultural Workers and the French Winegrowers Revolt of 1907," *Past and Present*, 79, 1978, pp. 101-25.

6. Henri Mendras, *La Fin des paysans* (Paris, 1967), *Sociologie de la campagne française* (Paris, 1971), and *Sociétés paysannes* (Paris, 1976); on the importance of mass communications, see Laurence Wylie, *Village in the Vaucluse* (Cambridge, Mass., 1957) and Valéry Giscard d'Estaing, *Démocratie française* (Paris, 1976).

7. For strikes and worker organization, see Michelle Perrot, *Les Ouvriers en grève: France, 1871-1890*, 2 vols. (Paris, 1974), as well as Yves Lequin,

Les Ouvriers de la région lyonnaise (1848-1914), 2 vols. (Lyon, 1977); see also Michael Hanagan, *The Logic of Solidarity: Artisans and Industrial Workers in Three French Towns, 1871-1914* (Urbana, 1980), and John M. Merriman's important forthcoming study of Limoges across the nineteenth century.

8. Eugen Weber, *Peasants into Frenchmen: The Modernization of Rural France, 1870-1914* (Stanford, 1976), p. 493.

9. Ibid., p. xv.

10. Examples of thoughtful and penetrating reviews of Weber's book include Maurice Agulhon in *Times Literary Supplement*, May 6, 1977; Tony Judt in *Social History*, Jan. 1978; Ted W. Margadant in *Agricultural History*, July 1979; and John M. Merriman in *The Journal of Modern History*, Sept. 1978.

11. Charles Tilly in John M. Merriman, ed., *Consciousness and Class Experience in Nineteenth Century Europe* (New York, 1979), p. 39.

12. G. M. Young, *Victorian England: Portrait of an Age* (London, 1974), p. vi.

13. Maurice Halbwachs, *Equisse d'une psychologie des classes sociales* (Paris, 1955), p. 52.

14. For works which stress the charismatic, Caesar-like quality of Boulanger, see Adrien Dansette, *Le Boulangisme* (Paris, 1946), and James Harding, *The Astonishing Adventure of General Boulanger* (New York, 1971). On the profound effect of Boulangism on Third Republic politics, see Zeev Sternhell, *La Droite révolutionnaire, 1885-1914: Les Origines françaises du fascisme* (Paris, 1978); Frederick Seager, *The Boulanger Affair: The Political Crossroad of France, 1886-1889* (Ithaca, 1969); and the excellent article by Patrick H. Hutton, "Popular Boulangism and the Advent of Mass Politics in France, 1886-1890," *Journal of Contemporary History*, 11, 1976, pp. 85-106.

15. Roger Martin du Gard, *Jean Barois*, trans. Stuart Gilbert (Indianapolis, 1978), p. 211.

16. Léon Lipschutz, *Une Bibliographie dreyfusienne: Essai de bibliographie thématique et analytique de l'affaire Dreyfus* (Paris, 1970). Among the most recent studies of the Affair are, Robert L. Hoffman's *More Than a Trial: The Struggle Over Captain Dreyfus* (New York, 1980), and Jean Denis Bredin's long and excellent synthesis, *L'Affaire* (Paris, 1983).

17. Stephen Wilson, in his recent important and thorough *Ideology and Experience: Antisemitism in France at the Time of the Dreyfus Affair* (Rutherford, 1982), confirms that we know little about how far the Affair "impinged on the lives of ordinary people, or how far it articulated their interests and desires" (p. 6). Wilson goes a long way in examining urban provincial reactions to the Affair, but does not treat the peasantry in any detail.

18. On Decazeville and Boulanger, see Jacques Néré, *La Crise industrielle de 1882 et le mouvement boulangiste* (Unpubl. thesis, Sorbonne, 1959), pp. 136ff., and the same author's *Les Elections Boulanger dans le département du Nord* (Unpub. thesis, Sorbonne, 1959), pp. 157-58, and *Le Boulangisme et*

la presse (Paris, 1964), p. 27; see also Eugène Fournière, "Physiologie du Boulangisme," *La Société nouvelle*, 4, t.1, 1888 ". . . la clientèle est en immense majorité composée d'ouvriers . . ." (p. 435); and Don Reid, "Decazeville: Company Town and Working Class Community, 1826-1914," in John M. Merriman, ed., *French Cities in the Nineteenth Century* (New York, 1981), p. 201.

19. Néré, *Les Elections Boulanger*, pp. 169, 175 and *passim*.

20. Ibid., pp. 26-27, 134-36, 150; Hutton supports Néré's observations on the important link between Boulangism and future socialist organization ("Popular Boulangism," pp. 85-106). On the Parti ouvrier and the Boulangist challenge in the Nord, see Claude Willard, *Le Mouvement socialiste en France (1893-1905): Les Guesdistes* (Paris, 1965), pp. 37-38.

21. Seager, *Boulanger Affair*, p. 3.

22. Friedrich Engels and Paul Lafargue, *Correspondance, 1887-1900*, vol. 2 (London, 1960).

23. Scores of similar comments from primary and secondary literature could be cited. These are taken from: René Rémond, *The Right Wing in France: From 1815 to de Gaulle*, trans. James Laux (Philadelphia, 1968), p. 214; "The Dreyfus Case: A Study of French Opinion," (n.a.), *Contemporary Review*, 74, Oct. 1898; F.W.J. Hemmings, *Culture and Society in France, 1848-1898* (New York, 1971), p. 8; William Shirer, *The Collapse of the Third Republic* (New York, 1969), p. 55; Nicholas Halasz, *Captain Dreyfus: The Story of Mass Hysteria* (New York, 1955), p. 6; Henri Mazel, *Histoire et psychologie de l'affaire Dreyfus* (Paris, 1934); and John McManners, *Church and State in France, 1870-1914* (New York, 1972), pp. 118, 121-22; see also Betty Schechter, *The Dreyfus Affair: A National Scandal* (Boston, 1965), p. 255; Hannah Arendt, *Origins of Totalitarianism* (New York, 1973), p. 114; and the comments of Dreyfus's lawyer, Labori, in *Le Siècle*, Dec. 11, 1901. Joseph Reinach insisted that "people talked only about the Affair. . . . It now preoccupied everyone" (quoted in Stephen Wilson, *Ideology and Experience*, p. 13).

24. Halasz, *Captain Dreyfus*, p. 5.

25. Hannah Lynch, *French Life in Town and Country* (New York, 1901), p. 237.

26. Lewis Namier in Fritz Stern, *The Varieties of History* (New York, 1956), p. 375.

27. The classic work is, Joseph Reinach's seven-volume *Histoire de l'affaire Dreyfus* (Paris, 1903-11); see also Bredin's *L'Affaire*; and for an excellent account in English, see Douglas Johnson, *France and the Dreyfus Affair* (London, 1966). On responses in provincial cities see Stephen Wilson, *Ideology and Experience*, especially Chap. III. For more on this and other works by Wilson, see below, Chaps. V and VI.

28. Robert Redfield, *Peasant Society and Culture* (Chicago, 1956), p. 25.

29. Richard Hofstadter, *The Paranoid Style in American Politics* (New York, 1965), p. viii.

30. For a brilliant correction to this in African history, see A. G. Hopkins, *Economic History of West Africa* (New York, 1973); and on a related subject in France, see Michael Marrus, "Folklore as an Ethnographic Source," in Jacques Beauroy et al., eds., *The Wolf and the Lamb: Popular Culture in France* (Sarasota, Calif., 1976); and William H. Sewell, Jr., *Work and Revolution in France: The Language of Labor from the Old Regime to 1848* (Cambridge, 1980): "French artisans cannot be treated as Trobriand islanders, as an isolated, static . . . society" (p. 12). Nor, as we shall see, can French peasants.

31. Jack Goody, *The Domestication of the Savage Mind* (Cambridge, 1978), pp. 16, 36.

32. Ibid., pp. 43-44.

33. Ibid., p. 37.

34. Dupeux, *Histoire sociale et politique*, p. 513. For André Siegfried, in politics words by themselves have no sense, they must be constantly reinterpreted; see *Tableau politique de la France de l'ouest sous la Troisième République* (Paris, 1913), p. xvi; see also Henri Mendras, *The Vanishing Peasant*, trans. Jean Lerner (Cambridge, Mass., 1970): the peasant "finds that in national politics even words themselves do not always have the same meaning" (p. 195).

35. Peter Brown, "The Rise of the Holy Man in Late Antiquity," *Journal of Roman Studies*, vol. 61, 1971, p. 81. On personalities and politics in rural France, see Eugen Weber, "Comment la Politique Vint aux Paysans: A Second Look at Peasant Politicization in France," *American Historical Review*, 87, April 1982, pp. 357-89; and on contemporary India, see *The New York Times*, July 25, 1979: ten million Jat peasants are "solidly behind Mr. Singh, having linked their recently increased prosperity and political leverage to his mounting prominence" (p. A2).

36. Emile Guillaumin, *Panorama de l'évolution paysanne* (Colombes, 1936), p. 7.

37. Marc Bloch, *French Rural History: An Essay on its Basic Characteristics*, trans., Janet Sondheimer (Berkeley, 1970), p. xxv. For more on the difficulty of defining "peasants," see Philippe Pinchemel, *Structures sociales et dépopulation rurale dans les campagnes picardes de 1836 à 1936* (Paris, 1957), p. 14.

38. Michel Augé-Laribé, *L'Evolution de la France agricole* (Paris, 1912), p. 7; Jacques Maho, *L'Image des autres chez le paysan* (Paris, 1974), p. 12.

39. Margadant, *French Peasants in Revolt*, p. 73 and *passim*. On the need to distinguish among peasants, artisans, and others in the 1851 insurrection, see Maurice Agulhon's review of Margadant in *European Studies Review*, vol. 11, 1981, pp. 555-62.

40. *Résultats statistiques du recensement de la population, 1891*, p. 65; on the 1846 "rural" and "urban" distinctions, see Georges Dupeux, "La Croissance urbaine en France au XIXe siècle," *Revue d'histoire économique et sociale*, 2, 52, 1974, pp. 173-89.

41. Meuriot, *Des Agglomérations urbaines dans l'Europe contemporaine* (Paris, 1898), pp. 40-42.

42. *Résultats statistiques, 1891*, pp. 61, 119-20; Gordon Wright, *Rural Revolution in France* (Stanford, 1968), p. 6; and Meuriot, *Agglomérations urbaines*, pp. 119-20.

43. Joseph Blanc, *Notes d'un curé de campagne* (?, 1911), p. 26; see also Theodore Zeldin, *France, 1848-1945*, vol. 1 (London, 1973), pp. 138-39.

44. Eric R. Wolf, *Peasants* (Englewood Cliffs, 1966), pp. 46-47.

45. Ibid., p. 16; see also pp. 11, 87-88.

46. Pierre Barral, "Note historique sur l'emploi du terme 'paysan'," *Etudes rurales*, 21, 1966, pp. 72-73. For a detailed analysis of how city dwellers defined "peasants," and how peasants viewed themselves, see Weber, *Peasants into Frenchmen*, p. 7 and *passim*; for an example of this vocabulary, see *Almanach des familles* (1887), p. 22; and for a rebuttal to these "false ideas," see Augé-Laribé, *L'Evolution de la France agricole*, pp. viii-ix.

47. "L'arrondisement et . . . le département sont des abstractions administratives, installées sur plusieurs régions géographiques . . ." (Pinchemel, *Structures sociales*, p. 21).

48. Johann von Grimmelshausen, "Simplicius Simplicissimus" in Andrew Lossky, ed., *The Seventeenth Century* (New York, 1969), p. 38.

CHAPTER I

1. ADI 55 M 2, telegram, May 27, 1895. The deputy, Basly, known for his close association with mining communities, was joined by the editor of the Lyon newspaper *Peuple*. Their topic was to have been "The Organization of Syndicates."

2. See Merriman, *Consciousness and Class*, pp. 129-48, and Merriman's forthcoming book on nineteenth-century Limoges.

3. Daniel Halévy, *Visites aux paysans du Centre* (Paris, 1921), p. 9.

4. Lequin, *Les Ouvriers de la région lyonnaise*, vol. 1, pp. vi, 43, 139 and *passim*; and Dupeux, "La Croissance urbaine," p. 177.

5. Discussed in Georges Friedmann, ed., *Villes et campagnes* (Paris, 1953), p. 119.

6. Karl Marx and Friedrich Engels, *The Communist Manifesto* (Harmondsworth, 1977), pp. 84-85.

7. See Richard Cobb referring parenthetically to 1918-39 in the *Police and the People*, p. 320. Discussing the second half of the nineteenth century in the Southwest, André Armengaud says that "la dualité politique villes-campagnes . . . est sans doute le trait le plus saillant de la sociologie électorale de cette époque." *Les Populations de l'est-aquitain au début de l'époque contemporaine, 1845-1871* (Paris, 1961), p. 461.

8. Margadant, *French Peasants in Revolt*, pp. 54-55; see also Agulhon, *La République au village, passim*.

9. Siegfried, *Tableau politique*, pp. 362-63; Judt, *Socialism in Provence*, p. 6; and Meuriot, *Agglomérations urbaines*, pp. 43, 60-64.

10. Emilie Carles, *Une Soupe aux herbes sauvages* (Paris, 1977), p. 20 and *passim*.

11. Guillaumin, *Panorama de l'évolution paysanne*, p. 85.

12. Serge Grafteaux, *Mémé Santerre* (Paris, 1975), p. 125.

13. Quoted in Friedmann, *Villes et campagnes*, p. 391.

14. On different perceptions of time in rural and urban settings, see Mendras, *Vanishing Peasant*, p. 66; E. P. Thompson, "Time, Work-Discipline, and Industrial Capitalism," *Past and Present*, 38, 1967, pp. 56-97; Georg Simmel, "The Metropolis and Mental Life," in Kurt Wolff, ed., *The Sociology of Georg Simmel* (London, 1950), pp. 409-24; and Weber, *Peasants into Frenchmen*, p. 483. On rural land greed and *morcellement*, see Emile Zola, *La Terre* (Paris, 1889).

15. *Le Petit Journal*, Oct. 5, 1898.

16. Paul Hohenberg, "Change in Rural France in the Period of Industrialization, 1830-1914," *Journal of Economic History*, 32, 1, March 1972, p. 227; see also pp. 222, 229, 239 (Hohenberg's emphasis). For more on low fertility, exodus and rural depopulation, see Pinchemel, *Structures sociales*, pp. 149, 183; Roger Brunet, *Les Campagnes toulousaines: Etude géographique* (Toulouse, 1965), p. 409; and Gabriel Désert, "Aperçu sur l'exode rural en Basse-Normandie à la fin du XIXe siècle," *Revue historique*, 507, July-Sept. 1973, pp. 107-18. Armengaud says that the rural birth rate was steady in the Est-Aquitain, and that depopulation must be explained "above all by emigration" (*Les Populations de l'est-aquitain*, p. 226).

17. Gabriel Désert, *Une Société rurale au XIXe siècle: les paysans du Calvados, 1815-1895* (Thèse, Université de Paris I, 1971), pp. 1230, 1218; and Hohenberg, "Change in Rural France," p. 228. For more on this and other rural economic factors in selected departments, see Chap. II below.

18. Brunet, *Campagnes toulousaines*, p. 174.

19. For a nation-wide view of this, see George W. Grantham, "Scale and Organization in French Farming, 1840-1880," in William N. Parker and Eric L. Jones, eds., *European Peasants and Their Markets: Essays in Agrarian Economic History* (Princeton, 1975), pp. 293-326; see also Pinchemel, *Structures sociales*, pp. 82-90; and Désert, "Aperçu sur l'exode," pp. 114-15.

20. Grantham, "Scale and Organization," pp. 295-96.

21. Weber, *Peasants into Frenchmen*, pp. 195-374.

22. Pinchemel, *Structures sociales*, pp. 208-209. For more on the marked contrast between towns and farmsteads late in the century, see Thabault, *Education and Change*, pp. 156-57. Hohenberg and others have discussed the "agriculturalization of the countryside" due to the loss of rural-based industries ("Change in Rural France," p. 223, n. 16 and 227).

23. Zeldin, *France, 1848-1945*, vol. 1, pp. 171ff.

24. Pinchemel, *Structures sociales*, p. 104.

25. Brunet, *Campagnes toulousaines*, p. 400; see also pp. 393-95 and *passim*; Désert, "Aperçu sur l'exode," p. 114.

26. Tilly, "Did The Cake of Custom Break?," in Merriman, ed., *Consciousness and Class*, p. 36.

27. *La Démocratie rurale*, Dec. 22, 1889; Emile Vandervelde, *Les Villes tentaculaires* (Paris, 1899), p. 19; Pinchemel, *Structures sociales*, pp. 152-55; and Brunet, *Campagnes toulousaines*, pp. 388, 409. For more on the higher incidence of elderly members in small, agricultural communes, see *Résultats statistiques, 1891*, p. 277; Meuriot, *Agglomérations urbaines*, p. 361; Armengaud, *Les Populations de l'est-aquitain*, pp. 498-99, 544, which includes graphs and statistics on the aging of the rural population after 1850; and Mendras, *Sociétés paysannes*, pp. 152ff. *Résultats statistiques du dénombrement de 1891* shows a higher proportion of older persons in towns under 5000 (p. 222), but given only partial statistics in the *Résultats* and other sources it is impossible to chart, by commune, the aging of village populations. Overwhelming qualitative and quantitative evidence suggests, however, that older peasants stayed on the land.

28. APP Ba 411, note dated Sept. 9, 1894; for more on why country people moved, see Dupeux, "La Croissance urbaine," pp. 188-89. Dupeux prefers the term "migration interne" to "exode rural."

29. Marc Bloch, "Les Transformations des techniques comme problème de psychologie collective," *Journal de psychologie normale et pathologique*, 12, 1948, p. 106.

30. Karl Mannheim, "The Problem of Generations," in *Essays on the Sociology of Knowledge* (London, 1972), p. 290.

31. Ibid., pp. 297, 303 (Mannheim's emphasis). For a discussion of Mannheim's theories applied to the World War I generation in France, see Robert Wohl, *The Generation of 1914* (Cambridge, Mass., 1979), p. 78 and *passim*. I thank Professor Wohl for his comments on generational change in rural France.

32. H. Stuart Hughes, *Consciousness and Society* (New York, 1961), p. 18. In Roger Martin du Gard's novel *Jean Barois* (Paris, 1913) one of the characters remarks: "The vast development of industry has drained our countryside of tens of thousands of young men who have thus broken completely with traditions of their elders." An exaggeration, but by no means wrong.

33. On how this transpired in a Lorraine village, see Claude Karnoouh, "Parenté et politique: La Démocratie impossible," *Etudes rurales*, 52, Oct. 1973, p. 51. An observer in the Gers said that peasants had become "the masters of the village and of the countryside" (quoted in Weber, *Peasants into Frenchmen*, p. 240). On how the social structure of the countryside was simplified, see Zeldin, *France: 1848-1945*, vol. 1, p. 173. In 1887 over 95 percent of French cultivators were "immobile," rarely moving beyond their commune; 90 percent of the conscripts that year lived with their families. After the completion of military service, however, many left the countryside for good (see Emmanuel Le Roy Ladurie and A. Zysberg, "Anthro-

pologie des conscrits français, 1868-87," *Ethnologie française*, 9, 1, 1979, pp. 51-52, 55).

34. For more regional examples of the "aging" of rural communities, see Thabault, *Education and Change*, p. 189; and Pierre Barral, *Les Agrariens français de Méline à Pisani* (Paris, 1968): "Les jeunes adultes . . . représentaient certainement une faible part de la [rural] population totale, car c'est eux surtout que l'exode touchait . . ." (p. 22).

35. John Merriman is right (see above, n. 2); it is ironic that the butchers' quarter in Limoges remained an atavistic community in the midst of a large provincial city. Outlying areas were changing more rapidly than some city enclaves; but the faubourgs of Limoges differed from thousands of agricultural villages, hamlets, and farmsteads with long-time residents and solid rural routines.

36. Karl Marx, *The Eighteenth Brumaire of Louis Bonaparte* (New York, 1972), p. 124.

37. See also Mannheim, "Problem of Generations": "Traditions bearing in a particular direction only persist so long as the location relationships of the group acknowledging them remain more or less unchanged" (p. 292).

38. Karnoouh, "Parenté et politique," pp. 54-55. For a similar though more folkloric view of Lorraine villages at the end of the nineteenth century, see Louis Marin, *Disparition des institutions traditionnelles . . . en Lorraine* (Paris, 1948), p. 56.

39. Karnoouh, "Parenté et politique," p. 32; see also Mendras, *Sociétés paysannes*, pp. 80-85, 167; Tina Jolas and Françoise Zonabend, "Tillers of the Fields and Woodspeople," in Robert Forster and Orest Ranum, eds., *Rural Society in France* (Baltimore, 1977), pp. 126-51; and Jacques Le Goff and Pierre Nora, eds., *Faire l'histoire*, 3, 1974: "La mentalité est ce qui change le plus lentement. Histoire des mentalités, histoire de la lenteur dans l'histoire" (p. 82).

40. E. Grenadou and A. Prevost, *Grenadou, paysan français* (Paris, 1978), p. 161.

41. See, for example, Pierre Jakez Hélias, *The Horse of Pride*, trans. June Guicharnaud (New Haven, 1978); Laurence Wylie, *Chanzeaux: A Village in Anjou* (Cambridge, Mass., 1974); Emile Guillaumin, *La Vie d'un simple* (Paris, 1904); Carles, *Une Soupe*; Thabault, *Education and Change*; and Grafteaux, *Mémé Santerre*.

42. André Siegfried quoted in Friedmann, *Villes et campagnes*, p. 123.

43. Augé-Laribé, *L'Evolution*, pp. 227ff. For example, on the *liste nominative* for the small commune of Saint Elix-Theux (Gers) seven rural domestics were also designated "laboureurs" which usually indicates "plowmen." Did they hire out to other farmers or plow exclusively for their full-time employer? (see ADG M 4874).

44. J. Harvey Smith, "Agricultural Workers," pp. 101-25.

45. Gustave Flaubert, *Madame Bovary*, trans. Lowell Blair (New York,

1972), pp. 129-30; ADI 138 M 2, July 10, 1890, report on Medailles d'honneur agricoles.

46. *Bulletin de la société des agriculteurs de France*, 27, 1888, p. 646.

47. Armand Depresseville, *Etude générale sur les ouvriers agricoles en Basse-Normandie: Manche, Calvados et Orne* (Saint Lô, 1914), p. 141, see also pp. iv-v.

48. Camille Besse, *Le Curé, l'instituteur, et le paysan* (Tulle, 1912); see also E. Doutté, *Situation agricole du département de la Marne en 1892* (Châlons-sur-Marne, 1893), pp. 44ff.; Siegfried in Friedmann, *Villes et campagnes*, pp. 123ff.; Mendras, *Sociétés paysannes*, p. 62; Zeldin, *France: 1848-1945*, vol. 1, p. 155; and Grenadou, *Grenadou, paysan français*, p. 167. On continuing patterns of rural sociability, see Charles Joisten, "Rites de terminaison des veillées en Dauphiné," *Folklore*, 135, 1969, p. 3.

49. Clarisse Bader, *Enseignement social: Nos paysans, les vétérans du travail agricole* (Paris, 1899), p. 7.

50. Arnold Van Gennep, "Surviances primitives dans les cérémonies agraires de la Savoie et du Dauphiné," *Studi e Materali di Storia delle Religion*, vol. 5, 1930, pp. 88, 94-95, 128; see the same author's *Manuel de folklore français contemporaine* (Paris, 1943), I, vol, 5, p. 2206; and *Le Folklore du dauphiné* (Paris, 1932), II, pp. 401ff.; Jolas and Zonabend, "Tillers," pp. 132, 151. For a contemporary view, see reports of *fêtes domestiques* in the Gers in *L'Avenir républicain*, March 28, April 9, May 2, 1898. In the Isère, *fêtes des agriculteurs* took place on the same day that Paris, Marseille, and other large cities were in the midst of anti-Dreyfus riots (see *Le Réveil du dauphiné*, Jan. 25, 1898).

51. On harvesters' demands and discontent, see Henry Verdié, "L'Evolution agricole, économique et sociale de la commune de Saint Brès (Gers)," *Bulletin de la société archéologique, historique, littéraire et scientifique du Gers*, 1959; and Van Gennep, *Manuel de folklore*, I, vol. 5, p. 2219. For general information on strikes throughout rural France, see Philippe Gratton, *Les Luttes de classe dans les campagnes* (Paris, 1971), pp. 148, 171, 245-47; and Augé-Laribé, *L'Evolution de la France agricole*, p. 250.

52. ADG M 2799, police report, May 5, 1888.

53. ADV 1 M 528, note to prefect, July 10, 1890.

54. ADS 9 M II 22, prefect, May 10, 1902. Also in the Savoie, Aillon-le-Vieux and Aillon-le-Jeune are carrying on a similar feud in the late twentieth century. These two villages, in clear view of one another, have maintained a hostile attitude ever since the young community split from the old. Accord has proved so impossible that separate mayors and councils are needed to attend to what should be communal interests (author's conversation with the mayor of Aillon-le-Jeune, Feb. 1980).

55. Siegfried, *Tableau politique*, p. 497; see also the chapter on "Feuds and Personalities," in Judt, *Socialism in Provence*.

56. Jean Dubarry, *Nouveau manuel des gardes-champêtres* (Paris, 1911), pp. 3-7, 33-35, 87ff.; André Lanchier, *Manuel encyclopédique des gardes-cham-*

pêtres (Grenoble, 1887), pp. v-vii; see also ADM 2 Z 30 for information on the background of rural guards, especially notes dated June 3, 12, 1900; on salaries, see ADM 43 M 60-67.

57. Dubarry, *Nouveau manuel*, pp. 10ff; for representative examples of the age and position of rural guards, see ADI 6 O 2; ADM 43 M 62, police report, Jan 14, 1890; and ADM 43 M 67, commune of Berzieux.

58. John Rothney, *Bonapartism After Sedan* (Ithaca, 1969), p. 163; and Vigier, *La Seconde République dans la région alpine*, vol. 2, p. 233.

59. ADV 4 M 11, June 12, 15, 1888; see also Nov. 7, 1890, subprefect report on the political activities of another rural guard.

60. L. Nocart, *Manuel à l'usage des agents de la police et des gardes-champêtres* (Tlemcen, 1899), p. 3.

61. Ibid.; for the Marne, see ADM 43 M 60, March 7, July 10, 12 and Nov. 3, 1888; and 43 M 67, Sept. 16, 1890 (Binarville).

62. L. Escaich, *Code formulaire des gardes-champêtres* (Paris, 1887), pp. 208-209; see also, Nocart, *Manuel à l'usage*, p. 27; on Cormontreuil, see ADM 13 M 4, Aug. 16, 1900.

63. ADM 43 M 60, guard report, Nov. 2, 1888; subprefect note, Nov. 12, 1888; guard to prefect, Sept. 10, 1888.

64. Louis Ducamp, *La Conquête républicaine du Gers, 1870-1893* (Unpub. thesis, 1971, on file ADG), p. 152.

65. ADV 4 M 11, Feb. 16, 1888.

66. Lucien Freynet, *Aide-mémoire du facteur des postes* (Paris, 1910), p. 43; Eugène Gallois, *La Poste et les moyens de communication* (Paris, 1894), pp. 193ff.; see also Pierre Zaconne, *La Poste anecdotique et pittoresque* (Paris, 1867), pp. 214-22; and on postmen as cultural mediators in the Vendée, see Armel de Wismes, *Histoire de la Vendée* (Paris, 1973), p. 256.

67. Besse, *Le Curé, l'instituteur*, p. xvi.

68. Roger Martin du Gard, *Vieille France* (Paris, 1933), pp. 31, 112, 127, 151.

69. ADG M 2799, Gimont police report to prefect, March 24, 1888; Dubarry, *Nouveau manuel*, p. 215; on singers and peddlers, see August Grise, *Coutumes du Trièves au XIXe siècle* (Grenoble, 1939), p. 22 and ADS 9 M III 23, lists requesting permission to travel and peddle in the department, 1881-1900; ADI 9 T 77, lists 1886-89; on barbers, see ADG M 2799, Nogaro police report, Oct. 12, 1889, and Grafteaux, *Mémé Santerre*, p. 133. (Professor Robert Herbert has told me that Breton peasants near Quimper were still receiving their news from the town crier in the 1950s.)

70. D. W. Brogan, *The Development of Modern France*, vol. 1 (Gloucester, Mass., 1970), p. 353.

71. ADI 9 U 441, Sept. 6, 1899.

72. ADM 43 M 63, prefect note, May, 1890, and Châlons-sur-Marne police report, May 28, 1890.

73. ADI 17 M 167, notes on municipal elections, May 1888; see also Ornon commune. For other conflicts over councils dominated by families

from 1884 to 1896, see ADM 13 M 2-5: communes of Passavant, Charmont, Courjeonnet and Cuisles, where, in 1888, four individuals named Mousses and two named Heucqs ran for council posts in this tiny village of 197 inhabitants, causing great confusion. See also AN C 5470 for more on electoral fraud and confusing family names in the Corrèze.

74. ADI 16 M 203, Venosc municipal council to prefect, May 4, 1896; ADI 123 M 29, *liste nominative* Venosc, 1896; and 4E 1 k 1, *liste électorale*, Venosc 1898. For similar examples, see the communes of Besse, Sassenage, and Veury. Another insight into the special nature of rural municipal councils is found in *Le Réveil dauphiné*, Jan. 23, 1888: an article asks whether council members should be literate.

75. ADM 43 M 60, guard to prefect, July 20, 1888.

76. Verdié, "Saint Brès," p. 272; see, for example, the commune of Blanquefort near Gimont where the de Reuble family was dominant and Père de Reuble, aged 92, was the local Cassagnac, overseeing 100 share-croppers (ADG M 4865, *liste nominative*, 1891).

77. Quoted in Raymond Belbèze, *La Neurasthénie rurale* (Paris, 1911), p. 30.

78. ADG M 1194, prefect note, Oct. 1, 1894; ADG M 107, letter dated July 24, 1884, Saint Arailles.

79. Carles, *Une Soupe*, p. 84.

80. Guillaumin, *Panorama*, p. 59.

81. Karnoouh, "Parenté et politique," pp. 34, 44.

82. Maho, *L'Image des autres*, p. 96; Jolas and Zonabend, "Tillers," p. 132.

83. How are we to imagine the Vieux Melchior family formed political opinions in the Isère? It comprised one small holding farmer, one glove maker, one quarryman, and one ambiguous *cultivateur* (ADI 123 M 48, *liste nominative*, Veury 1896). There are many examples of proprietors, day laborers, artisans and industrial workers in the same family, and chances are good that choices were not always based on class interests alone. On the importance of family ties in an industrial setting, see William Reddy, "Family and Factory: French Linen Workers in the Belle époque," *Journal of Social History*, 1975, pp. 102-12.

84. Mannheim, "Problem of Generations," p. 309.

85. For more on this, see Guy Palmade, *L'Evolution de l'opinion politique dans le département du Gers de 1848 à 1914* (Thesis, 1946, on file ADG), p. 22; and Siegfried, *Tableau politique*, p. 373.

86. Judt, *Socialism in Provence*, p. 214.

87. Communication from Professor John Merriman; for more on this, see Merriman's forthcoming book on Limoges.

88. Mannheim, "Problem of Generations," p. 299, note 1.

89. Mendras, *Sociologie de la campagne*, p. 37.

90. Weber, *Peasants into Frenchmen*, p. 67.

91. Patois was still heard in parts of the Isère until 1918, and in other

regions much later; see Pierre Barral, *Le Département de l'Isère sous la Tro-isième République* (Paris, 1962), p. 71. For a discussion of the importance of patois, see Weber, *Peasants into Frenchmen*, pp. 67-94; and Zeldin, *France: 1848-1945*, vol. 2, p. 204. On the significance of literacy, see Tilly in Merriman, ed., *Consciousness and Class*, pp. 18, 28; and Judt, *Socialism in Provence*, p. 187. We must look beyond general statistics to crucial differences among rural populations: conscripts in 1887 were only 10 percent illiterate overall, but 25 percent of the domestics, 19.2 percent of rural day laborers, and 15.3 percent of cultivators were illiterate; artisans and urban workers were three times more literate than cultivators (see Le Roy Ladurie and Zysberg, "Anthropologie," pp. 50-51). Gordon Wright believes that perhaps one-third of the peasantry was unable to read or write circa 1880 (*Rural Revolution*, p. 10). For more on "linguistic particularisms" in the countryside, see Armengaud, *Les Populations de l'est-aquitain*, pp. 429, 462.

92. Levi-Strauss commentary, Musée national des arts et traditions populaires, Paris.

93. *Le Réveil du dauphiné*, May 13, 1892.

94. Brunet, *Campagnes toulousaines*, p. 196.

CHAPTER II

1. Brunet discusses Febvre's point in *Campagnes toulousaines*, p. 14.

2. *Résultats statistiques du recensement, 1891*, pp. 65, 284-88, 362; and Maurice Bordes, ed., *Histoire de la Gascogne des origines à nos jours* (Roanne, 1977), p. 343.

3. ADG M 4863, *listes nominatives*, 1891; *Résultats statistiques, 1891*, pp. 400-403; and Ducamp, *La Conquête*, pp. 15-16.

4. *Résultats statistiques*, 1891, pp. 122-25; Ducamp, *La Conquête*, p. 14. It is important to repeat that statistics provide only department-wide information on average age; rural Gersois were older still than their urban neighbors.

5. Belbèze, *La Neurasthénie*; see, for example, p. 215, note 1.

6. *Appel au peuple*, Sept. 12, 1889.

7. Palmade, *L'Evolution de l'opinion*: ". . . le malaise économique que s'appesantissait depuis une dizaine d'années prend en 1885 justement des allures catastrophe" (p. 124, see also pp. 2-8, 164); *Annuaire administratif du Gers, 1898* for the impact of phylloxera; and Ducamp, *La Conquête*, pp. 22, 195. For more on cereals, livestock, and polyculture in general in the Southwest, see Brunet, *Campagnes toulousaines*, pp. 55, 332-38, 363-92 and *passim*.

8. Brunet, *Campagnes toulousaines*, pp. 402ff.

9. M. Luxembourg, "Problème de la démographie gersoise," *Bulletin de la société archéologique du Gers*, 2, 1948, p. 80; and ADG M 2799, police reports, April 7, July 7, 1888.

10. Verdié, "Saint Brès," p. 270.

11. Palmade, *L'Evolution de l'opinion*, p. 95; Ducamp, *La Conquête*, p. 284; Augé-Laribé, *L'Evolution de la France agricole*, pp. 132-33; Halbwachs, *Equisse d' une psychologie*, pp. 70-71. For a discussion of deproletarianization, see G. Chalvy, "Sur l'histoire occitane," *Annales: Economies, sociétés, civilisations*, July 1978, p. 871; and on the increasing wages of agricultural laborers, see Brunet, *Campagnes toulousaines*, p. 386.

12. Palmade, *L'Evolution de l'opinion*, pp. 11-12, 165; Brunet, *Campagnes toulousaines*, pp. 387-88.

13. Luxembourg, "Problème de la démographie," p. 81; on falling birthrates, see Brunet, *Campagnes toulousaines*, p. 409, and above chap. I, n. 27.

14. For example, see Bordes, *Histoire de la Gascogne*, pp. 360-61; and J. Dagnan, *Le Coup d'état et la répression*, p. 552.

15. Margadant, *French Peasants in Revolt, passim*; and Palmade, *L'Evolution de l'opinion*, pp. 66-67.

16. For a discussion of the conflicting interpretations of mid-century politics in rural France, see Eugen Weber, "The Second Republic, Politics, and the Peasants," *French Historical Studies*, vol. 11, 4, Fall 1980, pp. 521-50.

17. Margadant, *French Peasants in Revolt*, p. 73; on the weak participation of cultivators in the insurrection, see Ducamp, *La Conquête*, p. 35.

18. Emmanuel Labat, "En Gascogne," *Revue des deux mondes*, Aug. 1910, pp. 639-45; Bordes, *Histoire de la Gascogne*, p. 331.

19. Margadant, *French Peasants in Revolt*, p. 183.

20. Luxembourg, "Problème de la démographie," pp. 80-84.

21. *La République des paysans*, Dec. 1, 1889.

22. Judt says that in the late 1870s and 80s the Var did not "awaken after a generation of silence . . . [T]he events of the intervening years, the economic and political conjuncture, count for much" (*Socialism in Provence*, p. 20). This was true in the Gers, too.

23. Labat, "En Gascogne," p. 645.

24. *Résultats statistiques du dénombrement de 1891*, pp. 62, 67-68, 120-21, 362-66.

25. G. Bourdin, *Population-artisanat-industrie dans l'Orne de 1800 à 1914* (Caen, 1934), pp. 1-2; *Résultats statistiques 1891*, pp. 396-97: Arsène Dumont, "Note sur la démographie de l'Orne," *Revue normande et percheronne*, 1897, pp. 337-38; M. G. Callon, "Le Mouvement de la population dans le département de l'Orne, 1821-1920," *Bulletin des études locales du Gers*, 4, 1929.

26. Georges Duby et al., eds., *Histoire de la France rurale*, vol. 3 (Paris, 1976), p. 68.

27. See Bourdin, *Population-artisanat*, p. 39; and *La Diminution de la population dans le département de l'Orne et à Alençon* (Alençon, 1902), pp. 3-5.

28. Bourdin, *Population-artisanat*, pp. 11, 18, 71-74, 87ff.

29. René Jouanne, *La Révolution de 1848 dans le département de l'Orne* (Alençon, 1948), pp. 41-49.

30. A. E. Poëssel, *L'Orne et l'histoire* (?, 1963), p. 408; Jouanne, *La Révolution de 1848*, pp. 48-50.

31. Jouanne, *La Révolution de 1848*, pp. 14-15; see also Margadant, *French Peasants in Revolt*, for different roles played by artisans and cultivators in the insurrection.

32. Barral, *Le Département de l'Isère*, p. 27.

33. Honoré de Balzac, *The Country Doctor*, trans. Ellen Marriage (Philadelphia, 1898), pp. 16, 39.

34. *Résultats statistiques, 1891*, pp. 48-50, 65, 284-88, 362, 400-403; see also Raoul Blanchard, *Les Alpes occidentales*, t. 7 (Grenoble, 1956).

35. *Resultats statistiques, 1891*, pp. 378-79.

36. Barral, *Le Département de l'Isère*, p. 53. The population in rural areas dropped from 381,123 in 1872 to 314,801 in 1911, while the urban population went from 183,754 to 241,110. See also Lequin, *Les Ouvriers de la région lyonnaise*, vol. 1, p. 143; and *Résultats statistiques, 1891*, pp. 122-25.

37. On this interplay of agriculture and industry, see Néré, *La Crise industrielle*, pp. 114ff., 130, 140; M. Blanche in Friedmann, *Villes et campagnes*, p. 256; Lequin, *Les Ouvriers de la région lyonnaise*, vol. 1, pp. 129, 142 and the same author's "Sources et methodes de l'histoire des grèves dans la seconde moitié du XIXe siècle," *Cahiers d'histoire*, t. 12, 1967, pp. 215-31; ADI 53 M 17, Vienne police report, July 12, 1886. For similar transformations in a Southwest mining community, see Joan Scott, *The Glassworkers of Carmaux* (Cambridge, Mass., 1980).

38. Bernard Bligny, ed., *Histoire du dauphiné* (Toulouse, 1973), p. 354; Barral, *Le Département de l'Isère*, pp. 40-41.

39. Blanchard, *Les Alpes*, t. 7, pp. 250, 541-58.

40. Zeldin, *France: 1848-1945*, vol. 1, pp. 178-81.

41. Barral, *Le Département de l'Isère*, p. 8. On the early stages of this transformation, and the importance of mobility in shaping different mentalities of city dwellers and peasants, see Jesus Ibarrola, *Structure sociale et fortune dans la campagne proche de Grenoble* (Paris, 1966), p. 29.

42. Ardouin-Dumazet, *Voyage en France: Les alpes* (Paris, 1910), p. 3.

43. ADI III M 4, mayoral reports: Courtenay, Oct. 11, 1880; Saint Chef, Oct. 11, 1880; Chezeneuve, Oct. 5, 1880; Mazenne, Oct (?), 1880; Solaize, Oct. 5, 1880. I am grateful to Professor Susanna Barrows for bringing these reports to my attention.

44. Barral, *Le Département de l'Isère*, pp. 104, 124; Lequin, *Les Ouvriers de la région lyonnaise*, vol. 1, p. 143; see also ADI 137 M 38, and *Statistique agricole de la France, 1892* (Paris, 1897).

45. Vigier, *La Seconde République dans la région alpine*, vol. 1, pp. 23ff and vol. 2, pp. 26ff.

46. Ibid., vol. 1, p. 51.

47. Ibid., pp. 114-15.

48. Barral, *Le Département de l'Isère*, p. 389.

49. Vigier, *La Seconde République dans la région alpine*, vol. 2, p. 389; see

also pp. 295, 308, 324, 386; for a detailed study of the importance of secret societies, see Margadant, *French Peasants in Revolt*.

50. Bligny, *Histoire du dauphiné*, pp. 359, 373, 390-93; and the same author's *Histoire du diocèse de Grenoble* (Grenoble, 1979); and Barral, *Le Département de l'Isère*, pp. 243-70. Fava was the Isère's controversial Bishop until 1900. For an excellent analysis of local variations of anti-clericalism in Isère villages, see Roger Magraw in Theodore Zeldin, ed., *Conflicts in French Society: Anticlericalism, Education and Morals in the Nineteenth Century* (London, 1970), pp. 169-227.

51. Barral, *Le Département de l'Isère*, pp. 124-25. On Nov. 2, 1897 *Le Réveil du dauphiné* reported that vines, wheat, rye, and potatoes were good to excellent compared to previous years; see also *Le Petit dauphinois*, April 4, 1898, "Situation des recoltes."

52. Barral, *Le Département de l'Isère*, pp. 213ff.; Lequin, *Les Ouvriers de la région lyonnaise*, vol. 2, pp. 308-15.

53. Bligny, *Histoire du dauphiné*, pp. 379-81; Lequin, *Les Ouvriers de la région lyonnaise*, vol. 2, p. 358 and *passim*; ADI 56 M 1, report June 30, 1898. Skirmishes were taking place between French and Italian workers in the late 1880s, but major problems would come in the 90s and later; see ADI 53 M 17, various Grenoble police reports, 1888. Between 1890 and 1914 the Isère had a high rate of strikes, but with relatively few participants; see Charles Tilly and Edward Shorter, *Strikes in France* (London, 1968), p. 260.

54. Grise, *Coutumes du Trièves*, p. 25.

55. *Résultats statistiques, 1891*, p. 362.

56. Ibid., pp. 40-50, 65, 122-25, 278-79, 284-88, 374; see also Patrick Forbes, *Champagne* (New York, 1967), pp. 20-21.

57. ADM 30 M 42, prefect report, Oct. 16, 1894. In October, 1894, the prefect responded to the Minister of the Interior's request for detailed information on the social, economic, and political situation in the Marne. The report provides a rich analysis of public spirit in city and country. See also Néré, *La Crise industrielle*, pp. 150-51; and Forbes, *Champagne*, pp. 55-56.

58. Edmond Doutté, *Situation agricole du département de la Marne en 1892* (Châlons-sur-Marne, 1893), pp. 21-23; Gratton, *Les Luttes de classe*, pp. 210-13; Forbes, *Champagne*, pp. 165-76; and on the Dreyfus Affair in the Marne, see chap. VI below.

59. Doutté, *Situation agricole*, p. 7; *Statistique agricole décennale, 1893* in ADM 146 M.

60. Langlet, *La Population de Vitry le François* (Reims, 1905), p. 5.

61. ADM 138 M 9, prefect note, Dec. 1885; ADM 142 M 1, prefect note, May 23, 1898.

62. Langlet, *Vitry*, p. 69.

63. ADM 30 M 42, prefect, Oct. 16, 1894; see also Weber, *Peasants into*

Frenchmen: "The process of demographic decomposition helped those who stayed behind . . ." (pp. 281, 287).

64. ADM 122 M, *listes nominatives*, 1891. Scores of Marne communes were almost purely agricultural. For wood-cutters, see the communes of Pourcy and Nanteuil-la-Fosse.

65. This proximity also facilitated repression before and after the 1851 coup. There was no major uprising in the Marne, though some wine-growers and workers in Reims took part in anti-Bonapartist demonstrations. When Louis Napoleon demanded that Liberty Trees be leveled, the Procurer General reported: "In many communes the cutting of these trees is protested not because of their political significance, but because inhabitants want to retain the benefits that pruning yields." Perhaps some residents, fearing the consequences, found a non-political reason to save trees which had both practical and political significance; see Maurice Grigaut, *Autour du 2 Décembre dans le département de la Marne* (Châlons-sur-Marne, 1910), p. 27.

66. For example, upon hearing news of Dreyfus's arrest, Grenoble newspapers feared that "the traitor" was in league with nearby Italians; see *Le Petit dauphinois*, Nov. 2, 1894.

67. Forbes, *Champagne*, pp. 17, 66.

68. ADM 30 M 42, prefect, Oct. 18, 1894.

69. Ibid.

70. On anarchists, see AN F7 12506, "Anarchism en province," prefectoral reports, 1892-94. As late as 1908, voting ballots in Epernay were scrawled with anti-Semitic, anti-Dreyfusard slogans, as well as "Long live Anarchy: Down with the Army!" see ADM 13 M 16.

CHAPTER III

1. Engels and Lafargue, *Correspondence*, vol. 2, p. 109.

2. APP Ba 977, Nov. 3, 1899.

3. Quoted in Dansette, *Le Boulangisme*, p. 144.

4. Lt. Col. Villot, *Le Général Boulanger et le plebiscite* (Poiters, 1889), pp. 11-12, 24.

5. Raoul Frary, "Chronique politique," *La Nouvelle revue*, 54, 15, Sept. 15, 1888, p. 424; see also Susanna Barrows, *Distorting Mirrors: Visions of the Crowd in Late Nineteenth Century France* (New Haven, 1981), pp. 11-16.

6. Barrès quoted in Harding, *Astonishing Adventure*, p. 152.

7. Alexandre Zévaès, *Au Temps du boulangisme* (Paris, 1930), p. 80; see also p. 238.

8. Hutton, "Popular Boulangism," pp. 92, 95, 102.

9. Louis Marin, *Disparition des institutions traditionnelles en Lorraine* (Paris, 1948), p. 74.

10. Lequin, *Les Ouvriers de la région lyonnaise*, vol. 2, *passim*.

11. Hutton, "Popular Boulangism," p. 86.

12. On this, see Michael Hechter, *Internal Colonialism: The Celtic Fringe in British National Development, 1536-1966* (Berkeley, 1975).

13. APP Ba 971, note to prefect of police, Paris, July, 1889; AN F7 12448, special police, Le Mans, Aug. 29, 1887; Harding, *Astonishing Adventure*, p. 121.

14. In Zévaès, *Au temps*, p. 99; Harding, *Astonishing Adventure*, p. 167.

15. AN 156 Archives Privées (hereafter, AP) I 102.

16. Ibid.

17. AN 156 AP I 105, printers' bills and correspondence with Mackau, July-Sept., 1889.

18. On the unprecedented nature of Boulanger's propaganda see *Histoire générale de la presse française, III* (Paris, 1972), p. 256, note 1: "veritables campagnes de propagande à l'échelle nationale où la presse tint naturellement le rôle principal, mais où l'affiche, l'image et la brochure furent aussi très largement utilisées." It is interesting to note that Boulanger felt that his lack of success in the Midi and Southeast could be explained in part by weak propaganda campaigns in those areas (see *Mémoires du général Boulanger*, Paris, 1890). It is impossible to calculate the number of posters, ballots, brochures, and images which reached those regions, but in the Isère alone, as we shall see, it was tens of thousands. For more on Boulanger's propaganda see Zévaès, *Au temps*, p. 121.

19. *La Charge*, July 15, 1888. For more examples, see the rich collection in the BN Cabinet des estampes, Qb 1 1888, and N 3 "Boulanger."

20. *La Silhouette*, April 7, 1889.

21. *Le Jeune Garde*, Oct. 6, 1889; *Le Grelot*, April 22, 1888.

22. See "Dossiers Boulanger" held in the Musée Carnavalet, Paris.

23. *Le Figaro*, Oct. 22, 1890.

24. See the series of articles by John Grand-Carteret in *Revue encyclopédique: Scènes morales et politiques* (n.d. [1890s?]) in "Dossiers Boulanger," Musée Carnavalet. See also *La Vie parisienne*, May 5, 1888.

25. Advertisements for Boulangist watch chains were sent to a few "notables" in the Isère (ADI 51 M 25, police report Feb. 18, 1889), but it seems that for economic reasons, portability, and most important, custom, peasants received far more traditional views of the General. At the turn of the century the *Bauerbund* in Lower Austria adopted, perhaps unknowingly, many of Boulanger's modern publicity techniques, including soaps, candles, hats, and more carrying political messages; see Gavin Lewis, "The Peasantry, Rural Change, and Conservative Agrarism: Lower Austria at the Turn of the Century," *Past and Present*, 81, 1978, pp. 128-29.

26. Grand-Carteret, *Revue encyclopédique*; Harding, *Astonishing Adventure*, p. 121.

27. AN F7 12448, see note on Puy-de-Dôme, Sept. 11, 1888, and examples of images peddled in the countryside including "Russie et France" and "L'Alsace et la Lorraine."

28. AN F7 12448 and BN Cabinet des estampes, Qb 1: Jan.-March 1889.

29. AN 156 AP I 109, June 24, 1889.

30. *Le Petit Journal*, April 18, 1888, "Le Musée Boulanger." See two dozen variations on this common, "neutral" theme in BN Cabinet des estampes, N 2: Boulanger. See also Néré, *Le Boulangisme et la presse*, p. 10.

31. Timothy J. Clark, *Image of the People* (Greenwich, 1973), p. 15.

32. *Religions et traditions populaires* (Paris, 1979), p. 211.

33. Geneviève Bollème, *La Bibliothèque bleue* (Paris, 1971), pp. 7-26; Denise Lantiez, "Cinq siècles d'images populaires," *La France graphique*, 1957, p. 24.

34. Jean Mistler et al., *Epinal et l'imagerie populaire* (Paris, 1961), pp. 121, 128.

35. Ibid., pp. 27, 101.

36. For examples, see holdings of the "Iconothèque" at the MATP; for similar renderings of the Comte de Paris and Prince Victor Napoleon, see BN Cabinet des estampes, Qb 1: 1888.

37. André Varagnac, "L'Art et le peuple: Problèmes d'art populaire," *L'Amour de l'art*, Nov. 1938, p. 354.

38. On Napoleon I, see *Religions et traditions*, p. 57; Mistler, *Epinal*, pp. 97ff.; on Napoleon III, see MATP Iconothèque; and for examples of similar Boulangist images see AN F7 12448, especially the poster entitled "Faut-il qu'il revienne."

39. APP Ba 971 police report (no date) and examples of Boulangist lithographs; for older examples of vignettes, see *Religions et traditions*, p. 175, and MATP "Iconothèque." For more on Boulangist use of popular imagery, see *Le Figaro*, March 20, 1889, "Les Images et la politique;" Grand-Carteret, *Revue encyclopédique*; and "Dossier Boulanger," Musée Carnavalet.

40. *Religions et traditions*, pp. 181-86; see examples of devotional images in MATP "Iconothèque."

41. *Le Paris*, Aug. 10, 1889; see also AN F7 12448, police reports, July 6 and 12, 1889, Saint Malo, where small photos of Boulanger were found nestled between the pages of a local paper, *Le Bonhomme Breton*; or in Nevers where copies of *La Cocarde* included small photos of the General.

42. For a discussion of "associative composition," see Susan J. Delaney, " 'Atala' in the Arts," in Beauroy et al., eds., *The Wolf and the Lamb*, p. 221.

43. Mistler, *Epinal*, p. 62.

44. APP Ba 971, "La propagande boulangiste." In March 1889 prefects were told to keep an eye out for Boulangist propaganda, especially portraits and photographs; see *La Patrie*, March 30, 1889.

45. APP Ba 971, note to police prefect, Paris, August 27, 1889; AN F7 12448, Alençon police, April 30, 1888.

46. For examples, see the anonymous *Trois ans de conspiration, 1886-1889* (Paris, 1890), p.20.

47. AN F712448, special police, Le Mans, June 17, 1887.

48. Eugène Fournière, "Physiologie du boulangisme," *La Société nouvelle*, 4, t.1, 1888, p. 421.

49. *Réveil du dauphiné*, April 10, 1888; Néré, *Les Elections Boulanger*, p. 104; see also *Messager de Valence*, July 11, 1887.

50. On this, see Barrows, *Distorting Mirrors*, especially pp. 119ff.

51. Ibid., p. 124.

52. Gustave Le Bon, *The Crowd: A Study of the Popular Mind* (Harmondsworth, 1981), p. 75.

53. APP Ba 971, letter from local Boulangist in Moreuil, August 12, 1888.

54. *La Bataille*, June 6, 1889.

55. For Boulanger's thoughts on this, see *Mémoires du général Boulanger* p. 159.

56. Quoted in Harding, *Astonishing Adventure*, p. 162.

57. Paul Sébillot, *Le Folklore de France* (Paris, 1968), t.1, p. 472; t.4, pp. 403-404; see also Barral, *Le Département de l'Isère*, p. 55.

58. On the long history of the popular imagery industry, see Mistler, *Epinal*. At the time of the Dreyfus Affair very few political images were being sent to the provinces. We shall see that the written word—especially of Edouard Drumont and the Catholic newspaper *La Croix*—was attracting more support.

59. Roger Vaultier, "Un Colporteur d'images populaires en Bretagne il y a un siècle," *Passiflora*, 22, 1940(?), pp. 15-21.

60. APP Ba 497, "Embauchage de camelots;" Ba 970, police report Nov. 10, 1889; *La Presse*, Sept. 2, 1889; and AN 156 AP I 105.

61. Lantiez, "Cinq siècles d'images populaires," p. 25.

62. *Le Matin*, Sept. 30, 1890, "Coulisse du camelot."

63. Weber, *Peasants into Frenchmen*, p. 256.

64. BN Cabinet d'estampes, Qb 1: August 1888; see also Maurice Millot, *La Comédie boulangiste: Chansons et satires* (Paris, 1891), pp. 267-69.

65. APP Ba 971, see the 1888 "Conventions" with barely legible names of hawkers (sometimes signed with an X), their places of residence, and the communes they visited; see also police notes dated July 21 and Oct. 13, 1889, and the Jan. 1889 report on the Comité revisionniste. For more on hawkers, see *Bataille*, May 5, 1889; *Le Figaro*, Oct. 22, 1889; and Dansette, *Le Boulangisme*, p. 213. On Boulangist agents in Corsica, see AN F7 12445, police note, July 27, 1887.

66. AN F7 12445, Comité d'Amiens records, August 1888.

67. AN F7 12447, Tours, March 18, 1889; APP Ba 971, police summary of Boulanger in Tours, March 1889; *Le Matin*, June 11, 1889. For street hawkers in Paris, see *Le Petit Journal*, March 17, 1888.

68. *Le Démocratie du centre*, Dec. 4, 1888; for another report on hawkers in Nevers, see AN F7 12448, Jan. 28, 1890.

69. Harding, *Astonishing Adventure*, p. 172; for more examples of hawkers traveling with Boulanger, see the various reports in APP Ba 971.

70. AN 156 AP I 105.

71. AN 156 AP I 102, letters dated July 9 and Aug. 1, 1889.

72. AN 156 AP I 105, note dated Nov. 9, 1889 and *passim*.

73. See the long police report on the Orne dated August 23, 1889 in APP Ba 971; and chap. IV below.

74. AN F7 12448, police report, March 1, 1888.

75. Ibid., prefect Haute-Saône, Sept. 24, 1887.

76. Ibid., reports from Oise and Puy-de-Dôme, April 14 and August 27, 1889.

77. Ibid., Baisieux police report, June 3, 1888; also *Les Alpes républicaines*, May 18, 1889.

78. *Le Matin*, Sept. 30, 1890.

79. Grand-Carteret, *Revue encyclopédique* in "Dossiers Boulanger," Musée Carnavalet, Paris.

80. AN F7 12448, prefect Loire-Inférieure, April 16, 1889.

81. Zévaès, *Au temps*, p. 48 *passim*.

82. Engels and Lafargue, *Correspondence*, vol. 2, 1887-90, p. 117.

83. AN F7 12445, unsigned note dated May 2, 1888.

84. AN 156 AP I 104, May 19(?), 1889.

85. Ibid., AP I 108, Aug. 24 and Sept. 4, 1889.

86. Ibid., AP I 102, 105, 107, 109, and *passim* for various departmental reports from traveling agents to Baron Mackau.

CHAPTER IV

1. ADI 8 M 24, police report, Vienne, May 20, 1887; and subprefect report, La Tour du Pin, June 16, 1887.

2. Ibid., and subprefects Saint Marcellin and Vienne, June 8, 1887; see also various updated reports on M. Valentin, the agricultural candidate.

3. ADI 53 M 17, pamphlet of the Comité républicain cantonal de Voiron, 1886.

4. *Almanach de la France rurale et des syndicats agricoles* (1888), pp. 76-81.

5. He had also been wounded accompanying troops into Paris against the Communards, a fact keep under wraps so as not to upset early supporters on the Left. Scores of popular biographies of Boulanger carried no reference to the General's participation in the events of 1871. His wound, early in the attack, was fortuitous; it removed him from the carnage of "Bloody Week," and salvaged, for a while at least, his radical image. See, for example, *Almanach Boulanger* (1888), pp. 11ff.

6. The 1886 fête is described in every history of Boulangism: see Seager, *The Boulanger Affair*, p. 34; and Brogan, *Development of Modern France*, vol. 1, p. 184.

7. ADI 54 M 32, police report, July 23, 1887.

8. Ibid., note to Min. of Int., July 20, 1887.

9. Ibid., police report, Grenoble, July 15, 1887.

10. From its inception in February 1888, *Le Petit Grenoblois* focused on national politics, Grenoble news, and occasional articles concerning local glove and other industries. It contained no detailed cantonal news, agri-

cultural supplements, or any other features which might attract peasant readers.

11. ADI 8 M 25, police reports, Voiron, April 16, 1888; and April 20, 1888 note to prefect.

12. Ibid., subprefect Saint Marcellin, April 24, 1888.

13. *Le Petit Grenoblois*, April 18, 1888.

14. ADI 8 M 25, police reports, Grenoble, May 9 and 11, 1888.

15. *Le Petit Grenoblois*, May 9 and 10, 1888; see also APP Ba 977, "Aperçu politique relatif au Général Boulanger" on his Isère candidacy. At the moment that propaganda was flooding into the Isère, Boulanger, in Paris, was publicly withdrawing from the Isère contest. Peasants who were aware of this (and Boulangist agents were not acting as if their man were a non-candidate) might have voted for another on May 13, or might have abstained. In this light, as we shall see, the three-fold increase in Boulanger's tally is even more impressive. For events in Paris at this time, see Seager, *The Boulanger Affair*, p. 144. On the regional focus of Boulangist propaganda in the Isère, see ADI 8 M 25, police report, Grenoble to prefect, May 12, 1888. After the fact, Boulangist agents asserted that they would have rounded up 50-60,000 votes had the campaign begun five days earlier.

16. ADI 8 M 25, May 11, 1888.

17. See BMG V. 5504 for orders and receipts for posters and ballots sent to communes throughout the department, as well as for miscellaneous information pertaining to Girerd's campaign. See also the posters and ballots of all candidates in ADI 8 M 25.

18. BMG V. 5504, mayor Saint Egrève, May 4, 1888.

19. *Réveil du dauphiné*, March 1, 1888.

20. Ibid., May 9, 1888.

21. ADI 8 M 25, police and subprefect reports, Grenoble, Saint Marcellin, Vienne, and Voiron, May 11, 1888; ADI 51 M 25, police reports, Voiron, May 18, 1888; and note to Min. of Int., May 21, 1888; BMG V. 5504, telegram from Mens, May 11, 1888; *Le Petit Grenoblois*, May 30, 1888. On the Vienne hinterlands at mid-century, see Vigier, *La Seconde République dans la région alpine*, vol. 2, p. 399.

22. BMG V. 5504, note from Corps to Republican Congress, May 14, 1888.

23. On the League throughout France, see Peter Rutkoff, *Revanche and Revision: The Ligue des Patriotes and the Origins of the Radical Right in France, 1882-1900* (Athens, Ohio, 1981) passim; and Sternhell, *La Droite révolutionnaire*, pp. 96ff. Sternhell confirms that the League was weak in the Isère. See also, Hutton, "Popular Boulangism," p. 93. As a direct result of its involvement with Boulanger, the League was outlawed in March, 1889 (see the circular from the Min. of Int. in AN F7 12450).

24. Robert O. Paxton, *Vichy France* (New York, 1975), p. 18.

25. ADI 55 M I, police report, Grenoble, June 12, 1887; subprefect Saint

Marcellin, Nov. 21, 1887; note concerning Voiron, Feb. 21, 1888; and *Réveil du dauphiné*, May 13, 1888.

26. ADI 53 M 17, report to Sûreté, Sept. 28, 1888; police report, Grenoble, Sept. 3, 1889; see also ADI 52 M 57, response to Min. of Int., March 12, 1889.

27. AN F7 12449, Isère prefect to Min. of Int., Feb. 7, 1893.

28. *L'Intransigeant*, March 1888; for examples of Boulangist rhetoric, see Néré, *Boulangisme et la presse*.

29. For examples, see *L'Intransigeant*, Jan. 1, 9, 25; Feb. 22; April 17, 30; and May 18, 1888.

30. For detailed information on those newspapers which reached the Isère countryside in the late nineteenth century, see chap. V below.

31. Quoted in Néré, *La Crise industrielle*, p. 473.

32. *Le Petit Grenoblois*, May 10, 1888.

33. See below chap. V, n. 56.

34. Pierre Sorlin, *'La Croix' et les juifs* (Paris, 1967), pp. 57-58, 87.

35. *La Semaine religieuse du diocèse de Grenoble*, 1888.

36. ADI 51 M 25, "Affiche électorale boulangiste," May 1888.

37. It is unclear whether the pamphlets *Le Général Boulanger: Histoire populaire complète*, *Almanach des célébrités contemporaines: Le Général Boulanger*, or the General's own *L'Invasion Allemande* reached peasant communities in the Isère, but they are typical and capture the unrelenting themes of military preparedness, honor, and sacrifice for the Fatherland. *L'Invasion Allemande* proved such a failure in the provinces that booksellers requested that shipments be halted. But this commercial fare, sold rather than given away, might not have come to the attention of the peasantry. See AN F7 12448 for a copy of *L'Invasion Allemande* with note dated May 23, 1888; see also police report, Royot, May 9, 1888.

38. Weber, *Peasants into Frenchmen*, pp. 297-98.

39. A. Marchet, *Lettres de populus à Jacques Bonhomme* (n.d.).

40. ADI 8 M 25, election poster signed "Brenier de Montmorand (Père)."

41. Ibid., legislative election results, May 1888. For May 1887, see ADI 8 M 24-25, as well as a chart on earlier Isère elections in ADI 8 M 26.

42. ADI 8 M 25, police report to Isère prefect, May 12, 1888; for an account of other departmental elections, see Seager, *The Boulanger Affair*, chap. 5.

43. See the excellent appendix, "Les Résultats électoraux," in Barral, *Le Département de l'Isère*, pp. 548-65. For example, in the by-election of 1887 the turnout dropped by almost 10,000 on the second round. The discrepancy was even greater in 1885. In May 1888, however, the turnout increased from 76,008 to 96,489. On abstention in general, see Alain Lancelot, *L'Abstentionnisme électorale en France* (Paris, 1968).

44. ADI 8 M 25, election results, 1888.

45. Vigier discusses this aspect of the Isère at mid-century in *La Seconde République dans la région alpine*, vol. 2, p. 215. See a similar assessment of

mountains and lowlands in the Var in the 1880s in Judt, *Socialism in Provence*, and the indispensible Siegfried, *Tableau politique* for the West.

46. ADI 8 M 25, election results, 1888; on the population and economy of individual communes, see ADI 123 M, *listes nominatives* 1896 (1888 unavailable); ADI 137 M, *Statistique agricole*, 1892; and *Annuaire officiel du département de l'Isère, 1888*.

47. Vigier, *La Seconde République dans la région alpine*, vol. 2, pp. 389-91, 394-95.

48. Ibid., pp. 215, 396, 400; ADI 8 M 25, election results, 1888.

49. Vigier, *La Seconde République dans la région alpine*, vol. 2, p. 398.

50. Report to Republican Committee, May 27, 1887, quoted in Barral, *Le Département de l'Isère*, pp. 521-22.

51. AN F⁷ 12445, unsigned report, May 2, 1888; for the influence of the clergy in the Isère four decades earlier, see Vigier, *La Seconde République dans la région alpine*, vol. 2, p. 206: clergymen were often Bonapartist agents, "surtout dans les contrées montagneuse où son influence reste très forte" (see also pp. 392-93).

52. ADI 16 M 167, letter to Isère prefect, May 9, 1888.

53. ADI 54 M 32, notes to Isère prefect, July 18, Aug. 2, 1889.

54. For the 1888 election in Monestier d'Ambel, see ADI 8 M 25, Corps canton.

55. ADS M 342, election reports, Aug. 28, Sept. 5, 1889.

56. Carles, *Une Soupe*, p. 213.

57. Lancelot, *L'Abstentionnisme*, p. 129.

58. ADI 10 M 18, Conseil général elections, March 1888, Rousillon; ADI 8 M 25, election results, 1888. For contrasting participation in local elections in rural and urban settings, see Lancelot, *L'Abstentionnisme*, pp. 140ff.; Augé-Laribé, *L'Evolution de la France agricole*, p. 285; Barral, *Les Agrariens français*, p. 339; and on municipal council elections throughout France, see *Le Petit Journal*, May 10, 1888.

59. Patrick H. Hutton, "The Impact of the Boulangist Crisis upon the Guesdist Party at Bordeaux," *French Historical Studies*, 7, 2, 1971.

60. See Gratton, *Les Luttes de classe, passim*, and Augé-Laribé, *L'Evolution de la France agricole*, p. 252.

61. On local anti-Boulangist campaigns, see ADI 51 M 25, Sept. 1889 reports, and note from Morestel, Feb. 26, 1889; see also ADI 8 M 26, police report, Vienne, Sept. 16, 1889. On republican responses to the Boulangist challenge, see ADI 8 M 26, *professions de foi*, posters, and election results; and for more on Boulangist tactics in the rural Isère, see Baron Mackau's private papers, AN 156 AP I 109.

62. *La République des paysans: Organe indépendant de la démocratie du Gers*, Nov. 8, 1889.

63. ADG M 2844, note to subprefect, June 28, 1889.

64. ADG M 2799, police report, Gimont, Aug. 4, 1888.

65. On the Gers peasantry and Bonapartism, see Ducamp, *La Conquête*,

p. 93; Palmade, *L'Evolution de l'opinion*, pp. 77, 87-88, 118; and Bordes, *Histoire de la Gascogne*, p. 362. See also Lt. Col. Villot, *Le Général Boulanger*, pp. 12, 22.

66. Ducamp, *La Conquête*, p. 337; Bordes, *Histoire de la Gascogne*, pp. 351ff.

67. Brogan, *Development of Modern France*, vol. 1, pp. 109, 166.

68. For more on this, see the engaging article by James C. Hunt, "Peasants, Grain Tariffs and Meat Quotas: Imperial German Protection Reexamined," *Central European History*, 7, 4, 1974, pp. 311-31; and compare Siegfried's statement that the mass of voters in the West of France supported the Republic "because it has revived imperial prosperity" (*Tableau politique*, p. 106).

69. Pierre Barral, "L'Agrarisme de gauche et agrarisme de droite sous la Troisième République," in *L'Univers politique paysans* (Paris, 1972), p. 250.

70. Ducamp, *La Conquête*, pp. 221-28.

71. Quoted in Palmade, *L'Evolution de l'opinion*, p. 166. For more on Cassagnac, see Maurice Bordes, "L'Evolution politique du Gers sous la Troisième République," *Information historique*, 1, 1961, pp. 19-22.

72. Ducamp, *La Conquête*, p. 93.

73. ADG M 2799, police report, Gimont, May 12, 1888.

74. E. M. de Vogüé, *Les Morts qui parlent* (Paris, 1899), pp. 89-90.

75. Bordes, *Histoire de la Gascogne*, p. 345; Ducamp, *La Conquête*, p. 60 and *passim*.

76. ADG M 2799, police reports, Mirande, Dec. 6, 1888 and Jan. 6, 1889; police report, Nogaro, Jan. 27, 1889; and police report, Gimont, Nov. 16, 1889.

77. Ducamp, *La Conquête*, p. 281.

78. ADG M 2799, police report, Nogaro, Oct. 15, 1889.

79. The commune was Justian; see ADG M 4855, *liste nominative* 1886; on the election, see Ducamp, *La Conquête*, p. 267.

80. See Sept. 1888 issues of *Le Conservateur: Journal politique* for "Revision" without Boulanger; see also Palmade, *L'Evolution de l'opinion*: ". . . l'autorité personnelle de Cassagnac paraît avoir absorbé toutes les tendances plébiscitaires de l'opinion," pp. 150-51.

81. *L'Appel au peuple*, Jan. 29-30, 1889.

82. Cassagnac quoted in Ducamp, *La Conquête*, p. 247.

83. ADG M 2799, Cassagnac posters for 1889 elections; and *L'Appel au peuple*, Jan. 15, 1889.

84. ADG M 2799, police report, Isle-Jourdain, July 21, 1889.

85. See the long police report from Eauze, Sept. 24, 1889 in ADG M 2799.

86. APP Ba 977, note dated June 18, 1889.

87. For more details on these transformations, see Bordes, "L'Evolution politique du Gers," pp. 20-22.

88. Ducamp, *La Conquête*, p. 207.

89. AN F⁷ 12446 and 12450; including the series of reports to the Sûreté, March 3, 5, and April 13, 1889. See also ADI 51 M 25, Isère prefect report, Aug. 17, 1889; as well as Barral, *Les Agrariens français*, p. 87, and Ducamp, *La Conquête*, p. 103.

90. AN F⁷ 12447, note to Sûreté, April 5, 1889.

91. AN F⁷ 12446, police report, Mâcon, April 28, 1889.

92. Jouanne, *La Révolution de 1848*, pp. 31-41; Gabriel Désert, "Les Paysans bas-normands et la politique," *Annales de Normandie*, 3, Oct. 1976, pp. 214-15; on the fate of rural industries in the Orne, see above chap. II.

93. Brogan, *Development of Modern France*, vol. 1, pp. 200-203.

94. ADO M 1228, April 27, 1888.

95. On Mackau's propaganda, see AN 156 AP I 102-11; on agents in the rural Orne, see, for example, ADO M 414, various police reports, Aug.-Sept., 1889.

96. ADO M 1228, police report, Tinchebay, Aug. 7, 1887; and Pierre Flament, "Boulanger, 'l'Apprenti-Dictateur' et le département de l'Orne en 1888," *Société historique et archéologique de l'Orne*, 79, 1961, p. 88.

97. ADO M 1228, Domfront subprefect, April 21, 1888.

98. See ibid., prefect report, March 16, 1889; and on the limited scope of the League in neighboring regions, M. Boivin, "Le Boulangisme en Haute Normandie," *Annales de Normandie*, 3, Oct. 1976, pp. 232-34.

99. ADO M 1228, Domfront subprefect, Oct. 16, 1888.

100. AN 156 AP I 111; on the *Gazette des campagnes*, see AN 156 AP I 102, notes from editor, July 3, Aug. 12, 1889.

101. ADO M 1228, Domfront subprefect, Oct. 16, 1888.

102. It is important to note at this point that through 1889 Mackau never renounced Boulangism. Minister Constans launched his republican counteroffensive in the spring, but on the eve of the fall elections Mackau's speeches remained explicitly revisionist and Boulangist. His immense power and popularity in the Orne (and in the Chamber of Deputies) undoubtedly helped shield him from Constans' attacks (see AN 156 AP I 111).

103. For Mackau's comments on local agents, see AN 156 AP I 111, 132; for more on the type and cost of propaganda, see AN 156 AP I 102, 105, 109.

104. AN 156 AP I 109, local agent, Aug. 29, 1889.

105. ADO M 414, police reports, Sees, Aug. 24, Sept. 7, 1889.

106. AN 156 AP I 109, local agent, Aug. 29, 1889.

107. Ibid., Aug. 10, 1889; on the 1889 legislative elections, see ADO M 414.

108. ADO M 414; see also AN 156 AP I 112 for Mackau's notes on the Sept. 1889 elections.

109. For example, see ADO M 414, police report, Sept. 7, 1889.

110. Ibid., subprefect report, Aug. 31, 1889.

111. Désert, "Les Paysans bas-normands," p. 218.

112. ADM 47 M 52, police report, Mourmelon, March 16, 1888.

113. For the Feb. 1888 election, see ADM 7 M 58.

114. *L'Indépendant de la Marne et de la Moselle*, Feb. 23, 28, 1888.

115. ADM 7 M 58; see Boulangist appeals to voters.

116. Ibid., material on Léon Bourgeois; and *L'Indépendant de la Marne*, Feb. 14, 1888.

117. ADM 47 M 52, police report, Mourmelon, Feb. 25, 1888; and ADM 7 M 58.

118. ADM 30 M 41, Reims subprefect, Dec. 4, 1889.

119. Ibid., police report, Châlons-sur-Marne, Jan. 31, 1889; and *procès-verbal*, Feb. 12, 1889.

120. Ibid., police reports, Ay, Feb. 10, 1889.

121. Ibid., *procès-verbal*, Sept. 1889; and police report, Reims, Sept. 7, 1889.

122. For an example of the republican response, see ADM 77 M 21, Reims subprefect, Oct. 19, 1888.

123. *Le Réveil national de la Marne*, Sept. 9-10, 1889.

124. ADM 30 M 41, police report, Reims, Sept. 1, 1889.

125. Ibid., Sept. 8, 1889.

126. On the Mailly incident, see ADM 30 M 41, police report, Reims, Sept. 14, 1889; on Vienne-le Chateau, see Sept. 15, 1889.

127. APP Ba 971, telegram, June 5, 1889; for the prospectus with instructions, see ADM 43 M 61, May 26, 1889.

128. ADI 53 M 17, Isère prefect to mayors, June 6, 1889, and responses.

129. For details on the Courthiézy incident, see ADM 43 M 51, Epernay subprefect report, June 28, 1889; and the long *procès-verbal*, June 21-22, 1889.

130. *Le Réveil national de la Marne*, Sept. 22, 1889.

131. ADM 30 M 41, Epernay subprefect, Nov. 30, 1889.

132. AN 156 AP I 109, letter dated May 27, 1889.

133. Hutton, "Popular Boulangism," p. 101.

134. ADM 30 M 41, Boulangist manifesto seized in Reims, Sept. 21, 1889.

135. *Le Réveil national de la Marne*, Sept. 8-9, 15-17, 21, 1889.

136. ADM 4 Z 56, see copy of "Le Peuple souverain," and police report, Oct. 29, 1888.

137. See the Boulanger-Naquet correspondence in the BN, N.A.F. 23783.

138. *Le Réveil national de la Marne*, Sept. 7, 1889; for more on Boulangist anti-Semitism, see AN 156 AP I 102; and Boivin, "Le Boulangisme en Haute Normandie," pp. 243.

139. See above chap. III, n. l.

140. ADV 1 M 375, report to Min. of Int., May 16, 1889. For a thorough analysis of Boulangism in the Vendée, see other reports in the same file, as well as additional material on agents, propaganda, and electioneering

in ADV 1 M 442; 3 M 225, 254; and 4 M 11, 404, 442. On republican and royalist reactions to the General, see *L'Avenir et l'indicateur de la Vendée*, especially Jan. 2, 1889; and *L'Etoile de la Vendée*, 1889 *passim*. A Boulangist newspaper, *Le Révisionniste de la Vendée*, lasted only a few months in 1889 and attracted few readers; it confirms, however, the General's attempt to appeal to Vendée workers, not peasants (see, for example, Sept. 22, 1889). See also, L. Morauzau, "L'Equivoque boulangiste en Vendée," *Société d'émulation de la Vendée*, 1950, pp. 97-104.

141. AN C 5470, peasant report to commission investigating electoral fraud in the Vosges, Oct. 22, 1889; see similar testimonies in AN C 5469.

142. AN 156 AP I 109, report from local agent in the Landes.

143. This fits, though not in its timing, with Charles Tilly's engaging discussion of proactive, reactive, and modern forms of collective violence (see below, chap. VI, n. 16).

CHAPTER V

1. On Panama in general, see Robert Byrnes, *Anti-Semitism in Modern France* (New Brunswick, 1950), pp. 332-39; and Hannah Arendt, *Origins of Totalitarianism* (New York, 1973), pp. 95-99.

2. AN F7 12459, Agen police report, March 18, 1893; and Palmade, *L'Evolution de l'opinion*, p. 158. Although Stephen Wilson, citing Zévaès, suggests that "many peasants . . . were the victims of large scale embezzlements" (*Ideology and Experience*, p. 268), I have found no evidence showing significant peasant involvement or interest in the Panama scandal. On Jan. 17, 1889 a Panama-related rally took place in Saint Menehould (Marne), but was attended by municipal council members, architects and other urban folk (see ADM 47 M 33). It is clear, however, that more work is needed on the scope of the Panama crisis.

3. ADG M 2799, mayor of Gimont, note dated May 10, 1890 describing a local peasant.

4. George L. Mosse, *Toward the Final Solution: A History of European Racism* (New York, 1978), p. 150.

5. Arendt, *Origins*, p. xi.

6. See Wolff, ed., *Georg Simmel*, pp. 403-404.

7. For this in another historical and geographical context, see Crawford Young, *The Politics of Cultural Pluralism* (Madison, 1976), p. 65. Bernard Lazare believed that "at the bottom of the anti-Semitism of our own day [is] the fear of, and hatred for, the stranger"; see *Anti-Semitism: Its History and Causes* (New York, 1903), p. 361.

8. Jean Paul Sartre, *Anti-Semite and Jew*, trans George J. Becker (New York, 1965), p. 13.

9. Weber, *Peasants into Frenchmen*, p. 458.

10. J. Levaillant, "La Genèse de l'antisémitisme sous la Troisième République," *Revue des études juives*, 1907, p. LXXVII.

11. On the Wandering Jew, see Mosse, *Toward the Final Solution*, pp. 114-

15; Geneviève Bollème, *La Bibliothèque bleue: La littérature populaire en France du XVIe au XIXe siècle* (Paris, 1971), pp. 183-89; Wilson, *Ideology and Experience*, p. 298; and George Anderson, *The Legend of the Wandering Jew* (Providence, 1970).

12. Pierre Pierrard, *Juifs et catholiques français* (Paris, 1970), p. 17; see also Mosse, *Toward the Final Solution*, p. 155.

13. Sorlin, '*La Croix*' *et les juifs*, pp. 32, 95-96.

14. Joseph Blanc, *Notes d'un curé de campagne* (1911), pp. 134-42.

15. On the power of books and newspapers in rural France, see Weber, *Peasants into Frenchmen*, chap. 27; and E. Villane, *L'Opinion publique et l'affaire Dreyfus* (1898), pp. 11-12, 31-32.

16. Doris Ben Simon-Donath, *Socio-démographie des juifs de France et d'Algérie* (Paris, 1976), p. 43.

17. See *Drumont et Dreyfus* (n.a.) (1898), p. 12; and for circulation statistics of *Le Petit Journal*, see the Jan. 2, 1888 issue.

18. Pierrard, *Juifs et catholiques*, p. 62.

19. Halévy, *Visites aux paysans du Centre*, p. 42; see also Weber, *Peasants into Frenchmen*, p. 466.

20. For examples see *Chronique du sud-est*, Jan. 1898, p. 52, which carries an advertisement for the 142nd edition of *La France juive*; see also *Les Veillées des chaumières*, Dec. 26, 1888; and *La Démocratie rurale* (various editions in the 90s). *La Croix* was constantly quoting and publicizing Drumont: "It was the first newspaper to review *La France juive* in 1886, and it praised Drumont enthusiastically" (Byrnes, *Anti-Semitism in Modern France*, p. 196). On the widespread effects of a popular publication see Douglas Waples et al., *What Reading Does to People* (Chicago, 1940), especially p. 9: "The initial effect upon a few readers may be so diffused by the currents of group interest and by the ground swells of public opinion at large that the effects of a single publication may carry far indeed." So went *La France juive*.

21. Edouard Drumont, *La France juive devant l'opinion* (Paris, 1886), p. 4.

22. Edouard Drumont, *La France juive* (Paris, 1888), pp. XLIV-XLVI.

23. Ibid., p. 11.

24. Drumont, *La France juive devant l'opinion*, p. 147.

25. See above, chap. IV.

26. Gustave Flaubert, *Madame Bovary*, trans. Lowell Blair (New York, 1972), p. 163; see also Wilson, *Ideology and Experience*, p. 262.

27. Ben Simon-Donath, *Socio-démographie des juifs*, pp. 21-23. See also David Cohen, "L'Image du juif dans la société française en 1843 d'après les rapports des préfets," *Revue d'histoire économique et sociale*, 55, 1977, p. 90; Paul Leuilliot, *L'Alsace au début du XIXe siècle*, II (Paris, 1959), pp. 177-87; Wilson, *Ideology and Experience*, p. 268; and Patrick Girard, *Les Juifs de France de 1789 à 1860* (Paris, 1976) for more on usury in Alsace, pp. 72-75, 124.

28. Lazare, *Anti-Semitism*, p. 182.

29. Weber, *Peasants into Frenchmen*, pp. 38-40.

30. Vigier, *La Seconde République dans la région alpine*, vol. 1, pp. 38-40; see also vol. 2, pp. 60-62, 163-64, 332; and Ted W. Margadant in Roger Price, ed. *Revolution and Reaction: 1848 and the Second French Republic* (London, 1975), pp. 254-79; see also Zeldin, *France: 1848-1945*, vol. 1, p. 147.

31. For the Isère, see *Le Petit dauphinois*, April 16, 1889; and for the Var Judt, *Socialism in Provence*, p. 165.

32. For the Gers, see Jean François Bladé, *Contes populaires de la Gascogne*, t. 3 (1886); and Ducamp, *La Conquête*, p. 257. The *Annuaire administratif du Gers, 1898* lists no Jewish residents at all (see p. 165). Political campaigns of 1898 will show that there were a few Jewish residents in the capital, Auch, but there is no evidence of Jewish usury in the department; on "Christian Jews," see Rudolph Löwenstein, *Christians and Jews: A Psychoanalytic Study* (New York, 1951), p. 84.

33. Drumont, *La France juive*, p. 42.

34. Michael Marrus, *The Politics of Assimilation: A Study of the French Jewish Community at the Time of the Dreyfus Affair* (Oxford, 1971), pp. 30-35; and Ben Simon-Donath, *Socio-démographie des juifs*, p. 69. Robert Byrnes points out that in "1900 only two percent of the Jewish population *in the world* lived on the land" (my emphasis). See *Anti-Semitism in Modern France*, p. 78.

35. *Le Temps*, Jan. 25, 1898; Stephen Wilson, "Catholic Populism in France at the Time of the Dreyfus Affair: The *Union Nationale*," *Journal of Contemporary History*, 10, Oct. 1975, pp. 674, 697; Marrus, *Politics of Assimilation*, p. 41.

36. For the make-up of anti-Semitic leagues and Catholic groups see Zeev Sternhell, *La Droite révolutionnaire*, p. 224; Pierrard, *Juifs et catholiques*, p. 147; on urban limits of Leagues see Byrnes, *Anti-Semitism in Modern France*, p. 253; Stephen Wilson, "The Anti-Semitic Riots of 1898 in France," *The Historical Journal*, 16, 1973, pp. 794-95; and AN F⁷ 12459, Aug. 1889 report on the Ligue antisémitique showing most members "inscrits à Paris," and the same author's *Ideology and Experience*, pp. 179-93.

37. For examples of priests mixing politics and religion, see Sorlin, *'La Croix' et les juifs*, pp. 40, 219; Jacques Liber, *Enseignements de l'affaire Dreyfus* (Poligny, 1899), p. 40; Magraw in Zeldin, ed., *Conflicts in French Society*; and Besse, *Le Curé, l'instituteur, passim*. See also Felix Pradel, *Le Curé de campagne et les oeuvres rurales* (Saint Maixent, 1905): "We are lost if the French clergy does not address itself resolutely to social issues" (p. 8). In 1898 a Dreyfusard reporting on the provinces cautions that the press is not the only instigator of anti-Dreyfus agitation. One must look to the clergy who "influence men in two ways: first, directly [in the confessional], and then in a more sure and insinuating manner, through their wives." See Michel Colline, *Affaire Dreyfus: Billets de la province* (Paris, 1898). Priests also got mixed up in industrial relations in curious ways: in the Gard crafty

patrons paid a local vicar to sound the angelus earlier than usual in the morning and later at night in order to make the work day longer and get the most from laborers; see Van Gennep, *Manuel de folklore français* t.1, 5, p. 2220.

38. AN F7 12315, "Congrégations non-autorisées," Gers, June 1880.

39. ADG M 1227, various reports from Eauze and Condom, especially prefect note, Nov. 18, 1881, and subprefect Lombez note, Dec. 17, 1881; see also Palmade, *L'Evolution de l'opinion*, p. 26.

40. ADG M 1227, letter to the Secrétaire général, July 15, 1881.

41. Stephen Wilson, "The Anti-Semitic Riots," pp. 789-806; in *Ideology and Experience*, Wilson suggests that this was less an example of peasant anti-Semitism than of country folk responding to pressures from local notables (p. 735).

42. Bligny, ed., *Histoire du diocèse de Grenoble*, p. 230ff.; and Pierrard, *Juifs et catholiques*, p. 29.

43. AN F7 12316, Isère prefect to Sûreté, Sept. 1888. The situation was similar in the Loire-Inférieure, where Trappists maintained close links with nearby peasants.

44. Désert, *Une Société rurale*, pp. 1191-93; ADV 1 M 375, prefect report, June 2, 1889, and 41 M 31, prefect report, Nov. 26, 1881; on the Finistère, see AN C 5573, 1897 *enquête* on electoral fraud.

45. On an anti-Semitic campaign in Reims in June 1896, see ADM 30 M 42, "Affaire Mirman-Gobréaux;" on population statistics see *Annuaire de la Marne 1898*, and Marrus, *Politics of Assimilation*, pp. 31-32.

46. *L'Univers israélite*, Feb. 18, 1898.

47. Mosse, *Toward the Final Solution*, p. 114 and *passim*.

48. Drumont, *La France juive*, p. LIV; Pierrard, *Juifs et catholiques*, p. 18.

49. Pierrard, *Juifs et catholiques*, p. 104; see also Stephen Wilson, "Le Monument Henry," *Annales*, 2, March-April, 1977, pp. 265-91.

50. *La Croix* comment quoted in Sorlin, *'La Croix' et les juifs*, pp. 95-96.

51. Ibid., p. 48, and for nation-wide circulation, pp. 42-44; see also *Histoire générale de la presse française*, III p. 256; Byrnes, *Anti-Semitism in Modern France*, pp. 195-96; and *La Croix du Gers*, which reported on Jan. 23, 1898 that total sales in France had reached 600,000 copies.

52. On "general" and "political" populations in rural France, see Weber, *Peasants into Frenchmen*, p. 244.

53. *La Croix du Gers* reported a circulation of 4,000 on Jan. 9, 1898, and *La Croix de l'Orne* had "thousands" of readers, 2,000 in the Vire area alone (*La Croix de l'Orne*, Jan. 2, 1898).

54. On June 30, 1899, police in Grenoble said that 22,000 copies had been distributed (ADI 52 M 59); for the Savoie see *Chronique du sud-est*, Feb. 1898, p. 68. *La Croix* was extremely popular in the Savoie, but no statistics are given; the same publication mentions that circulation in the Ain had reached 13,000. For the Marne, see Sorlin, *'La Croix' et les juifs*: circulation was 8,000 in 1893 and growing (p. 43).

55. *Chronique du sud-est*, May 1898, p. 179, and Feb. 1898, p. 70.

56. See above, note 54.

57. ADI 9 T 39, Sardieu, Jan. 8, 1893; and Beaufort mayor's report, Jan. 8, 1893.

58. Ibid., mayoral reports from Rencurel and La Murette, Jan. 16, 1893; and Chormanche, Jan. 10, 1893; ADV 4 M 176, police report, June 13, 1896, and 1 M 444, June 28, 1898.

59. Blanc, *Notes d'un curé*: Blanc was a priest in an unnamed anticlerical commune at the turn of the century. In order to gain the confidence of suspicious peasants, he offered each farmer a subscription to *La Croix*. According to Blanc, it worked (p. 61).

60. ADI 9 T 39, Varacieux, peddlers' report, Feb. 2, 1893; for Têche see Jan. 6, 1893 report.

61. ADI 52 M 57, Séchilienne mayor to prefect, Sept. 1, 1890.

62. *Chronique du sud-est*, Feb. 1898, p. 68.

63. ADS 9 M III 123, mayor Saint Paul-sur-Yenne, Nov. 20, 1892.

64. Ibid., mayor Héry-sur-Ugine, Dec. 27, 1904.

65. *Chronique du sud-est*, Feb. 1898, "Dans l'Ain;" ADV 4 M 163, police report, June 9, 1896.

66. Sorlin, *'La Croix' et les juifs*, p. 48. In 1899 anti-Semites in Epinal printed colored confetti destined for peasants in outlying communes: "Peasants!!! Who exploits you? The Jew! Peasants do no more business with the Jews!" (see AN F7 12463).

67. ADM 77 M 21, Colportage. Excluding Vitry le François, the great majority of *La Croix* peddlers' requests came from communes with less than 1,000 inhabitants.

68. ADM 5 Z 30, Conseiller général, June 12, 1900.

69. Maurice Bordes, "L'Evolution politique du Gers," p. 22.

70. Sorlin, *'La Croix' et les juifs*, p. 46.

71. On Guillaumin and *La Croix*, see Gratton, *Les Luttes de classe*, pp. 260-61.

72. Byrnes, *Anti-Semitism in Modern France*, p. 193. The 1885 break with the Bonapartists might have made life difficult for *La Croix* in the Gers (see Sorlin, *'La Croix' et les juifs*, p. 56). Unfortunately, unlike the Marne, Isère, and Savoie there is no available information on peddling in the Gers.

73. Sorlin, *'La Croix' et les juifs*, p. 54.

74. Ibid., p. 256 note 213. In 1897 there were 20 departmental newspapers in the Gers, 49 in the Isère, 45 in the Marne, and 26 in the Savoie (see *Annuaire de la presse française 1897*, p. 230). Again, in peddlers' requests, none appears so often as *La Croix*.

75. *La Croix de l'Isère*, Dec. 22, 1897. On the importance of addressing a specific readership using relevant and understandable material, see Waples et al., *What Reading Does*: ". . . many readers are attracted to publications which increase their self-respect by many and ingenious forms of flattery" (p. 75).

76. *La Croix du Gers*, Aug. 7, 1898. For the Marne see *La Croix de la Marne*, Dec. 4, 1898: an old peasant reads "Le Dreyfusard" and remarks, "Nothing but slander and all for one *sou*. . . . Manure is cheap in Paris!"

77. A glance at any of these papers in the tumultuous years of 1897-99 will reveal its tone, format, and priorities. For example, *Le Petit dauphinois* is full of Dreyfus-related news and analyses of Parisian events, whereas *Réveil agricole* devotes only a few lines to the Affair at its height in January 1898, and mentions it not at all after February.

78. Like everything else, Cassagnac dominated journalism in the Gers. Republican papers came and went through the 1880s and 90s, a sign of uneasy political footing. Much of *La Croix*'s anti-Semitic, anti-government impact in the Gers must have been upstaged by Cassagnac's own brand of politics. Still, *La Croix du Gers* did well (see note 51 above).

79. For example, see the republican, but anti-Dreyfus, *Le Réveil de Marne: Indépendant de la Marne et de la Moselle*, especially Jan. 15, 1898.

80. See *Chronique du sud-est* which was affiliated with the Union Nationale organization and spiritual partners with *La Croix*. It was, however, more concerned with urban workers (especially in Lyon) than peasants. See also *La République des paysans*, a Gers weekly with rural as well as national news, which, however, stopped publication in 1893; and *Le Démocratie rurale*, a mildly anti-Semitic, strongly anti-government paper which tried desperately to enlist peasant support throughout France in the 1890s.

81. Siegfried, *Tableau politique*, p. 505.

82. *La Croix de l'Isère*, Jan. 30, 1897. *La Croix* also published an *Annuaire-almanach catholique du dauphiné* with agricultural advice and anti-Semitic commentary (see *La Croix de l'Isère*, Dec. 3, 1897).

83. *La Croix Vendéenne*, Jan. 16, 1898; for another example see *La Croix de la Marne*, Feb. 13, 1898.

84. Wilson, *Ideology and Experience*, pp. 90-91.

85. *La Croix de l'Isère*, Nov. 15, 1897, "Le Laboureur dauphinois."

CHAPTER VI

1. ADM 5 Z 45, police reports Jan. 25-27, 1898, Vitry le François.

2. *Le Républicain . . . de Vitry le François*, Jan. 25, 1898.

3. *La Libre parole*, Feb. 12, 1898.

4. AN F7 12467, "Manifestations en province, Jan. 1898"; Wilson, "Anti-Semitic Riots," pp. 789-806; and by the same author, "Catholic Populism in France," pp. 667-705. See also Wilson's recent *Ideology and Experience*; his analysis of provincial reaction is cogent, though it does not include material from departmental archives on peasant politics.

5. *La Croix de la Marne*, Feb. 4, 1898.

6. Ibid., March 4, 1898.

7. Ibid., Jan. 28, 1898; for Reims see AN F7 12467, "Manifestations."

8. *La Croix de la Marne*, Jan. 26, 1898.

9. AN F7 12467, "Manifestations"; for Grenoble see ADI 51 M 26, police

report, Jan. 23, 1898; for Nantes see AN F⁷ 12467, prefect report, Jan.
20, 1898; and for Caen see AN F⁷ 12460, unsigned report, Jan. 25, 1898;
see also Wilson, "Anti-Semitic Riots," *passim*.

10. Byrnes, *Anti-Semitism in Modern France*, p. 271.

11. Thabault, *Education and Change*: "The *affaire Dreyfus* which aroused
so much passion throughout France left Mazières practically unmoved . . ."
(p. 167); AN F⁷ 12467, Loire prefect, Jan. 23, 1898; Narbonne police,
Sept. 26, 1899; ADI 53 M 18, see various Rapports de quinzaine, 1898-
99.

12. For Saint-Brieuc, see AN F⁷ 12467, police report, Jan. 28, 1898; for
La Tour du Pin, ADI 51 M 26, subprefect report, Jan. 26, 1898; for
Montereau, AN F⁷ 12466, police report, Oct. 8, 1898; for Limoges AN F⁷
12466, police report, Nov. 18, 1898; for Vienne and Bourgoin ADI 53 M
18, Rapports de quinzaine, June 30, 1898 and May 15, 1899. The overwhelming majority of Rapports de quinzaine in the Isère archives for 1898-
99 contain no reference whatsoever to the Affair. Of more than 100 reports
still available in the Isère, only seventeen cite the Affair at all, and almost
half of these are from Grenoble; there was even less interest in the Vendée
(see ADV 4 M 25).

13. Cobb, *Police and the People*, p. 50.

14. Paul Stapfer, "Qu'est-ce que le public?," *La Grande revue*, June, 1899,
pp. 529-47.

15. *L'Univers israélite*, Jan. 7, 1898, pp. 485-89.

16. Following Charles Tilly, the term "reactive" indicates those responses
which were marked by personal rivalries, tyrannies, and feuds within a
specific locality; "proactive" demonstrations were organized and directed
toward national political goals; see Charles Tilly et al., *The Rebellious Century*
(Cambridge, Mass., 1975), pp. 50-55.

17. The phrase is Jean Paul Sartre's, quoted in André Decouflé, *La
Commune de Paris (1871), révolution populaire et pouvoir révolutionnaire* (Paris,
1969), p. 25.

18. Agulhon, *La République au village*, p. 267.

19. Robert Bezucha, "Masks of Revolution: A Study of Popular Culture
During the Second French Republic," in Roger Price, ed. *Revolution and
Reaction* (London, 1975), pp. 236-37.

20. Levaillant, "La Genèse de l'antisémitisme, p. XCIX.

21. Weber, *Peasants into Frenchmen*, pp. 377-78.

22. On ceremonies, rituals, and superstitions surrounding the *tirage au
sort*, see Van Gennep, *Manuel de folklore français*, t. 1, vol. 1, pp. 213ff.;
Raymond Rousseau, "Les Conscrits de la Belle époque," *Bulletin de la société
d'études folkloriques au centre-ouest*, t. 3, Aug.-Sept. 1968, pp. 104-105; Emile
Dave, *Le Tirage au sort* (Namur, 1934); Geneviève Massignon, "Coutumes
et chants de conscrits," *Revue du Bas-Poitu*, 1960, pp. 170-92; René Thie-
baut, "Le Numéro du tirage au sort," *Artisans et paysans de France*, 3, 1948,
pp. 157-64; for survival of ceremonies in the 1970s see Michel Bozon,

"Conscrits et fêtes de conscrits à Villefranche-sur-Saône," *Ethnologie française*, t. 9, 1, 1979, pp. 29-46: "The permanence and popularity of conscript demonstrations in certain regions indicates that they constitute above all secular rites of passage, profoundly linked to the life and sociability of the community" (p. 29).

23. *La Croix de l'Isère*, March 4, 1898.

24. Van Gennep, *Le Folklore du dauphiné* (Paris, 1932), vol. 1, pp. 246ff; and by the same author, "Le Cycle cérémonial du carnaval et du carême en Savoie," *Journal de psychologie*, 22, 5, May 15, 1925, pp. 430-31; Weber, *Peasants into Frenchmen*, p. 378; and "Brandon" in the *Dictionnaire historique de l'ancien langage français* (1877).

25. AN 156 AP 109, Sept. 6, 1889.

26. ADI 8 M 31, police report, Feb. 24, 1898; 8 M 32, police report, May 10, 1898; and *La Croix de l'Isère*, March 4, 1898.

27. Pierrard, *Juifs et catholiques*, p. 100.

28. On Maurennais priests, see Pierrard, *Juifs et catholiques*, p. 104; on the schoolteacher, see *La Croix de la Savoie*, Feb. 13, 1898; for a further description of the Saint Jean de Maurienne incident, see AN F7 12461, police report, Feb. 23, 1898; and Wilson, "Anti-Semitic Riots," p. 793.

29. Redfield, *Peasant Society and Culture*, p. 25.

30. ADM 49 M 56, *procès-verbal*, Feb. 28, 1898.

31. ADM 122 M 268, *liste nominative*, Pogny.

32. *Le Réveil de la Marne*, Feb. 17, 1898, *La Croix de Marne*, Feb. 23 and March 11, 1898.

33. Van Gennep, *Le Folklore du Dauphiné*, t. 1, pp. 270-71.

34. Ibid., p. 243; on Dauphiné "vogues," see Grise, *Coutumes du Trièves*, p. 27.

35. Natalie Zemon Davis, *Society and Culture in Early Modern France* (Stanford, 1975), p. 159.

36. AN F7 12467, "Chanson des youpins," *L'Anti-Juif*, March 5, 1899. In a pamphlet signed "Marthe," Zola is depicted as a "filthy corrupter," and the author believes that France should turn to her heroine, Joan of Arc, for "purification"; see *Protestation des femmes françaises . . . contre soulèvements Zola-Dreyfus* (Paris, 1898), pp. 3-5; see also Fore-Fauré, *Face aux juifs!: Essai de psychologie sociale et contemporaine* (Paris, 1891), pp. 21-22.

37. Van Gennep, *Manuel de folklore français*, t. 1, vol. 3, pp. 950, 994.

38. See Louis Sebastien Mercier's utopian novel *L'An 2440* (Paris, 1770); for exorcistic ceremonies during the Commune, see Michel Winock and Jean-Pierre Azéma, *Les Communards* (Paris, 1970), pp. 123-24, and Decouflé, pp. 58-59. On January 18, 1898, students burned a Dreyfus mannequin in the streets of Rennes; they were sending a symbolic message to detested university faculty members who were Dreyfusards (AN F7 12460). To this day effigies are incinerated in urban demonstrations and village fêtes, but, again, they have lost their original significance. For a Champagne village

in 1965, see G. Railliet, "Incineration de mannequins," *Bulletin du comité du folklore champenois*, 90-92, 1968.

39. See below, note 81.

40. AN F7 12467, police report, Montmorillon, Jan. 21, 1898.

41. For "Departure masses" in the Dolomieu, Montcarra, and Le Passage communes of the Isère, see *La Croix de l'Isère*, Nov. 9-10, 1897; for similar ceremonies in the Vendée, see ADV 4 M 170, police report, Nov. 12, 1897.

42. *La Croix de l'Isère*, Nov. 10, 1897.

43. ADI 51 M 26, Jan. 26, 1898; see also *Le Moniteur de Bourgoin*, Feb. 5, 1898, "Tirage au sort."

44. *La Croix de la Savoie*, Feb. 6, 1898; *La Croix Vendéenne*, Jan. 30, 1898.

45. *La Croix du Gers*, Feb. 6, 1898: On Jan. 30 the paper had run a small illustration of a young conscript drawing his number in front of a panel of three men, one a caricature of a Jew. The caption read: "J'ai le numéro 22 M. le souspréfect." The Jewish director responds: "Pon bour drois ans de serfice; Fife la Vrance!" And the conscript says to himself: "Ben, il parle comme un youpin, not' souspréfect."

46. *Le Réveil de la Marne*, Jan. 31, 1898. Stephen Wilson mentions the importance of conscripts in many anti-Semitic demonstrations, but does not elaborate ("Anti-Semitic Riots," p. 792).

47. ADV 4 M 2, police reports, Jan. 24, 28, 1898.

48. AN F712448, *procès-verbal*, Jan. 23, 1889.

49. ADM 5 Z 42, prefect letter, Feb. 21, 1893.

50. See above, Intro., n. 29.

51. Dave, *Tirage au sort*, pp. 5-6.

52. Van Gennep, *Manuel du folklore français*, t. 1, vol. 1, p. 216.

53. Rousseau, "Les Conscrits de la Belle époque," pp. 103-104.

54. Gwynn Lewis in Douglas Johnson, ed., *French Society and the Revolution* (Cambridge, 1976).

55. P. Joutaud, *La Légende des Camisards* (Paris, 1977), p. 314.

56. On Feb. 2, 1898, *Le Réveil du dauphiné* described the Mens *tirage*; it was a lively event with much patriotic speechmaking, but no reported references to the Dreyfus Affair.

57. *La Démocratie rurale*, Jan. 23, 1898.

58. Anatole France, *The Amethyst's Ring*, trans., B. Brillien (London, 1924), p. 252.

59. Mosse, *Toward the Final Solution*, p. 146.

60. AN F7 12463, especially police report, Morteau, Nov. 10, 1898.

61. Guy Chapman, *The Dreyfus Trials* (London, 1972), pp. 127-28; see also AN F7 12549, note dated Nov. 3, 1898; and ADI 51 M 25, poster hung in Grenoble on Feb. 17, 1899.

62. AN F7 12463, police report, Laval, Sept. 17, 1898.

63. Wilson, "Anti-Semitic Riots," p. 802; see also AN F7 12463, Vesoul (Haute-Sâone) police, Nov. 18, 1898.

64. On Pressensé speeches in Toulouse, Marseille, and Montpellier, see

AN F7 12465, Nov. 30, 1898; on Jaurès in Grenoble, see AN F7 12466, May 12, 1899; and on Zévaès in Grenoble, see ADI 51 M 25, Feb. 1899 report.

65. ADI 51 M 25, police report, Grenoble, May 20, 1899.

66. Agulhon in *European Studies Review*, Vol. II, 1981, p. 559.

67. Carles, *Une Soupe*, pp. 20, 29, 184.

68. Arendt, *Origins*, p. 25.

69. Quoted in Sorlin, '*La Croix' et les juifs*, p. 101.

70. Raymond Lacan, *Histoire des juifs: Leurs trahisons de Judas à Dreyfus* (Paris, 1898).

71. *La Croix du Gers*, June 5, 1898; see Wilson, *Ideology and Experience*, p. 735 on the persistant influence of local notables in the Southwest.

72. *La Croix de l'Isère*, Nov. 5, 1897.

73. Ibid., March 20, 1898, "L'Agriculture et l'impôt."

74. M. Kergall's *La Démocratie rurale* and the Catholic *Chronique de su-dest* echoed *La Croix*'s theme of equating high taxes and agricultural ruin with Jewish influence. For more on *La Démocratie rurale*, see Zeldin, *France: 1848-1945*, vol. 1, p. 176.

75. Dupeux, *Histoire sociale et politque*, p. 497.

76. Wilson, "Anti-Semitic Riots," p. 275.

77. Barral, *Les Agrariens français*, p. 156.

78. Lazare, *Anti-Semitism: Its History and Causes*, p. 208.

79. Mosse, *Toward the Final Solution*, pp. 166-67.

80. Levaillant, "La Genèse de l'antisémitisme," p. LXXXVIII.

81. On rural perceptions of, and reactions to, Méline's protectionist policies, see Eugene Owen Golob, *Méline* (New York, 1944), p. 244, and Mendras, *The Vanishing Peasant*, p. 281. On the growth of rural syndicates see Barral, *Les Agrariens*, p. 108 for the Union du sud-est, and Golob, *Méline*, p. 93 for the increasing strength of syndicates in the Southwest; see also Edouard Cohen, *La Politique agricole: Appel aux électeurs* (Paris, 1898), p. 13. All these sources stress the continuing democratization of agricultural syndicates at the close of the nineteenth century, but add that real progress comes after 1900. On technological improvements see Charles Talon, "Migrations et moissoneurs à la faux en Bas Dauphiné 1890-1914," *Evocations*, 3, 1964, pp. 79-83; A. Collard, *La Main d'oeuvre et l'outillage agricole dans le département de la Marne* (Vitry le Francois, 1894); *Statistique agricole de la France* (1897), pp. 254-57; and Guillaumin, *Panorama de l'évolution paysanne* on the dawn of the twentieth century as an important moment of *machinisme* (especially, pp. 30-1). Reapers, binders, and steam-powered machines appear in many rural communes circa 1900, but are generalized after 1918. The relation between the increased use of farm machinery and the drop in the number of laborers is, of course, crucial (see Golob, *Méline*, p. 67). But for those peasants who stayed on the land the 1890s was an improvement over the previous decade; see Edmond Doutté, *Situation agricole du département de la Marne en 1892* (Châlons-sur-

Marne, 1893), p. 44; *Statistique agricole*, p. 413 on relief after 1895; and Augé-Laribé, *L'Evolution de la France agricole*, p. 20. For a personal view of all this, see Thabault, *Education and Change*, p. 186: a new religion of "Progress" became "deeply rooted" in Mazières-en-Gâtine.

82. Pierre Barral, "Agrarisme de gauche, agrarisme de droite sous la Troisième République" in *L'Univers politique paysan*, p. 250; and *Statistique agricole*, 1897, p. 413.

83. *Le Réveil du dauphiné*, Nov. 2, 1897; and *L'Avenir républicain* (Gers), Feb. 2, 1898. On the political impact of protection, see François Goguel-Nyegaard, *La Politique des partis sous la IIIe République* (Paris, 1958), p. 76.

84. Eugen Weber, "Jews, Anti-Semitism, and the Origins of the Holocaust," *Historical Reflections*, 5, 1, Summer 1978, p. 7; Tony Judt adds that for Socialists "International Jewry" was "a depressingly common target of a certain tendancy on the European left in this period" (*Socialism in Provence*, p. 183).

85. On Zévaès meeting, see ADI 51 M 25, Grenoble report, Feb. 16, 1899; on socialists and anti-Semitism, see APP Ba 411, Jan. 23, 1890 note on a Paris meeting with anti-Semitic references.

86. See Gratton, *Les Luttes de classe*, p. 57 and *passim*; and Judt, *Socialism in Provence*, passim.

87. See the reprint from *Revue socialiste* entitled "Lettre aux paysans" (1896) by Georges Renard; and *La Lanterne*, Dec. 10, 1899 on the Socialist Congress and "le prolétariat agricole."

88. See note 77 above. For more on socialists, anti-Semitism and the Affair, see Wilson, *Ideology and Experience*: In mid-1898 Jean Jaurès could still say that ". . . the Jewish race, concentrated and clever, always devoured by the drive to make a profit, manipulates the capitalist system with great skill" (pp. 66-68). But Jaurès would rally to Dreyfus, a victim of the bourgeois state, and more important for our purposes, socialists would concentrate on other issues in the countryside.

89. Siegfried, *Tableau politique*, p. 391.

90. Wilson, *Ideology and Experience*, pp. 692-730; see also Byrnes, *Anti-Semitism in Modern France*, p. 96; and Sternhell, *La Droite révolutionnaire*, p. 224.

91. Weber, *Peasants into Frenchmen*, p. 357.

92. During the Second World War Protestant inhabitants in the nearby Haute-Loire sheltered Jews fleeing Fascist tyranny. These villagers, descendants of Camisards, were remaining true to a long, heroic tradition; see Philip Hallie, *Lest Innocent Blood Be Shed* (New York, 1979); and Michael Marrus and Robert Paxton, *Vichy France and the Jews* (New York, 1981).

93. Dupeux, *Histoire sociale et politique*, pp. 618, 540-41; Margadant, *French Peasants in Revolt, passim*.

94. Bruno Bettelheim and Morris Janowitz, *Social Change and Prejudice* (New York, 1964), p. 165.

95. Hoffman, *More Than a Trial*, p. 199; for rural anti-Semitism in central

Europe at this time, see Mosse, *Toward the Final Solution*, pp. 166-67; and Arendt, *Origins*, p. 38.

96. AN F7 12466, Oct. 2, 1898; for more reports on indifference, see above, note 12.

97. Marcel Proust, *Jean Santeuil*, trans. G. Hopkins (New York, 1956), pp. 354, 320.

98. Julie Manet quoted in Arthur Gold and Robert Fizdale, *Misia: The Life of Misia Sert* (New York, 1980), p. 81.

99. Like Proust and Renoir, Sigmund Freud was fascinated by the Affair: "Zola keeps us breathless," he wrote Wilhelm Fliess in February 1898, "The disgusting behavior of the French reminded me of what you said . . . about the degeneracy of France, which at first I could not believe!"; *The Origins of Psychoanalysis: Letters to Wilhelm Fliess, 1877-1902* (New York, 1954), p. 245.

100. Mina Curtiss, ed., *Letters of Marcel Proust* (New York, 1966), p. 51.

CONCLUSION

1. Tilly in Merriman, ed., *Consciousness and Class*, p. 37; Weber, *Peasants into Frenchmen, passim*; and Margadant, *French Peasants in Revolt*, p. 57.

2. Fernand Braudel, *On History*, trans. Sarah Matthews (Chicago, 1980), p. 34.

3. E. P. Thompson in Ralph Miliband and John Saville, eds., *The Socialist Register* (London, 1965).

4. David M. Potter, *The Impending Crisis, 1848-1861* (New York, 1976), p. 333.

5. Peter Stansky, *Gladstone: A Progress in Politics* (Boston, 1979), p. 25.

6. AN C 565, proposition 2974, Feb. 12, 1902; for more on this, see Hutton, "Popular Boulangism," pp. 85-106.

7. Geoffrey Barraclough, *An Introduction to Contemporary History* (Harmondsworth, 1967).

8. Gratton, *Les Luttes de classe*, p. 64.

9. *Indépendant Normand*, Aug. 4, 1889.

10. See "On the Jewish Question" in *Karl Marx: Early Writings*, trans. T. B. Bottomore (New York, 1964).

11. Stanley Hoffmann et al., eds., *In Search of France* (New York, 1965), p. 7.

12. Maurice Barrès, *Les Déracinés*, vol. 1 (Paris, 1922), p. 9.

13. Zeldin, *France: 1848-1945*, vol. 1, p. 171. For more on the constrasts, real or imagined, between urban and rural anxieties during this period, see Peter Gay in Merriman, ed., *Consciousness and Class*, pp. 189-90.

14. Thabault, *Education and Change*, pp. 176-79. See also Weber, *Peasants into Frenchmen*: ". . . optimism, hope, and sense of progress so evident among the masses" (p. 478).

15. Brunet, *Campagnes toulousaines*, p. 398; see also Hohenberg, "Change in Rural France," p. 239.

16. *Le Petit Journal*, Jan. 1, 1888.

17. See above, Intro., n. 23.

18. Interview from *Le Figaro* quoted in Guy Chapman, *The Dreyfus Case* (London, 1972), p. 219.

19. Engels quoted in an excellent and timely article by Philip Abrams, "History, Sociology, Historical Sociology," *Past and Present*, 87, May 1980, pp. 3-16.

20. Richard Cobb, *Reactions to the French Revolution* (London, 1972).

21. William Sewell, Jr., *Work and Revolution in France: The Language of Labor from the Old Regime to 1848* (New York, 1980).

22. APP Ba 411, note dated Jan. 12, 1888.

23. E. P. Thompson, " 'Rough Music': Le Charivari anglais," *Annales: Economies, sociétés, civilisations*, 27, 2, March-April, 1972, p. 309 (Thompson's emphasis).

24. Ibid., p. 308.

25. See Brunet, *Campagnes toulousaines*, pp. 401, 197; Wismes, *Histoire de la Vendée*, pp. 258-59; for a survey, Duby et al., eds., *Histoire de la France rurale*, vols. 3 and 4.

26. George W. Grantham in Parker and Jones, eds., *European Peasants*, pp. 293-326.

BIBLIOGRAPHY

BIBLIOGRAPHY

I. ARCHIVES AND LIBRARIES

Students of Third Republic France who have worked in the Archives Nationales are aware of the paucity of material dealing with politics and public spirit in the three decades preceding the First World War. Despite the lacunae, however, the F7 series has some useful information on Boulangism and the Dreyfus Affair in the countryside, and offers a good, if random, selection of miscellaneous images, posters, songsheets, and photos. The C series contains invaluable testimonies by country people on electoral fraud in rural communities, and the Archives Privées at the AN hold the rich and abundant private papers of Baron Mackau, one of Boulanger's most influential supporters in the provinces. For more police reports (many anonymous) on Boulangist organizations and Dreyfus-related demonstrations in Paris and the provinces, the Ba series in the Archives de la préfecture de police, Paris, is an excellent source.

Most of the archival material for this study comes from the M series of the departmental archives of the Isère, Marne, Gers, Orne, and, to a lesser degree, the Vendée and Savoie. The Isère, with one of the most thorough and well-organized collections in provincial France, is now in the process of transferring municipal and communal records to its Grenoble headquarters. Additional material on local politics may be found in the "Fonds dauphinois" at the Bibliothèque municipale de la ville de Grenoble. The Marne archives—a smaller installation than the Isère—has good political and demographic data, and its Z series on subprefectures is a fine source for the historian interested in outlying regions of the department. The departmental archives of the Gers, housed in a picturesque monastery in the old quarter of Auch, offers an interesting but uneven collection: one may find a carton with excellent police reports, then be unable to locate general statistics on legislative elections. I am sure, however, that under the guidance of its director, M. Lemée, it will soon provide scholars with a superb and as yet relatively untapped source. The Orne has some instructive material on Boulangism in its M series, as well as a number of regional journals and periodicals which cover rural politics in the department. In La Roche-sur-Yon, the Vendée archives are complemented by rich newspaper holdings in the nearby municipal library. The Savoie, of course, became part of France—and fair game for its meticulous archivists—only after 1860. Students of the 1880s and 90s, however, will find good police and prefectoral reports on politics and public spirit in that majestic region.

Back in Paris, the Cabinet des estampes at the Bibliothèque Nationale holds a fine assortment of lithographs, photos, and illustrated publications on Boulangism and the Dreyfus Affair; the Manuscript room contains Boulanger's correspondence with his friend and political ally, Alfred Naquet—essential reading for those who wish to go beyond the movement to the man. Material in the Musée Carnavalet deals almost exclusively with Paris, of course, but its Boulanger "Dossier" has rare examples of popular imagery, including anonymous (though, alas, uninspired) anti-Boulangist pornography. The library at the Musée national des arts et traditions populaires is an excellent source for books and provincial pamphlets and periodicals on folklore and ethnography; and its archives and iconothèque are superb repositories of popular imagery. Historians working on almost any aspect of rural France are advised to spend a good deal of time at this friendly and well-equipped center.

Below is an annotated list of materials consulted at archives and libraries in Paris, Grenoble, Châlons-sur-Marne, Auch, Alençon, La Roche-sur-Yon, and Chambéry.

A. Archives Nationales, Paris

SERIES AP (156 AP I: Baron Mackau)
156 AP I 102-10, Boulangism
156 AP I 111-12, 131-32: Orne elections

SERIES C
5469-70: 1889 election enquête, Vosges and Corrèze; and propositions for electoral reform
5510: elections, 1889
5571-72: 1893 election enquête, Ardèche and Corrèze
5573: 1897 by-election enquête, Finistère
5650-52: propositions de loi, electoral reforms, Chamber of Deputies, 1898-1902

SERIES F7
12315-8: Unauthorized assemblies in the Gers, Isère, and Marne, 1880-1900
12445-8: Boulangist propaganda and imagery
12449-50: League of Patriots in provincial France, 1893-97
12459-60: Anti-Semitism and related meetings in provincial France, 1898
12463-5: Dreyfus Affair: anti-Semitism, posters, images
12466-7: Dreyfus Affair, 1898 meetings
12468-9: Dreyfus Affair: 1901-1903
12506: Anarchism, 1890s
12885: Socialism, 1894-1900
12923: Dreyfus Affair: camelots

B. *Archives de la préfecture de police, Paris*

SERIES Ba
> 119: 1889 Exposition, delegates from the provinces
> 190, 193: The Panama Affair
> 411: The "political situation" in France, 1880s-90s
> 497: Boulangism
> 626-28, 640: 1889 Legislative elections
> 648: 1893 Legislative elections
> 906: Count Dillon
> 970-1, 975, 977: General Boulanger
> 1042, 1049: Dreyfus Affair: newspaper articles
> 1052: Dreyfus Affair: political demonstrations; Rennes trial
> 1447: 1889 elections, Boulangism
> 1475-77: Socialism in the provinces

C. *Bibliothèque Nationale, Paris*

MANUSCRITS
> N.A.F. 23783: Boulanger-Naquet Correspondance, 1887-1890

CABINET DES ESTAMPES
> N 2-3: Boulanger; Dreyfus
> Qb 1: "History of France," 1888-89, 1898
> $\dfrac{\text{Qe 89}}{\text{fol}}$: Dreyfus Affair
> $\dfrac{\text{Qe 368, 441-42}}{40}$: Dreyfus Affair

D. *Musée Carnavalet, Paris*

Dossier "Boulanger"

E. *Musée national des arts et traditions populaires, Paris*

Library, archives, and *iconothèque* for popular imagery catalogued by location of manufacture, as well as by province and department

F. *Archives départementales*

ISÈRE
> 4E 1 F, 4E 1 K1: Venosc commune; electoral lists
> 8 M 24-27: Legislative elections, 1887-89
> 8 M 31-32: Legislative elections 1898
> 10 M 18: Cantonal elections, 1886-88
> 10 M 22, 12 M 14: Elections by arrondisement, 1898
> 15 M 18, 27-8: Mayors, general information, 1882-1919

16 M 167-8, 172-3, 203, 206: Municipal council elections, 1888-89

51 M 25: Boulangism

51 M 26: Dreyfus Affair

52 M 57-60: General police information; political affairs; correspondence; posters, 1880-1900

52 M 66: Press, 1892-1906

52 M 69: Trade union propaganda, posters, 1896-1922

53 M 17-18: Police reports, 1886-99

54 M 32: July 14 Festivities, 1880-1900

55 M 1-2: Police reports, 1850-1908

55 M 1, 4: Police administration; local fêtes, 1864-1898

123 M 39-40, 48, 50, 53, 58; Census lists by commune, 1896

137 M 23, 28-30: Agricultural statistics by commune, 1888, 1892

139 M 2-3: Miscellaneous agricultural information, 1897-1905

141 M 3, 5: Agricultural fairs, markets

142 M 1: Agricultural syndicates and associations

1 O 2-3, 6 O 1-2: *Gardes-champêtres*

9 T 39, 77: Press, *colportage*

9 U: Miscellaneous police reports, Corps canton, 1888, 1898

Subseries J: 1 J 357, 710, 1027, 1091, 1140: Miscellaneous letters

Newspapers and periodicals:
La Croix de l'Isère
Droit du peuple
Journal de Gresivaudan
Moniteur de Bourgoin
Petit Dauphinois
Petit Grenoblois
Réveil agricole des alpes
Réveil du dauphiné
Le Semaine religieuse du diocèse de Grenoble

Bibliothèque municipale de la ville de Grenoble (Isère):
Fonds dauphinois, III:

17003-4, 17006: Isère agricultural syndicates, 1800s-90s

17273, 17277, 17279, 17297: Rural almanachs, 1883-1900

18383-86: Legislative elections, 1888-1902. See especially subheading V. 5504 for posters, ballots, and miscellaneous documents concerning the 1888 by-election

18390: Legislative elections, 1889

18400: Legislative elections, 1898

MARNE

7 M 58-61: Legislative elections, correspondence, 1888-89, 1893, 1898

13 M 4-6, 10, 12: Municipal elections, protests, by commune

30 M 41-2: Boulangist meetings and propaganda, 1889-91

30 M 56: Public meetings, 1864-1907

30 M 3-4: July 14 festivities 1888-1898

43 M 60-2, 67: *Gardes-champêtres*, 1888-90, 1896-1905
47 M 33, 44, 49, 52: Police reports
49 M 53, 56: Police reports, 1888-89, 1898-99.
77 M 21-3: *Colportage*, 1882-1906
122 M 231, 242, 249, 255-6, 265-6, 268: *listes nominatives* by commune, 1891
138 M 9: Agricultural associations; *procès verbaux*
140 M 2: Agricultural syndicates, 1885-99
142 M 1: Agricultural labor
146 M 167-170: Agricultural statistics, 1892

Series Z (Subprefectures):
Epernay:
2 Z 73: Legislative elections, police reports, 1885-1910
2 Z 157: Public meetings, police reports, 1895-1932
2 Z 319: Harvest information, 1884-90
2 Z 731: *Colportage* 1881-1940
Sainte Menehould:
4 Z 56: Political affairs, Boulangism, 1860-1905
Vitry le François:
5 Z 30: Police personnel, *gardes-champêtres*, 1898-1918
5 Z 42: Police reports, politics, XIII-1929
5 Z 45: Dreyfus Affair 1897-98
5 Z 46: Strikes, 1890-1936
5 Z 498: Religion, XII-1914

Newspapers:
La Croix de la Marne et de la Champagne
La Croix de Vitry
Indépendent de la Marne et de la Moselle
Républicain de Vitry le François
Réveil national de la Marne

GERS
M 107: July 14 festivities, 1884-5
117: Subprefectoral notes, 1811-1913
137: Public opinion, posters, press, political meetings, 1883-86
1194, 1202: Municipal personnel, correspondence, 1888-95
1227: Reports on political activities of priests, 1880-81
1828: Police investigations and arrests, 1893-95
1834: General police information, 1884-88
1865: Public spirit, miscellaneous correspondence, 1849-1938
1888: Political affairs, newspapers, 1884-1919
2088: Miscellaneous police information
2799: Police reports, public spirit, crimes, 1884-90
4184: Elections results, municipalities, 1892-1947
4855, 4863-5, 4874: *listes nominatives* by canton and commune, 1886

Newspapers:
Appel au peuple
Avenir républicain
Conservateur
La Croix du Gers
République des paysans
République des travailleurs

ORNE

M 414: Legislative elections, 1889
M 1228: Police reports, Boulangism
M 1268: Fêtes, 1892-1908
M 1590-1692: *Listes nominatives* by commune
17 V 2: Religion

Newspapers and periodicals:
Annuaire du département de l'Orne (1898)
L'Avenir de l'Orne de la Mayenne
Le Bonhomme Normand
La Croix de l'Orne
L'Eclaireur de l'Orne
La Semaine catholique du diocèse de Seez

VENDÉE

1 M 375: Prefect reports, 1889-90
1 M 442-44: Politics, 1886-1901
1 M 528: *Fête nationale*
4 M 11-12: *Gardes-champêtres*, 1880-1918
4 M 14-15: *Gardes-particuliers*; politics; 1891-1904
4 M 25, 27: Police reports, 1873-1899
4 M 163: Rural priests, 1880-1905
4 M 167, 170: Religion, 1894-1913
4 M 175-76, 179, 182-83: Politics, 1893-1915
4 M 404: Politics; Boulangism
6 M: *Listes nominatives* by commune

Newspapers:
L'Avenir et l'indicateur de la Vendée
La Croix Vendéenne
L'Etoile de la Vendée
Le Révisionniste de la Vendée

SAVOIE

9 M II 7-8: Police and politics, 1860-88
9 M II 22: Press, 1892-1904
9 M III 8, 21: Police investigations
9 M III 23: *Colporteurs*
9 M V 5: July 14 festivities, 1880-92

M 85: *Procès-verbâux*, 1885-1903
M 342: Legislative elections, 1889

Newspapers:
La Croix de la Savoie
Courrier des alpes

G. Other newspapers, periodicals, annuals, statistical reports:

Annuaire de la Marne, 1888, 1898
Annuaire de la presse française, 1890, 1897
Annuaire du Gers, 1888, 1898
Annuaire officiel du département de l'Isère, 1888, 1898
Annuaire statistique de la France, 1898
Archives israélites
Bulletin de la société des agriculteurs de France
Chronique du sud-est
La Cocarde
La Croix (Paris)
Le Démocratie rurale
L'Intransigeant
La Libre parole
La Presse
Le Petit Journal
Le Pilori
Résultats statistiques du recensement de la population, 1891
Statistique agricole de la France, 1892
L'Univers israélite
Les Veillées des chaumières

II. Selected Primary and Secondary Material

A study which examines peasant political culture and the impact of two events as familiar as Boulangism and the Dreyfus Affair cannot hope to include a complete list of primary and secondary materials. Presented below, therefore, are only those titles I have found most helpful.

In recent years more and more French peasants have followed Emile Guillaumin's example (*La Vie d'un simple*, 1904, now available in translation, *The Life of a Simple Man*, [Univ. of New England Press, 1983]) and have recorded their recollections of rural life; especially instructive are works by Emilie Carles, E. Grenadou, Pierre Hélias, and Serge Grafteaux on Mémé Santerre; as well as Daniel Halévy's famous 1921 account of his visit to the peasants of the Centre. Roger Thabault was not a peasant, but his superb study of his Deux-Sévres village is invaluable and it helped inspire Eugen Weber to write *Peasants into Frenchmen*, the richest, most provocative analysis of the late nineteenth-century rural world available in English or

French (trans., *La Fin des terroirs* [Paris, 1983]). For more on rural customs and folklore, see the many volumes by Arnold Van Gennep (especially on the Dauphiné and Savoie) and Paul Sébillot. Among eye-witness accounts those by Camille Besse, Joseph Blanc and Raymond Belbèze reveal much about peasants, priests, and rural neurasthenics.

Economic issues in the countryside are covered by contemporary observers Michel Augé-Laribé, Auguste Souchon, and Emile Vandervelde, and in the classic though very different works of Karl Kautsky and Jules Méline. More recently, André Armengaud, Pierre Barral, Raoul Blanchard, Roger Brunet, Gabriel Désert, Paul Hohenberg, Claude Karnoouh and Henri Mendras have contributed a number of significant studies on the economics, culture, and politics of rural societies. For an excellent survey of French rural history, see the four volumes of *Histoire de la France rurale*, edited by Georges Duby et al.

An analysis of politics in the countryside must start with André Siegfried's classic *Tableau politique de la France de l'ouest sous la Troisième République*. His most notable recent followers, whose works have been important to this study, are Philippe Vigier and Barral on the Isère, Guy Palmade and Louis Ducamp on the Gers, and Brunet and Armengaud on the Southwest region. On Normandy, Désert and G. Bourdin should be consulted. Unfortunately, there is no thorough recent account of early Third Republic rural politics and culture in the Marne or Vendée. The most outstanding studies of nineteenth-century rural politics have focused on 1848-51. The work of Maurcie Agulhon, Charles Tilly, John Merriman, Peter McPhee and Ted Margadant's superb account of the insurrection, *French Peasants in Revolt*, have been most helpful and thought-provoking. Important recent works on late nineteenth-century rural politics include those by Tony Judt, J. Harvey Smith, and Weber. In addition, the novels of Balzac, Zola, and de Vogüé provide instructive literary (urban) views of rural life, and, used carefully, offer rich and entertaining peasant portraits.

The most thorough study of Boulangism was written in 1959 but never published: Jacques Néré's two-part account examines the industrial crisis of the 1880s throughout France, then focuses on Boulangism in the Nord. It is essential reading for any student of the Boulangist movement. Adrien Dansette's *Le Boulangisme* and Frederick Seager's *The Boulanger Affair* are good studies, and Patrick Hutton's articles on the Boulangist years are outstanding, as is his recent book on the Blanquists. The General's own memoirs shed interesting light on campaign strategy; among his contemporaries, the insights of Charles Chincholle and Lt. Col. Villot are useful though biased. After 1890, Boulanger's monarchist connections were exposed by a former associate in *Les Coulisses du boulangisme*. Alexandre Zévaès, a socialist deputy from the Isère, gives us another biased but well-informed view in *Au Temps du boulangisme*. The movement also provided material for two important novels of the period: Maurice Barrès's *Appel au soldat* and Paul Adam's *Le Mystère des foules*.

Works on propaganda and popular imagery I have found most helpful include Champfleury's classic *Histoire de l'imagerie populaire* and more recent studies by Jean Mistler, Geneviève Bollème and Denise Lantiez. M. Millot's *La Comédie boulangiste* contains scores of popular Boulangist songs, Grand-Carteret's works examine imagery during both the Boulangist and Dreyfus epochs, and Gustave Le Bon provides some telling, if tendentious, information on the hypnotic effect Boulangist propaganda had on impressionable crowds.

The famous contemporary analysis of the Dreyfus Affair is the seven-volume work by Joseph Reinach. For Captain Dreyfus's own thoughts, see his *Cinq années de ma vie* and *Souvenirs et correspondance*. Zola's *La Verité en marche* and works by Paul Marin and E. Villaine also deal with popular aspects of the Affair, though none bothers with rural reactions. Michel Colline's *Affaire Dreyfus: Billets de la province* is a thin account with only a few insights on the Affair outside Paris. The best recent works are by Marcel Thomas, Douglas Johnson, Pierre Paraf and, above all, Jean Denis Bredin's excellent synthesis, *L'Affaire* (1983). Stephen Wilson's many articles on the Affair are superb.

For this study, the most helpful secondary works on French anti-Semitism during the Affair include those by Robert Byrnes, Michael Marrus, Pierre Pierrard, Léon Poliakov, Pierre Sorlin, and especially Stephen Wilson's recent *Ideology and Experience: Antisemitism in France at the Time of the Dreyfus Affair*, a learned and thorough social history. For accounts by those who lived through the Affair and often fueled the controversy, see Bernard Lazare, Emile Zola, Alfred Dreyfus's letters, Mathieu Dreyfus's memoirs, J. Levaillant's article on anti-Semitism, and those scores of vicious tracts which helped set the stage for the Affair: for example, Fore-Fauré's *Face aux juifs!* and Edouard Drumont's *La France juive*, an enormously influential work by the most successful popularizer of late nineteenth-century anti-Semitism.

Selected Primary Material:

Adam, Paul. *Le Mystère des foules*. Paris: P. Ollendorff, 1895.

Almanach Boulanger. Paris: Marot, 1888.

Almanach de la France rurale et des syndicats agricoles. 1888.

Almanach des familles. 1887.

Anon., *Trois ans de conspiration, 1886-1889*. Paris, 1890.

Ardouin-Dumazet, Victor-Eugène. *Voyage en France: Les alpes*. Paris, 1910.

————. *Voyage en France: Normandie*. Nancy: Berger-Lerault, 1921.

Bader, Clarisse. *Enseignement social: Nos paysans, les vétérans du travail agricole*. Paris: X. Rondelet, 1899.

Balzac, Honoré de. *The Country Doctor*, trans. Ellen Marriage. Philadelphia: The Gebbie Pub. Co., 1898.

————. *Les Paysans: Scènes de la vie de campagne.* Paris: Calmann-Levy, n.d.

Barrès, Maurice. *L'Appel au soldat.* Paris: Plon-Nourrit, 1926.

Bazin, René. *La Terre qui meurt.* Paris: C. Levy, 1899.

Belbèze, Raymond. *La Neurasthénie rurale.* Paris: Vigot, 1911.

Besse, Camille. *Le Curé, l'instituteur, et le paysan.* Tulle: Librarie d'études provinciales, 1912.

Bladé, Jean François. *Contes populaires de la Gascogne.* Paris: Maisonneuve frères et C. Leclerc, 1886.

Blanc, Joseph. *Notes d'un curé de campagne.* n.p.: (?), 1911.

Blum, Léon. *Souvenirs sur l'affaire.* Paris: Gallimard, 1935.

Boulanger, Georges. *Mémoires du général Boulanger.* n.p.: G. Edinger, 1890.

————. *L'Invasion Allemande.* Paris: J. Rouff, 1888.

Champfleury. *Histoire de l'imagerie populaire.* Paris: E. Dentu, 1886.

Chincholle, Charles. *Le Général Boulanger.* Paris: A. Savine, 1889.

Cohen, Edouard. *La Politique agricole: Appel aux électeurs ruraux.* Paris: Guillaumin, 1898.

Collard, Albert. *La Main d'oeuvre et l'outillage agricole dans le département de la Marne.* Vitry le François: J. Denis, 1894.

Colline, Michel. *Affaire Dreyfus: Billets de la province.* Paris: P. V. Stock, 1898.

Compère-Morel. *La Verité aux paysans par un campagnard.* Paris: Librairie de la "Revue Socialiste," 1897.

Doutté, Edmond. *Situation agricole du département de la Marne en 1892.* Châlons-sur Marne: Imprimerie de l'Union Républicaine, 1893.

Dreyfus, Alfred. *Cinq années de ma vie, 1894-1899.* Paris: François Maspero, 1982.

————. *Souvenirs et correspondance publiés par son fils.* Paris: Grasset, 1936.

"The Dreyfus Case: A Study of French Opinion," *Contemporary Review.* 74, October, 1898.

Dreyfus, Mathieu. *L'Affaire telle que je l'ai vécue.* Paris: Grasset, 1978.

Drumont, Edouard. *La France juive.* 2 vols. Paris: C. Marpon & F. Flammarion, 1886.

————. *La France juive,* Illustrated edition. Paris: C. Marpon & F. Flammarion, 1887.

————. *La France juive devant l'opinion.* Paris: C. Marpon & F. Flammarion, 1886.

Dumont, Arsène. "Note sur la démographie de l'Orne," *Revue Normande et Percheronne,* 1897, pp. 337-348.

Engels, Friedrich. "La Question paysanne en France et en Allemagne," *Mouvement socialiste.* November 15 and December 1, 1901.

Engels, Friedrich, and Lafargue, Paul. *Correspondence.* vol. 2, 1887-1900 London: 1960.

Fore-Fauré. *Face aux juifs!: Essai de psychologie sociale et contemporaine.* Paris: A. Savine, 1891.

Fournière, Eugène. "Physiognomie du boulangisme," *Société nouvelle*, Brussels, 1888, 4, 1, pp. 420-36.

Frary, Raoul. "Chronique politique," *La Nouvelle revue*, 54, September 15, 1888.

Garnier, J. M. *Histoire de l'imagerie populaire et des cartes à jouer à Chartres.* Chartres: Garnier, 1869.

Grand, Antoine. *Une Promenade en Dauphiné.* Lyon: Mougin-Rusand, 1896.

Grand-Carteret, John. *L'Affaire Dreyfus et l'image.* Paris: E. Flammarion, 1898.

————. "Boulangisme," *Revue encyclopédique: Scènes morales et politiques.* n.d.: 1891?.

Granoux, Xavier. "L'Affaire Dreyfus": *Catalogue déscriptif des cartes postales illustrées.* Paris: H. Daragon, 1903.

Guillaumin, Emile. *La Vie d'un simple.* Paris: P. V. Stock, 1904.

Jupilles, Fernand de. *Le Général Boulanger, histoire populaire.* Paris, L. Baudot, 1887.

Kautsky, Karl. *La Question agraire.* Paris: V. Giard, 1900.

Labat, Emmanuel. "En Gascogne," *Revue des deux mondes*, August, 1910, pp. 639-45.

Lacan, Raymond. *Histoire des juifs: Leurs trahisons de Judas à Dreyfus.* Paris: A. Pierret, 1898.

Lazare, Bernard. *L'Antisémitisme, son histoire et ses causes.* Paris: L. Chailley, 1894.

Le Bon, Gustave. *Psychologie des foules.* Paris: F. Alcan, 1895.

Le Roy, Eugène. *Jacquou le Croquant.* Paris: Calmann-Levy, 1899.

Letizia de Rute, Marie. "Les Femmes dans l'affaire Drefus," *Nouvelle revue internationale*, October, 1899, pp. 401-413.

Levaillant, J. "La Genèse de l'antisémitisme sous la Troisième République," *Revue des études juives*, 1907.

Liber, Jacques. *Enseignements de l'affaire Dreyfus.* Poligny: A. Jacquin, 1899.

Marin, Paul. *Histoire populaire de l'affaire Dreyfus.* Paris: P. V. Stock, 1898.

Martin du Gard, Roger. *Jean Barois.* Paris: Ed. de la Nouvelle Revue Française, 1913.

————. *Vieille France.* Paris: Gallimard, 1933.

Marx, Karl. *The Eighteenth Brumaire of Louis Bonaparte.* New York: International Pub., 1972.

Maury, Louis. *M. Boulanger devant l'opinion publique.* Poitiers: Imprimerie de Millet, Descoust, et Pain, 1888.

Mazelin, Abbé. "Un Curé et ses oeuvres rurales," *Action populaire.* Lille: 1903.

Méline, Jules. *Le Retour à la terre et la surproduction industrielle.* Paris: Hachette, 1905.

Mermeix. *Les Coulisses du boulangisme.* Paris: L. Cerf, 1890.

Meuriot, Paul. *Des Agglomérations urbaines dans l'Europe contemporaine.* Paris: Belin frères, 1898.

Millot, Maurice. *La Comédie boulangiste: Chansons et satires.* Paris: J. B. Ferreyrol, 1891.

Monod, Gabriel. "Contemporary Life and Thought in France," *Contemporary Review,* 52, September, 1887, pp. 430-31.

Pecheux, Théodule. *Les Elections générales de 1889.* Paris: Imprimerie de Baudu, 1889.

Pradel, Abbé Felix. *Le Curé de campagne et les oeuvres rurales.* Saint Maixent: Maison de la Bonne Presse de l'Ouest, 1905.

Proust, Marcel. *Jean Santeuil.* Paris: Gallimard, 1952.

Quillard, Pierre. *Le Monument Henry, listes des souscripteurs.* Paris: P. V. Stock, 1899.

Reinach, Joseph. *Histoire de l'affaire Dreyfus.* 7 vols. Paris: Editions de la Revue Blanche, 1903-11.

Sébillot, Paul. *Le Folklore de France.* Paris: Libraire orientale & américaine. E. Guilmoto, 1904-07.

Sorel, Georges. *La Révolution dreyfusienne.* Paris: M. Rivière, 1911.

Souchon, Auguste. *La Crise de la main d'oeuvre agricole en France.* Paris: A. Rousseau, 1914.

———. *La Propriété paysanne.* Paris: L. Larose, 1899.

Stapfer, Paul. "Qu'est-ce que le public?," *La Grande revue,* June, 1899, pp. 529-47.

Vandervelde, Emile. *L'Exode rurale et le retour aux champs.* Paris: Alcan, 1910.

———. *Les Villes tentaculaires.* Paris: G. Bellais, 1899.

Viau, Raphael, *Vingt ans d'antisémitisme.* Paris: E. Fasquelle, 1910.

Villane, E. *L'Opinion publique et l'affaire Dreyfus.* Paris: P. V. Stock, 1898.

Villot. Lt. Col. *Le Général Boulanger et le plébiscite.* Poitiers, 1889.

Vogüé. E. M. de. *Les Morts qui parlent.* Paris: E. Plon, Nourrit, 1889.

Zola, Emile, *L'Affaire Dreyfus: La Verité en marche.* Paris: Charpentier, 1901.

———. *Germinal.* Paris: G. Charpentier, 1885.

———. *La Terre.* Paris: G. Charpentier, 1887.

Selected Secondary Material:

Abrams, Philip. "History, Sociology, Historical Sociology," *Past and Present,* 87, May 1980, pp. 3-16.

Ackerman, Evelyn B. *Village on the Seine: Tradition and Change in Bonnières, 1815-1914.* Ithaca: Cornell Univ. Press, 1978.

Agulhon, Maurice. *1848 ou l'apprentissage de la République, 1848-1852.* Paris: Seuil, 1973.

———. *Marianne au combat: L'imagerie et la symbolique républicaines de 1789 à 1880.* Paris: Flammarion, 1979.

———. *La République au village.* Paris: Plon, 1970.

Arendt, Hannah. *The Origins of Totalitarianism.* New York: Harcourt Brace Jovanovich, 1973.

Armengaud, André. *Les Populations de l'est—aquitain au début de l'époque contemporaine, 1845-1871*. Paris: Mouton, 1961.

Augé-Laribé, Michel. *L'Evolution de la France agricole*. Paris: A. Colin, 1912.

———. *La Politique agricole de la France 1880-1940*. Paris: Presses Universitaires de France, 1950.

Barlatier, P. *L'Aventure tragi-comique du grand général Boulanger*. Paris: Editeurs réunis, 1949.

Barral, Pierre. *Les Agrariens français de Méline à Pisani*. Paris: A. Colin, 1968.

———. *Le Département de l'Isère sous la Troisième République, 1870-1940*. Paris: A. Colin, 1962.

———. "Note historique sur l'emploi du terme 'paysan'," *Etudes rurales*, 21, 1966.

Barrows, Susanna. *Distorting Mirrors: Crowd Psychology in Late Nineteenth-Century France*. New Haven: Yale Univ. Press, 1981.

Beauroy, Jacques et al., eds. *The Wolf and the Lamb: Popular Culture in France*. Saratoga, California: Anma Libri, 1976.

Bellanger, Claude et al., eds. *Histoire générale de la presse française, III, de 1871 à 1940*. Paris: Presses Universitaires de France, 1972.

Ben Simon-Donath, Doris. *Socio-démographie des juifs de France et d'Algérie*. Paris: 1976.

Berger, Suzanne. *Peasants Against Politics*. Cambridge, Mass.: Harvard Univ. Press, 1972.

Bertaut, Jules. *Ce qu'était la province avant la guerre*. Paris: La Renaissance du livre, 1918.

Bezucha, Robert. "Masks of Revolution: A Study in Popular Culture During the Second French Republic," in Roger Price, ed., *Revolution and Reaction*. London: C. Helm, 1995.

Bibesco, Princesse. *Images d'Epinal*. Paris: Plon, 1937.

Blanchard, Raoul. *Les Alpes occidentales*. t. 7. Grenoble: B. Arthaud, 1956.

Bligny, Bernard, ed. *Histoire du Dauphiné*. Toulouse: Privat, 1973.

———, ed. *Histoire du diocèse de Grenoble*. Paris: Beauchesne, 1979.

Bloch, Marc. *French Rural History: An Essay on Its Basic Characteristics*, trans. Janet Sondheimer. Berkeley: Univ. of California Press, 1970.

———. "Les Transformations des techniques comme problèmes de psychologie collective," *Journal de psychologie normale et pathologique*, 12, 1948, pp. 104-20.

Boivin, M. "Le Boulangisme en Haute Normandie," *Annales de Normandie*, 3, October, 1976, pp. 225-62.

Bollème, Geneviève. *La Bibliothèque bleue*. Paris: Julliard, 1971.

Bordes, Maurice, ed. *Histoire de la Gascogne des origines à nos jours*. Roanne: Horvarth, 1977.

Bourdin, G. *Population-artisanat-industrie dans le département de l'Orne, 1821-1920*. Caen: Imprimerie Normandie, 1934.

Braque, René. "Aux origines du syndicalisme dans les milieux ruraux," *Mouvement social*. 42, January-March, 1963, pp. 79-116.

Bredin, Jean Denis. *L'Affaire*. Paris: Julliard, 1983.

Brown, Peter. "The Rise and Function of the Holy Man in Late Antiquity," *Journal of Roman Studies*, vol. 61, 1971, pp. 80-101.

Brown, Richard Maxwell and Fehrenbacher, Don Edward, eds. *Tradition, Conflict, and Modernization*. New York: Academic Press, 1977.

Brunet, Roger. *Les Campagnes toulousaines: Etude géographique*. Toulouse: Imprimerie Boisseau, 1965.

Burns, Michael. "Qui ça, Dreyfus?: The Affair in Rural France," *Historical Reflections*, 5, 1, 1978, pp. 99-115.

Byrnes, Robert. *Anti-Semitism in Modern France*. New Brunswick: Rutgers Univ. Press, 1950.

Callon, M. G. "Le Mouvement de la dépopulation dans le Gers, 1821-1920," *Bulletin des études locales du Gers*, 4, 1929.

Carles, Emilie. *Une Soupe aux herbes sauvages*. Paris: J. C. Simoën, 1977.

Chapman, Guy. *The Dreyfus Case: A Reassessment*. London: R. Hart-Davis, 1955.

———. *The Dreyfus Trials*. New York: Stein and Day, 1972.

Chatelain, Abel. *Les Migrants temporaires en France, 1800-1914*. Lille: Université de Lille, n.d.

Cobb, Richard. *Paris and Its Provinces, 1792-1802*. London: Oxford Univ. Press, 1975.

———. *The Police and the People: French Popular Protest, 1789-1820*. London: Oxford Clarendon Press, 1970.

———. *Reactions to the French Revolution*. London: Oxford Univ. Press, 1972.

Cohen, David. "L'Image du Juif dans la société française en 1843 d'après les rapports des préfets," *Revue d'histoire économique et sociale*, 55, 1977, pp. 70-91.

Combe, Paul. *Niveau de vie et progrès technique en France, 1860-1939*. Paris: Presses Universitaires de France, 1955.

Corbin, Alain. *Archaïsme et modernité en Limousin au XIXe siècle, 1845-1880*. 2 vols. Paris: M. Rivière, 1975.

Cuisenier, Jean. *L'Art populaire en France*. Fribourg: 1975.

Dagnan, Jean. *Le Gers sous la Seconde République*. 2 vols. Auch: Imprimerie F. Cocharaux, 1928-29.

Dansette, Adrien. *Le Boulangisme*. Paris: A. Fayard, 1946.

Dauvergne, Robert. "L'Iconographie et l'étude des sentiments populaires," *Revue de synthèse*, 9, 2, 1935, pp. 85-90.

Dave, Emile. *Le Tirage au sort*. Namur: Imprimerie Nave, 1934.

Davis, Natalie Zemon. *Society and Culture in Early Modern France*. Stanford: Stanford Univ. Press, 1975.

Désert, Gabriel. "Les paysans bas-normands et la politique," *Annales de Normandie*, 3, October, 1976, pp. 195-223.

————. *Une Société rurale au XIXe siècle: Les paysans du Calvados, 1815-1895.* 3 vols. Thèse: Université de Paris I, 1971.

Duby, Georges. "L'Urbanisation dans l'histoire," *Etudes rurales,* 49-50, 1973, pp. 10-13.

Duby, Georges et al., eds. *Histoire de la France rurale.* 4 vols. Paris: Seuil, 1975-76.

Ducamp, Louis. *La Conquête républicaine du Gers, 1870-93.* Unpub. ms. on file, ADG, 1971.

Duffour, J. "Démographie et dépopulation dans le Gers," *Revue de Gascogne,* 1914, pp. 193-216.

Dupeux, Georges. "La Croissance urbaine en France aux XIXe siècle," *Revue d'histoire économique et sociale,* 2, 52, 1974, pp. 173-89.

————. *Aspect de l'histoire sociale et politique du Loir-et-Cher, 1848-1914.* Paris: Imprimerie Nationale, 1962.

Faucher, Daniel. *Le Paysan et la machine.* Paris: Editions de minuit, 1954.

————. "Routine et innovation dans la vie paysanne," *Journal de psychologie normale et pathologique,* 1948, pp. 89-103.

Fauvet, Jacques and Mendras, Henri, eds. *Les Paysans et la politique dans la France contemporaine.* Paris: A. Colin, 1958.

Ferrand, Louis, and Magnac, Edmond. *Guide bibliographique de l'imagerie populaire.* Auxerre: Imprimerie moderne, 1956.

Forster, Robert, and Ranum, Orest, eds. *Rural Society in France.* Baltimore: Johns Hopkins, 1977.

Friedmann, Georges, ed. *Villes et campagnes.* Paris: 1953.

Furet, François, and Sachs, Wladimar. "La Croissance de l'alphabétisation en France, XVIII-XIXe siècles," *Annales: Économies, sociétés, et civilisations,* 29, 1974, pp. 714-37.

Gaucher, Michel. *L'Agriculture vendéenne: Son évolution aux XIX et XXᵉ siècle.* Les Sables d'Olonne: Pinson, 1976.

Girard, Patrick. *Les Juifs de France de 1789 à 1860.* Paris: Calmann-Lévy, 1976.

Girault, J. and Saillet, J. "Les Mouvements vignerons de Champagne," *Mouvement social.* April-June, 1969.

Goguel-Nyegaard, François. *La Politique des partis sous la IIIe République.* Paris: Seuil, 1948.

Golob, Eugene Owen. *The Méline Tariff: French Agriculture and Nationalist Economic Policy.* New York: Columbia Univ. Press, 1944.

Goody, Jack. *The Domestication of the Savage Mind.* Cambridge, England: Cambridge Univ. Press, 1978.

Grafteaux, Serge. *Mémé Santerre.* Paris: Editions du Jour, 1975.

Grantham, George, "Scale and Organization in French Farming," in William N. Parker and Eric L. Jones, eds., *European Peasants and Their Markets: Essays in Agrarian Economic History.* Princeton: Princeton Univ. Press, 1975.

Gratton, Philippe. *Les Luttes de classe dans les campagnes*. Paris: Anthropos, 1971.

Grenadou, E. and Prevost, A. *Grenadou, paysan français*. Paris: 1978.

Grise, Auguste. *Coutumes du Trièves au XIXe siècle*. Grenoble: 1939.

Guillaumin, Emile. *Panorama de l'évolution paysanne, 1875-1935*. Colombes: Cahiers de la quinzaine, 1936.

Halasz, Nicholas. *Captain Dreyfus: The Story of Mass Hysteria*. New York: Simon and Schuster, 1955.

Halbwachs, Maurice. *Equisse d'une psychologie des classes sociales*. Paris: M. Rivière, 1955.

Halévy, Daniel. *Visites aux paysans du Centre*. Paris: B. Grasset, 1921.

Hanagan, Michael. *The Logic of Solidarity: Artisans and Industrial Workers in Three French Towns, 1871-1914*. Urbana: Univ. of Illinois Press, 1980.

Harding, James. *The Astonishing Adventure of General Boulanger*. New York: W. H. Allen, 1971.

Hegel, S.W.F. "Qui pense abstrait?" *Mercure de France*, 349, 1963, pp. 746-51.

Hélias, Pierre Jakez. *The Horse of Pride: Life in a Breton Village*, trans. June Guicharnaud. New Haven: Yale Univ. Press, 1978.

Herbert, Robert L. "City vs. Country: The Rural Image in French Painting from Millet to Gauguin," *Artforum*, February 1970, pp. 44-55.

Hoffman, Robert L. *More Than a Trial: The Struggle Over Captain Dreyfus*. New York: Free Press, 1980.

Hofstadter, Richard. *The Paranoid Style in American Politics*. New York, 1965.

Hohenberg, Paul. "Change in Rural France in the Period of Industrialization," *Journal of Economic History*, 32, 1, March, 1972, pp. 219-40.

Hunt, James C. "Peasants, Grain Tariffs, and Meat Quotas: Imperial German Protectionism Reexamined," *Central European History*, 7, 4, December, 1974, pp. 311-31.

Hutton, Patrick, H. *The Cult of the Revolutionary Tradition: The Blanquists in French Politics, 1864-1893*. Berkeley: Univ. of California Press, 1981.

———. "Popular Boulangism and the Advent of Mass Politics in France, 1886-1890," *Journal of Contemporary History*, 11, 1976.

———. "The Impact of the Boulangist Crisis Upon the Guesdist Party at Bordeaux," *French Historical Studies*, 7, 2, 1971.

Ibarrola, Jesus. *Structure sociale et fortune dans la campagne proche de Grenoble en 1847*. Paris: Mouton, 1966.

Johnson, Douglas. *France and the Dreyfus Affair*. London: Blandford, 1966.

Joisten, Charles. "Rites de terminaison des veillées en Dauphiné," *Folklore*, 135, 1969.

Jollivet, Marcel, ed. *Sociétés paysannes ou lutte de classe au village*. Paris: Colin, 1974.

Joutard, Philippe. *La Légende des camisards*. Paris: Gallimard/Julliard, 1976.

Judt, Tony. "The Origins of Rural Socialism in Europe: Economic Change of the Provençal Peasantry, 1870-1914," *Social History*, January, 1976, pp. 45-65.

———. *Socialism in Provence*. New York: Cambridge Univ. Press, 1979.

Karnoouh, Claude. "La Démocratie impossible: Parenté et politique dans un village lorrain," *Etudes rurales*, 52, October 1963, pp. 24-56.

Kayser, Jacques, ed. *La Presse de province sous la Troisième République*. Paris: A. Colin, 1958.

Lancelot, Alain. *L'Abstentionnisme électoral en France*. Paris: A. Colin, 1968.

Lantiez, Denise. "Cinq siècles d'images populaires," *La France graphique*, 1957.

Le Goff, Jacques and Nora, Pierre, eds. *Faire l'histoire*, vol. 3. Paris: Gallimard, 1974.

Lehning, James. *The Peasants of Marlhes: Economic Development and Family Organization in Nineteenth Century France*. Chapel Hill: Univ. of North Carolina Press, 1980.

Lequin, Yves. *Les Ouvriers de la région lyonnaise (1848-1914)*, 2 vols. Lyon: Presses Universitaires de Lyon, 1977.

Le Roy Ladurie, Emmanuel, and Zysberg, A. "Anthropologie des conscrits français, 1868-87," *Ethnologie française*, 9, 1, 1979.

Leuilliot, Paul. *L'Alsace au début du XIXe siècle*, vol. 2. Paris: S.E.V.P.E.N., 1959.

Levillain, Philippe. *Boulanger: Fossoyeur de la Monarchie*. Paris: Flammarion, 1982.

Lewis, David L. *Prisoner of Honor: The Dreyfus Affair*. New York: William Morrow, 1973.

Lewis, Gavin. "The Peasantry, Rural Change, and Conservative Agrarism: Lower Austria at the Turn of the Century," *Past and Present*, 81, 1978, pp. 119-43.

Lipschutz, Léon. *Une Bibliographie dreyfusienne: Essai de bibliographie thématique et analytique de l'affaire Dreyfus*. Paris: Editions Fasquelle, 1970.

Loubère, Leo. *Radicalism in Mediterranean France: Its Rise and Decline*. Albany: Albany State, New York Univ. Press, 1974.

Luxembourg, M. "Problème de la démographie Gersoise," *Bulletin de la société archéologique du Gers*, 2, 1948, pp. 79-82.

MacGraw, Roger. "Pierre Joigneux and Socialist Propaganda in the French Countryside, 1849-51," *French Historical Studies*, 10, 4, Fall 1978, pp. 599-640.

McPhee, Peter. *The Seed-Time of the Republic: Society and Politics in Pyrénées-Orientales*. Unpub. diss., Univ. of Melbourne, 1977.

Maho, Jacques. *L'Image des autres chez le paysan*. Paris: le Champ du possible, 1974.

Mannheim, Karl. *Essays on the Sociology of Knowledge*. London: 1972.

Margadant, Ted. *French Peasants in Revolt: The Insurrection of 1851*. Princeton: Princeton Univ. Press, 1979.

Marcilhacy, Christiane. "Emile Zola, 'historian' des paysans beauçerons," *Annales: Économies, sociétés, et civilisations.* 1957.

Marin, Louis. *Les Contes traditionnels en Lorraine.* Paris: Imprimerie Jouve, 1946.

———. *Disparition des institutions traditionnelles.* Paris: 1948.

Marrus, Michael. *The Politics of Assimilation: A Study of the French Jewish Community at the Time of the Dreyfus Affair.* Oxford: Clarendon Press, 1971.

Marrus, Michael and Paxton, Robert. *Vichy France and the Jews.* New York: Basic Books, 1981.

Massignon, Geneviève. "Coutumes et chants de conscrits," *Revue du Bas Poitu,* 1960, pp. 170-92.

Mendras, Henri. *La Fin des paysans.* Paris: S.E.D.E.I.S., 1967.

———. *Sociétés paysannes.* Paris: A. Colin, 1976.

———. *Sociologie de la campagne française.* Paris: Presses Universitaires de France, 1971.

Merriman, John M. *The Agony of the Republic: Repression of the Left In Revolutionary France, 1848-1851.* New Haven: Yale Univ. Press, 1978.

———. ed., *Consciousness and Class Experience in Nineteenth Century Europe.* New York: Holmes-Meier, 1979.

Mistler, Jean et al., *Epinal et l'imagerie populaire.* Paris: Hachette, 1961.

Moore, Barrington. *Social Origins of Dictatorship and Democracy: Lord and Peasant in the Making of the Modern World.* Boston: Beacon Press, 1966.

Mosse, George. *Toward the Final Solution: A History of European Racism.* New York: H. Fertis, 1978.

Néré, Jacques. *Le Boulangisme et la presse.* Paris: A. Colin, 1964.

———. *La Crise industrielle de 1882 et le mouvement boulangiste.* Paris: Unpub. thesis, Sorbonne, 1959.

———. *Les Elections Boulanger dans le département du Nord.* Paris: Unpub. thesis, Sorbonne, 1959.

Palmade, Guy. "Le Département du Gers à la fin du Seconde Empire," *Bulletin de la société archéologique du Gers,* 1961.

———. *L'Evolution de l'opinion politique dans le département du Gers de 1848 à 1914.* Unpub. ms., on file ADG, 1946.

Paraf, Pierre. *La France de l'affaire Dreyfus.* Paris: Editions Droit et Liberté, 1978.

Perrot, Michelle. *Les Ouvriers en grève: France, 1871-1890,* 2 vols. Paris: Mouton, 1974.

Pierrard, Pierre. *Juifs et catholiques français de Drumont à Jules Isaac.* Paris: Fayard, 1970.

Piganiol, Georges. *Le Mouvement de la population dans le Gers.* Toulouse: Thesis, Université de Toulouse, 1924.

Pinchemel, Philippe. *Structures sociales et dépopulation rurale dans les campagnes picardes de 1836 à 1936.* Paris: A Colin, 1957.

Poliakov, Léon. *Histoire de l'antisémitisme,* 3 vols. Paris: Calmann-Lévy, 1955-68.

Ponty, J. "La Presse quotidienne et l'affaire Dreyfus, 1898-99," *Revue d'histoire moderne et contemporaine*, 21, 1974, pp. 201-14.

Price, Roger, ed. *Revolution and Reaction: 1848 and the Second French Republic*. London: C. Helm, 1975.

Rebérioux, Madeleine. "Histoire, historiens et dreyfusisme," *Revue historique*, 255, 1976, pp. 407-32.

Redfield, Robert. *Peasant Society and Culture*. Chicago: Chicago Univ. Press, 1956.

Reddy, William. "Family and Factory: French Linen Workers in the *Belle époque*," *Journal of Social History*, 1975, pp. 102-12.

Rémond, René, ed. *Atlas historique de la France contemporaine, 1800-1965*. Paris: A. Colin, 1966.

————. *The Right Wing in France: From 1815 to de Gaulle*, trans. James Laux. Philadelphia: Univ. of Pennsylvania Press, 1968.

Roblin, L-H. "Le Mouvement bûcheron," *Revue socialiste*, 38, 1903, pp. 712-33.

Rossel, André, ed. *Napoléon, imagerie, affiches*. Paris: Editions des yeux ouverts, 1969.

Rothney, John. *Bonapartism After Sedan*. Ithaca: Cornell Univ. Press, 1969.

Rousseau, Raymond. "Les Conscrits de la Belle Epoque," *Bulletin de la société d'études folkloriques du centre-ouest*, 3, 1968.

Rutkoff, Peter. *Revanche and Revision: The Ligue des Patriotes and the Origins of the Radical Right in France, 1882-1900*. Athens, Ohio: Ohio Univ. Press, 1981.

Sartre, Jean Paul. *Réflexions sur la question juive*. Paris: Gallimard, 1962.

Scott, Joan. *The Glassworkers of Carmaux: French Craftsmen and Political Action in a Nineteenth Century City*. Cambridge, Mass.: Harvard Univ. Press, 1974.

Seager, Frederick. *The Boulanger Affair: Political Crossroad of France, 1886-1889*. Ithaca: Cornell Univ. Press, 1969.

Sewell, William H., Jr. *Work and Revolution in France: The Language of Labor from the Old Regime to 1848*. New York: Cambridge Univ. Press, 1980.

Siegfried, André. *Tableau politique de la France de l'ouest sous la Troisième République*. Paris: A. Colin, 1913.

Smith, J. Harvey. "Agricultural Workers and the French Winegrowers Revolt of 1907," *Past and Present*, 79, 1978, pp. 101-25.

Sorlin, Pierre. *'La Croix' et les juifs*. Paris: B. Grasset, 1967.

————. *Waldeck-Rousseau*. Paris: A. Colin, 1966.

Sternhell, Zeev. *La Droite révolutionnaire, 1885-1914: Les Origines françaises du fascisme*. Paris: Seuil, 1978.

Talon, Charles. "Migrations et moissoneurs à la faux en Bas-Dauphiné, 1890-1914," *Evocations*, 3, 1964, pp. 79-83.

Thabault, Roger. *Education and Change in a Village Community: Mazières-en-Gâtine, 1848-1914*, trans. Peter Tregear. New York: Schocken, 1971.

Thomas, Marcel. *L'Affaire sans Dreyfus*. Paris: A. Fayard, 1961.

Thompson, E. P. " 'Rough Music': Le Charivari anglais," *Annales: Economies, sociétés, civilisations*, 27, 2, March-April, 1972, pp. 285-312.

——. "Time, Work-Discipline, and Industrial Capitalism," *Past and Present*, 38, 1967, pp. 56-97.

Tilly, Charles. *As Sociology Meets History*. New York: Academic Press, 1981.

——. "The Changing Place of Collective Violence," in Melvin Richter, ed., *Essays in Theory and History: An Approach to the Social Sciences*. Cambridge, Mass.: Harvard Univ. Press, 1970.

——. "How Protest Modernized in France, 1845-1855," in W. Aydelotte et al., *The Dimensions of Quantitative Research in History*. Princeton: Princeton Univ. Press, 1971.

—— et al., *The Rebellious Century, 1830-1930*. Cambridge, Mass.: Harvard Univ. Press, 1975.

Van Gennep, Arnold. "Le Cycle cérémonial du carnaval et du carême en Savoie," *Journal de psychologie*, 22, 5, May 5, 1925.

——. *Le Folklore du dauphiné*, 2 vols. Paris: Librairie orientale et américaine, 1932-33.

——. *Manuel de folklore français contemporaine*, 9 vols. Paris: A Picard, 1937-58.

——. "Surviances primitives dans les cérémonies agraires de la Savoie et du Dauphiné," *Studi e materiali di storia delle religion*, vol. 5, 1930.

Varagnac, André. "L'Art et le peuple: Problèmes d'art populaire," *L'Amour de l'art*, Nov. 1938.

Vaultier, Roger. "Un Colporteur d'images populaires en Bretagne il y a un siècle," *Passiflora*, 22, 1940 (?), pp. 15-21.

Vauthier, Paul. "Towards a Geography of French Historical Demography," *French Historical Studies*, 11, 1, 1979, pp. 108-30.

Verdès-Leroux, Jeannine. *Scandale financier et antisémitisme catholique: Le Krach de l'Union Générale*. Paris: Editions du Centurion, 1969.

Verdié, Henry. "L'Evolution agricole, économique et sociale de la commune de Saint Brès (Gers)," *Bulletin de la société archéologique, histoire, littéraire et scientifique du Gers*, 1959.

Vigier, Philippe. *La Seconde République dans la région alpine*, 2 vols. Paris: Presses Universitaires de France, 1963.

Weber, Eugen. "Comment la Politique Vint aux Paysans: A Second Look at Peasant Politicization in France," *American Historical Review*, 87, April, 1982, pp. 357-89.

——. "Jews, Anti-Semitism, and the Origins of the Holocaust," *Historical Reflections*, 5, 1, Summer 1978, pp. 1-17.

——. *Peasants into Frenchmen: The Modernization of Rural France, 1870-1914*. Stanford: Stanford Univ. Press, 1976.

——. "The Second Republic: Politics and the Peasant," *French Historical Studies*, 11, 4, Fall 1980, pp. 521-50.

Willard, Claude. *Le Mouvement socialiste en France (1893-1905) Les Guedistes*. Paris: Editions sociales, 1965.

Wilson, Stephen. "The Anti-Semitic Riots of 1898 in France," *Historical Journal*, 16, 1973, pp. 789-806.

———. "Catholic Populism in France at the Time of the Dreyfus Affair: The *Union Nationale*," *Journal of Contemporary History*, 10, Oct. 1975, pp. 667-705.

———. *Ideology and Experience: Antisemitism in France at the Time of the Dreyfus Affair*. Rutherford: Fairleigh Dickinson Press, 1982.

———. "Le Monument Henry: La Structure de l'antisémitisme en France, 1898-1899," *Annales: Economies, sociétés et civilisations*, 32, 2, March-April, 1977, pp. 265-91.

Winock, Michel. *Edouard Drumont et Cie: Antisémitisme et fascisme en France*. Paris: Seuil, 1982.

Wismes, Armel de. *Histoire de la Vendée*. Paris: Hachette, 1975.

Wohl, Robert. *The Generation of 1914*. Cambridge, Mass.: Harvard Univ. Press, 1979.

Wolf, Eric R. *Peasants*. Englewood Cliffs: Prentice-Hall, 1966.

Wolff, Kurt, ed. *The Sociology of Georg Simmel*. London: Free Press, 1950.

Wright, Gordon. *Rural Revolution in France*. Stanford: Stanford Univ. Press, 1968.

Wylie, Laurence. *Chanzeaux, A Village in Anjou*. Cambridge, Mass.: Harvard Univ. Press, 1966.

———. *Village in the Vaucluse*. Cambridge, Mass.: Harvard Univ. Press, 1957.

Zeldin, Theodore, ed. *Conflicts in French Society*. London: Allen and Unwin, 1970.

———. *France: 1848-1945*, 2 vols. Oxford: Clarendon Press, 1973, 1977.

Zévaès, Alexandre. *Au Temps du boulangisme*. Paris: Gallimard, 1930.

INDEX

Library of Congress Cataloging in Publication Data

Burns, Michael, 1947-
   Rural society and French politics.

   Bibliography: p.
   Includes index.
   1. France—Politics and government—1870-1940.
2. France—Rural conditions. 3. Boulanger, Georges-Ernest-
Jean-Marie, 1837-1891. 4. Dreyfus, Alfred, 1859-1935.
5. Peasantry—France—Political activity. I. Title.
DC348.B87   1984   306'.0944   84-3253
ISBN 0-691-05423-1 (alk. paper)